Electric and Hybrid Vehicles

▶ The first book on electric and hybrid vehicles (EVs) written specifically for automotive students and vehicle owners

▶ Clear diagrams, photos and flow charts outline the charging infrastructure, how EV technology works, and how to repair and maintain electric and hybrid vehicles

▶ Optional IMI online eLearning materials enable students to study the subject further and test their knowledge at www.theimi.org.uk/elearning

Full coverage of IMI Level 2 Award in Hybrid Electric Vehicle Operation and Maintenance, IMI Level 3 Award in Hybrid Electric Vehicle Repair and Replacement, IMI Accreditation, C&G and other EV/Hybrid courses.

The first book on electric and hybrid vehicles (endorsed by the IMI) starts with an introduction to the market, covering the different types of electric vehicle, costs and emissions, and the charging infrastructure, before moving on to explain how electric and hybrid vehicles work. A chapter on electrical technology introduces learners to subjects such as batteries, control systems and charging, which are then covered in more detail within their own chapters. The book also covers the maintenance and repair procedures of these vehicles, including fault-finding, servicing, repair and first-responder information. Case studies are used throughout to illustrate different technologies.

Tom Denton is the leading UK automotive author with a teaching career spanning lecturer to head of automotive engineering in a large college. His range of automotive textbooks published since 1995 are bestsellers and led to his authoring of the Automotive Technician Training multimedia system that is in common use in the UK, USA and several other countries. Tom now works as the eLearning Development Manager for the Institute of the Motor Industry (IMI).

Electric and Hybrid Vehicles

Tom Denton   BA, FIMI, MSAE, MIRTE, Cert. Ed.

First published 2016
by Routledge
2 Park Square, Milton Park, Abingdon, Oxon OX14 4RN

and by Routledge
711 Third Avenue, New York, NY 10017

Routledge is an imprint of the Taylor & Francis Group, an informa business

British Library Cataloguing in Publication Data
A catalogue record for this book is available from the British Library

Library of Congress Cataloging in Publication Data
Names: Denton, Tom, author.
Title: Hybrid and electrical vehicles / Tom Denton.
Description: New York, NY : Routledge, 2016.
Identifiers: LCCN 2015046989 | ISBN 9781138842373 (pbk. : alk. paper) | ISBN 9781315731612 (ebook)
Subjects: LCSH: Electric vehicles. | Hybrid electric vehicles.
Classification: LCC TL220 .D4443 2016 | DDC 629.22/93--dc23
LC record available at http://lccn.loc.gov/2015046989

ISBN: 978-1-138-84237-3 (pbk)
ISBN: 978-1-315-73161-2 (ebk)

Typeset in Univers
by Servis Filmsetting Ltd, Stockport, Cheshire
Printed and bound in Great Britain by CPI Group (UK) Ltd, Croydon, CR0 4YY

Contents

v

Contents

Preface

In this book you will find lots of useful and interesting information about electric and hybrid vehicles (EVs). This book is the fourth in the 'Automotive Technology: Vehicle Maintenance and Repair' series, which includes:

▶ *Automobile Mechanical and Electrical Systems*
▶ *Automobile Electrical and Electronic Systems*
▶ *Advanced Automobile Fault Diagnosis*

Ideally, you will have studied some automotive technology, or have some experience, before starting on this book. If not, don't worry, it does start with the basics. The book looks at electrical and electronic principles as well as EV and hybrid technologies using comprehensive case studies and examples. It will cover everything you need to advance your studies to a higher level, no matter what qualification (if any) you are working towards.

I hope you find the content useful and informative. Comments, suggestions and feedback are always welcome at my website, www.automotive-technology.co.uk, where you will find new articles, links to online resources and much more.

Good luck and I hope you find automotive technology as interesting as I still do.

Acknowledgements

Over the years, many people have helped in the production of my books. I am therefore very grateful to the following companies who provided information and/or permission to reproduce photographs or diagrams:

AA
AC Delco
ACEA
Alpine Audio Systems
Autologic Data Systems
BMW UK
C&K Components
Citroën UK
Clarion Car Audio
CuiCAR
Delphi Media
Eberspaecher
Fluke Instruments UK
Flybrid Systems
Ford Motor Company
FreeScale Electronics
General Motors
GenRad
HaloIPT (Qualcomm)
Hella
HEVT
Honda
Hyundai

Institute of the Motor Industry
Jaguar Cars
Kavlico
Loctite
Lucas UK
LucasVarity
Mazda
McLaren Electronic Systems
Mennekes
Mercedes
Mitsubishi
Most Corporation
NGK Plugs
Nissan
Oacridge National Labs
Peugeot
Philips
PicoTech/PicoScope
Pioneer Radio
Porsche
Renasas
Robert Bosch Gmbh/Media
Rolec

Rover Cars
Saab Media
Scandmec
SMSC
Snap-on Tools
Society of Motor
  Manufacturers and
  Traders (SMMT)
Sofanou
Sun Electric
Tesla Motors
Thrust SSC Land Speed Team
T&M Auto-Electrical
Toyota
Tracker
Unipart Group
Valeo
Vauxhall
VDO Instruments
Volkswagen
Volvo Media
Wikimedia
ZF Servomatic

If I have used any information or mentioned a company name that is not listed here, please accept my apologies and let me know so it can be rectified as soon as possible.

CHAPTER 1

Electric vehicles introduction

1.1 EVs and hybrids

1.1.1 Types of electric vehicle

Electric Vehicle (EVs) or **Electrically Chargeable Vehicles (ECVs)** usually refers to any vehicle that is powered, in part or in full, by a battery that can be directly plugged into the mains. This textbook concentrates on car technologies, but larger vehicles are similar. We will use EV as the 'catch all' phrase as this in turn includes the following technologies:

> **Definition**
> EV is used as the general description for all types of electric vehicle.

Pure-Electric Vehicles (Pure-EVs) are electric vehicles powered only by a battery. At present, most manufacturers of standard performance cars offer pure-electric cars with a range up to about 100 miles.[1]

Plug-In Hybrid Electric Vehicles (PHEVs) have an internal combustion engine (ICE) but also a battery range in excess of 10 miles. After the battery range is utilized, the vehicle

Figure 1.1 Nissan LEAF – pure-EV (Source: Nissan Media)

reverts to the benefits of full hybrid capability (utilizing both battery and ICE power) without compromising the range.

> **Definition**
> ICE: internal combustion engine.

Extended-Range Electric Vehicles (E-REVs) are similar to pure-EVs but with a shorter battery range of 50 miles. However, range is extended by an ICE-driven generator providing

Figure 1.2 Volkswagen Golf GTE – PHEV

Figure 1.4 Toyota Prius – HEV (Source: Toyota Media)

many additional miles of mobility. With an E-REV, the propulsion is always electric, unlike a PHEV where the propulsion can be electric or full hybrid.

Figure 1.3 Chevrolet Volt – E-REV (Source: GM Media)

We will also cover standard **Hybrid Electric Vehicles (HEVs)** where it is not possible to charge the battery externally – there are a number of variations as outlined in Table 1.1. In addition we will examine EVs that use hydrogen fuel cells.

A phrase often used in connection with EVs is 'range anxiety'. This refers to the fear about the distance an EV can drive and the worry that it may not be enough to reach our destination!

However, an interesting point to note is that the average individual journey in the UK is less than 10 miles. The average total daily distance travelled is about 25 miles. In Europe, more than 80% of drivers cover less than 63 miles in a typical day. These distances can therefore be achieved using pure-electric cars and many journeys can be made with plug-in hybrid or extended-range electric cars without using the ICE.

Key Fact

The average individual journey in the UK is less than 10 miles.

1.1.2 Electric vehicle market

At the time of writing (2015), ECV sales were on the increase. All available data suggest that this will continue and grow even further. During 2014, over 75,000 new EVs were registered in the EU, a 36.6% rise. Looking at the EU's major markets, the UK saw the largest increase over the year (+300%), followed by Germany (+70%) and France (+30%). In the European Free Trade Association countries, Norway ended the year in first place with almost 20,000 registrations, more than doubling the registrations recorded in 2013 (+141%) (Source: ACEA).

Table 1.1 Summary of EVs and HEVs and their alternative names

Electric Vehicle/Car (EV), Electrically Chargeable Vehicle/Car	Generic terms for a vehicle powered, in part or in full, by a battery that can be plugged into the mains
Pure-EV, Pure-Electric Car, All Electric, Battery Electric Vehicle (BEV), Fully Electric	A vehicle powered only by a battery charged from mains electricity. Currently, typical pure-electric cars have a range of about 100 miles
Plug-In Hybrid Electric Vehicle (PHEV), Plug-In Hybrid Vehicle (PHV)	A vehicle with a plug-in battery and an internal combustion engine (ICE). Typical PHEVs will have a pure-electric range of 10–30 miles. After the pure-electric range is used up, the vehicle reverts to the benefits of full hybrid capability
Extended-Range Electric Vehicle (E-REV), Range-Extended Electric Vehicle (RE-EV)	A vehicle powered by a battery with an ICE-powered generator on board. E-REVs are like pure-EVs but with a shorter battery range of around 50 miles. Range is extended by an on-board generator providing additional miles of mobility. With an E-REV the vehicle is still always electrically driven and is known as a series hybrid (more on this later)
Hybrid Electric Vehicles (HEV), Full/Normal/Parallel/Standard hybrid	A hybrid vehicle is powered by a battery and/or an ICE. The power source is selected automatically by the vehicle, depending on speed, engine load and battery charge. This battery cannot be plugged in, so charge is maintained by regenerative braking supplemented by ICE-generated power
Mild Hybrid	A mild hybrid vehicle cannot be plugged in, or driven solely on battery power. However, it does harvest power during regenerative braking and uses this during acceleration (current F1 cars are a type of mild hybrid)
Micro Hybrid	A micro hybrid normally employs a stop-start system and regenerative braking which charges the 12-V battery
Stop-start Hybrid	A stop-start system shuts off the engine when the vehicle is stationary. An enhanced starter motor is used to support the increased number of engine starts
Alternative Fuel Vehicle (AFV)	Any vehicle that is not solely powered by traditional fuels (i.e. petrol or diesel) is referred to as alternative fuel
Internal Combustion Engine (ICE)	Petrol or diesel engine, as well as those adapted to operate on alternative fuels
Electric quadricycle	This is a four-wheeled vehicle that is categorized and tested in a similar way to a moped or three-wheeled motorcycle
Electric motorcycle	Battery only, so full electric drive motorcycles can have a range of up to 60 miles. However, a new range of Irish-built electric bikes have a claimed range of up to 136 miles. The Volt 220, which takes its name from its range of 220 km, will do up to 60 mph according to the manufacturer

Key Fact

During 2014, over 75,000 new EVs were registered in the EU.

It is expected that trends in development of different vehicle types will be as shown in Figure 1.5.

1.1.3 The EV experience

Cars running on electric drive are easy to use. They are also smooth, quiet and acceleration is good. Pure-EVs do not have a gearbox so are similar to driving an automatic. Plug-in hybrids (PHEVs) have a gearbox but this will be automatic, even though it can be controlled manually.

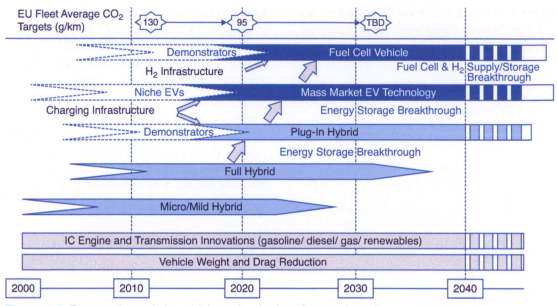

Figure 1.5 Expected trends in vehicle technologies (Source: http://www.smmt.co.uk)

Electricity, when produced from sustainable sources, is easy to supply and produces no emissions from the vehicle (often described as tailpipe emissions). EVs therefore have significant environmental benefits, particularly when used in urban environments. Some of the benefits of EVs when operating solely on battery power are:

▶ zero tailpipe emissions
▶ quiet driving
▶ easy to drive, particularly in stop–start traffic
▶ home charging avoids fuel station queues.

Electric vehicles can now achieve similar speeds to ICE vehicles during normal driving. Some pure-electric cars can reach speeds over 125 mph where permitted. Power is delivered by the electric motor as soon as the vehicle begins to move, which gives smooth and swift acceleration.

Key Fact

Some pure-electric cars can reach speeds over 125 mph.

The range of an EV depends on the type and how it is driven. At present, most pure-electric cars offer a range of 100 miles and over. They are ideal for short to medium length journeys. For journeys over 100 miles, an E-REV or PHEV is more suitable.

Key Fact

The range of an EV depends on the type and how it is driven.

EVs have to comply with the same safety standards as conventional cars by obtaining 'whole vehicle type approval'. Particular attention is paid during crash testing to ensure the EV-specific safety features operate correctly. Individual components such as the battery pack are also subjected to additional impact and other mechanical tests.

EVs typically use an inertia switch or a signal from the airbag system to disconnect the traction battery if the vehicle is involved in a collision. This is very similar to conventional vehicles, where an inertia switch is provided to stop the fuel supply in a crash. Battery packs are also designed with internal contactors so that if the 12 V supply is cut for any reason, the traction supply is also shut off.

Although EVs still generate tyre noise, the level of noise is much lower than an ICE car, particularly at low speed. Sight- and hearing-impaired people can be particularly vulnerable, so drivers need to be aware of this and take extra care.

> ### Safety First
> Sight- and hearing-impaired people can be particularly vulnerable, so drivers need to be aware of this and take extra care.

As with any vehicle, EV range depends on several factors, such as driving style, environmental conditions and the use of auxiliary systems in the vehicle. Manufacturers' performance claims should be seen as an indication of the capabilities of the vehicle – not what will happen in the real world![2] However, it is important to note how much driving style affects these performance figures and maximum range is unlikely to be achieved in a usage style based on rapid acceleration, high speeds and heavy use of auxiliary systems, such as heating and air conditioning.[3]

Specifically for EVs, UNECE Regulation 101 measures range, and the result of the electric energy consumption, which must be expressed in watt hours per kilometre (Wh/km). The test uses the same driving cycle (NEDC) as that which is used for measuring the fuel consumption, emissions and CO_2 of ICE cars.

> ### Definition
> NEDC: new European driving cycle.

1.1.4 History

The history of the EV is interesting and actually started earlier than many people think. A good way to look at it is in time periods or 'ages'. Table 1.2 outlines just some of the key events, numbers and trends in these periods.

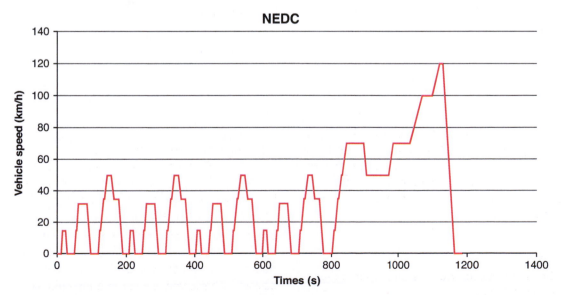

Figure 1.6 New European driving cycle (NEDC)

1 Electric vehicles introduction

Table 1.2 Key stages of EV development

Beginning – 1801–1850	First Age – 1851–1990	Boom and Bust – 1901–1950	Second Age – 1951–2000	Third Age – 2001–present
The earliest electric vehicles were invented in Scotland and the USA. **1832–39** – Robert Anderson of Scotland built the first prototype electric carriage. **1834** – Thomas Davenport of the USA invented the first direct current electrical motor in a car that operates on a circular electrified track.	Electric vehicles enter the market and start to find broad appeal. **1888** German engineer Andreas Flocken built the first four-wheeled electric car. **1897** – The first commercial EVs entered the New York City taxi fleet. The Pope Manufacturing Company became the first large-scale EV manufacturer in the USA. **1899** The 'La Jamais Contente' (The Never Happy!), built in France, became the first electric vehicle to travel over 100 km/h. **1900** Electricity-powered cars were the best-selling road vehicle in the USA with about 28% of the market.	EVs reach historical peaks of production but are then displaced by petrol-engine cars. **1908** The petrol-powered Ford Model T was introduced to the market. **1909** William Taft was the first US President to buy an automobile, a Baker Electric. **1912** The electric starter motor was invented by Charles Kettering. This made it easier to drive petrol cars because hand-cranking was not now necessary. The global stock of EVs reached around 30,000. **1930** By 1935, the number of EVs dropped almost to zero and ICE vehicles dominated because of cheap petrol. **1947** Oil rationing in Japan led carmaker Tama to release a 4.5 hp electric car. It used a 40V lead-acid battery.	High oil prices and pollution created a new interest in electric vehicles. **1966** US Congress introduced legislation recommending EVs as a way of reducing air pollution. **1973** The OPEC oil embargo caused high oil prices, long delays at fuel stations, and therefore renewed interest in EVs. **1976** The French government launched the 'PREDIT', which was a programme accelerating EV research and development. **1996** To comply with California's Zero Emission Vehicle (ZEV) requirements of 1990, GM produced the EV1 electric car. **1997** In Japan, Toyota began sales of the Prius, the world's first commercial hybrid car. Eighteen thousand were sold in the first year.	Public and private sectors now commit to vehicle electrification. **2008** Oil prices reached record highs. **2010** The Nissan LEAF was launched. **2011** The world's largest electric car sharing service, Autolib, was launched in Paris with a targeted stock of 3,000 vehicles. **2011** The global stock of EVs reached around 50,000. The French government fleet consortium committed to purchase 50,000 EVs over four years. Nissan LEAF won the European Car of the Year award. **2012** The Chevrolet Volt PHEV outsold half the car models on the US market. The global stock of EVs reached around 180,000. **2014** Tesla Model S, Euro NCAP 5-star safety rating, autopilot-equipped, available all-wheel drive dual motor with 0–60 mph in as little as 2.8 seconds and a range of up to 330 miles.

6

Beginning – 1801–1850	First Age – 1851–1990	Boom and Bust – 1901–1950	Second Age – 1951–2000	Third Age – 2001–present
				2015 Car manufacturers were caught cheating emission regulations making EVs more prominent in people's minds as perhaps the best way to reduce consumption and emissions.[4] (I purchased a VW Golf GTE (PHEV) and I love it!) The global stock of EVs reached around 700,000 and continues to grow (22,000 in the UK and 275,000 in the USA).

(Primary Source: Global EV outlook)

1.1.5 Formula-e

In the first season of Formula-e (2014–15), all 10 teams had to use identical single-seater cars. These were designed and built by Spark Racing Technology. McLaren, Williams, Dallara, Renault and Michelin also contributed their extensive expertise to the project.

Figure 1.7 Formula-e car

In season two, Formula-e becomes an open championship. This means that manufacturers and teams can develop their cars. To start with, they will be allowed to develop the powertrain, which includes the motor, inverter and transmission. It is expected that regulations will continue to change, for example to allow the battery to be developed.

The monocoque chassis made from carbon fibre and aluminium (by Dallara) is super lightweight and incredibly strong. It fully complies with the same FIA (Fédération Internationale de l'Automobile) crash tests that are used to regulate Formula One. McLaren Electronics Systems provide the electric powertrain and electronics. Williams Advanced Engineering supply the batteries. These are able to produce 200 kW, which is the equivalent of 270 bhp. Hewland supply a five-speed paddle shift sequential gearbox. It has fixed ratios to help keep costs down.

Figure 1.8 Formula-e race

A key part of any motorsport is the tyres. Treaded tyres designed for wet or dry use are fitted to 18-inch wheels. They can produce optimum performance in a range of conditions. The tyres, designed by Michelin, are very durable so they last throughout an entire race event.

The championship's technical partner, Renault, oversees the integration of all these systems.

A clear benefit of this is that the technical developments will greatly benefit the EVs and hybrids used on the roads. For this reason the use of latest technology is encouraged to push the boundaries for the future.

The amount of energy that can be delivered to the motor from the battery is limited to 28 kWh and this is closely monitored by the FIA. The performance, however, is still impressive:

▶ acceleration: 0–100 km/h (0–62 mph) in 3 seconds
▶ maximum speed: 225 km/h (140 mph).

For the second season, the power was raised from 150 kW to 170 kW.

In the first season, all teams used identical cars, but they now have some leeway to make modifications. Teams are allowed to use their own designs for motors, inverters, gearboxes and cooling systems. They will continue to use the same Spark-Renault chassis, with batteries supplied by Williams Advanced Engineering.

And finally, a big shout out to our British driver Sam Bird of Virgin Racing, who won the first London Formula-e event – we were there cheering him on! (http://www.virginracing.com)

Figure 1.9 London 2015 Formula-e: Sam Bird of Virgin Racing was a worthy winner

1.2 Costs and emissions

1.2.1 Electricity costs

The cost of charging an EV depends on the size of the battery, how discharged the battery is and how quickly you charge it. As a guide, charging a pure-electric car from flat to full will cost from as little as £1.00 to £4.00 (2015). This is for a typical pure-EV with a 24 kWh battery that will offer around 100 miles range.

The average cost of 'electrical fuel' therefore will be approximately £0.03 per mile.[5] Similar costs will apply to PHEVs and E-REVs, and because the batteries are smaller, it will cost less to charge them. See also the data in Table 1.3.

In some cases it may be possible to charge overnight and take advantage of cheaper

Table 1.3 Comparison of costs

Term, mileage, fuel cost	ICE	Pure-EV	PHEV	Notes
Annual mileage	10,000	10,000	10,000	
Cost of fuel (£/gallon or £kW/h)	£5.70	£0.05	£5.70/£0.05	Electricity (£/kWh). Higher value used for calculation. Lower if overnight charge or solar is used
Official combined cycle mpg	68 mpg	150 Wh/km	166 mpg	Electricity consumption (Wh/km)
'Real world' mpg	50 mpg	175 Wh/km 0.28 kWh/mile	100 mpg[6]	Real-world consumption
Total fuel costs	£1,140	£140	£570	(annual miles × fuel cost/mpg) (annual miles × fuel cost × kWh/mile)
Vehicle cost information				
Purchase price	£28,000	£34,000	£35,000	Estimates based on current list prices
Plug-in car grant		–£5,000	–£5,000	A grant to reduce cost by 25% (up to £5,000)
Net purchase price	£28,000	£29,000	£30,000	
Depreciation cost/year	£8,400	£8,700	£9,000	30% used – this will vary however
Residual value	£19,600	£21,300	£21,000	
Service, maintenance and repair	£190	£155	£190	Based on average of published figures
Other information				
Vehicle Excise Duty and Registration Fee	£30	£0	£0	
TOTAL COST	**£9,760**	**£8,995**	**£9,760**	**First year**

electricity rates. Other options include charging from domestic solar panels. At this time it is calculated that the total cost of ownership of an electric car is similar to an ICE because of the additional purchase costs. However, this will change and if other advantages are included such as congestion charges (£11.50 per day in London for ICE but zero for EVs in 2015), the EV will be significantly cheaper in the longer term.

Important note: the figures used in this table are 'best guesses', selected to give a reasonable comparison. The bottom line is that the three cars have broadly the same overall total cost even though the pure-EV and the PHEV have much lower fuel costs. The key factor will be how the depreciation cost of the EVs pans out. However, over subsequent years the fuel savings associated with the EVs will become more significant. The development of smart metering systems that can automatically select charging times and tariffs may also become common because they help to manage demand on the grid.

Figure 1.10 Photo voltaic (PV) solar panel

1.2.2 End of life

European legislation known as the End of Life Vehicle (ELV) Directive 2000/53/EC ensures that manufacturers of all cars and light vans have 95% of the vehicle re-used, recycled or recovered at the end of its life. Special authorized treatment facilities (ATFs) carry this out by stripping the vehicles after de-polluting them of all environmentally hazardous components such as batteries, tyres and oil. The ELV Directive also encourages good product design. For example, avoiding the use of harmful heavy metals, increasing the use of recycled materials and in general designing the car components and materials for easy reuse or recycling.

EV batteries could have significant value after automotive use. Various organizations are exploring ways in which these batteries could be used, such as extra domestic electricity storage where the battery could work in conjunction with home solar panels to store electricity.

Key Fact

EV batteries could have significant value after automotive use.

1.2.3 CO_2 emissions

A report by the Committee on Climate Change suggests that the reduction of CO_2 due to EV use will be modest. However, as the grid becomes cleaner, so do all the vehicles recharged from it and as a result the benefit is cumulative. The Committee on Climate Change has also stated that the widespread uptake of EVs is necessary if carbon reduction targets beyond 2030 are to be met. EVs cannot solve the climate change problem, but an increased uptake of EVs is an important step to help meet UK carbon reduction targets. The improvement in city air quality will be significant. Figure 1.11 shows the sources of CO_2 and the 2050 target.

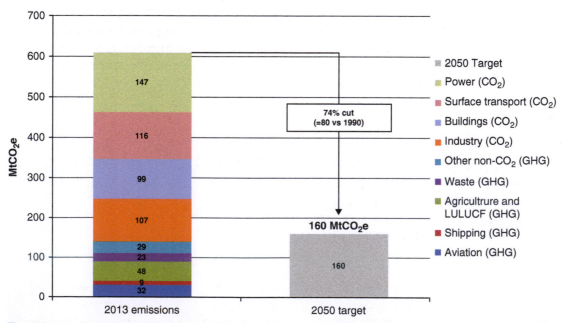

Figure 1.11 Sources of CO_2 (Source: UK Committee on Climate Change (UKCCC) https://www.theccc.org.uk/)

The Global EV Outlook 2015, produced by the International Energy Agency (IEA), shows significant growth in the use of EVs and therefore the reduction of CO_2 emissions (Source: http://www.iea.org).

1.2.4 Emissions

Electric vehicles have zero emissions at the point of use, so-called 'tank-to-wheel', when powered only by the battery. The 'well-to-wheel' analysis includes the CO_2 emissions during electricity generation, which depends on the current mixture of fuels used to make the electricity for the grid. To make a correct comparison with emissions from all cars, it is necessary to use the 'well-to-wheel' figure, which includes the CO_2 emissions during production, refining and distribution of petrol/diesel.

> **Key Fact**
> Electric vehicles have zero emissions at the point of use, so-called 'tank-to-wheel'.

To demonstrate the most extreme case, below is an example of typical pure-electric car emissions compared with emissions from small-to-medium-sized ICE cars.

Electricity production continues to decarbonize because of reduced reliance on oil and coal, so the overall emission figure for running an EV will drop further. Tailpipe emissions also include oxides of nitrogen (NOx) and particulate matter (tiny particles of solid or liquid matter suspended in a gas or liquid) that contribute to air pollution. This is why any vehicle operating only on battery power will play a significant role in improving local air quality.

1.3 Autonomous cars

1.3.1 Introduction

An autonomous car, also known as a driverless car, self-driving car and robotic car, is an autonomous vehicle capable of fulfilling the main transportation capabilities of a traditional car. It is capable of sensing its environment and navigating without human input. Of course, the vehicle does not have to be electrically powered, but almost all are, hence the reason for this short section.

Autonomous vehicles sense their surroundings with such techniques as RADAR, LIDAR, GPS and computer vision. Advanced control systems interpret sensory information to identify appropriate navigation paths, as well as obstacles and relevant signage. Autonomous vehicles are capable of updating their maps based on sensory input, allowing the vehicles to keep track of their position even when conditions change or when they enter unknown environments.

> **Key Fact**
> Lidar (LIDAR, LiDAR or LADAR) is a sensing technology that measures distance by illuminating a target with a laser and analysing the reflected light. The term LIDAR was created as a portmanteau of 'light' and 'radar'.

Legislation was passed in several US states (starting in 2012) allowing driverless cars. The number continues to increase. A Department of Transport report in the UK called *The Pathway to Driverless Cars* determined that current UK legislation is not a barrier to their

	Tank-to-wheel	Well-to-tank	Well-to-wheel
Pure-EV	0 g CO_2/km	77 g CO_2/km	77 g CO_2/km
ICE	132.3 g CO_2/km	14.7–29.0 g CO_2/km	147.0–161.3 g CO_2/km

(Source: SMMT)

use and a Code of Practice was produced in 2015. The intention is that this will facilitate developments.[7]

Figure 1.12 Audi autonomous car in development

1.3.2 Google self-driving car

The Google Self-Driving Car, commonly abbreviated as SDC, is a project by Google X that involves developing technology for autonomous cars, mainly electric cars.

Figure 1.13 Google car

In May 2014, Google presented a new concept for their driverless car that had neither a steering wheel nor pedals, and unveiled a fully functioning prototype in December of that year that they planned to test on San Francisco Bay Area roads beginning in 2015. Google plans to make these cars available to the public in 2020.

Google's autonomous cars include about $150,000 in equipment, including a $70,000 LIDAR system. This is the range finder mounted on the top that uses a 64-beam laser. This laser allows the vehicle to generate a detailed 3D map of its environment. The car then takes these generated maps and combines them with high-resolution maps of the world, producing different types of data models that allow it to drive itself.

Heavy rain or snow produce safety concerns for all autonomous vehicle. Other issues are that the cars rely primarily on pre-programmed route data and as a result do not obey temporary traffic lights and, in some situations, revert to a slower 'extra cautious' mode in complex unmapped intersections.

The vehicle has difficulty identifying when objects, such as trash and light debris, are harmless, causing the vehicle to veer unnecessarily. Additionally, the LIDAR technology cannot spot some potholes or discern when humans, such as a police officer, are signalling the car to stop.

All developers of autonomous vehicles face these issues – Google aims to fix them by 2020. In June 2015, Google announced that their vehicles had driven over 1 million miles, and that in the process they had encountered 200,000 stop signs, 600,000 traffic lights and 180 million other vehicles (Source: http://www.google.com/selfdrivingcar).

1.3.3 Hacking

As more systems on vehicles are connected to the outside world by radio waves of some sort, or they scan the world outside of the car, then more opportunities are presented to hackers. Of course manufacturers are working very hard to reduce the likelihood of cars being hacked and are helped in this process by what can be described as ethical hackers. There have been several interesting examples in the news recently, and here are two examples that illustrate why this is an important area.

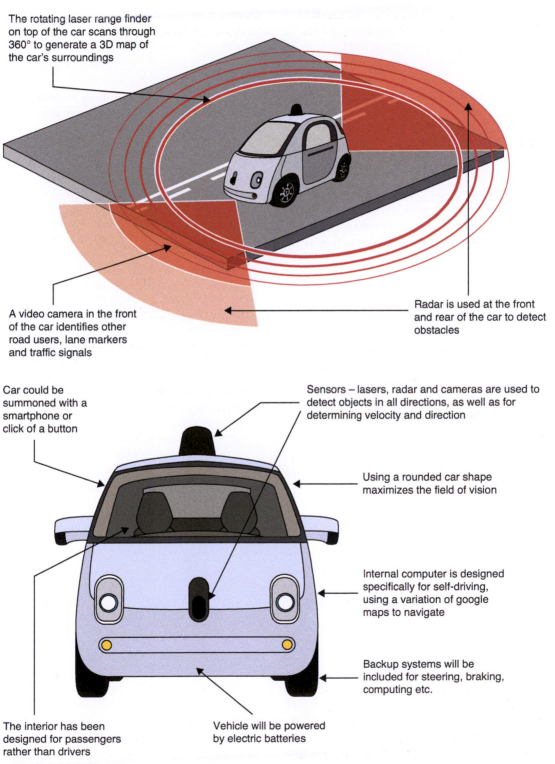

The rotating laser range finder on top of the car scans through 360° to generate a 3D map of the car's surroundings

A video camera in the front of the car identifies other road users, lane markers and traffic signals

Radar is used at the front and rear of the car to detect obstacles

Car could be summoned with a smartphone or click of a button

Sensors – lasers, radar and cameras are used to detect objects in all directions, as well as for determining velocity and direction

Using a rounded car shape maximizes the field of vision

Internal computer is designed specifically for self-driving, using a variation of google maps to navigate

Backup systems will be included for steering, braking, computing etc.

The interior has been designed for passengers rather than drivers

Vehicle will be powered by electric batteries

Figure 1.14 SDC features (Source: Google)

In 2015 Fiat Chrysler recalled 1.4 million vehicles in the USA because hackers had proved they could take control of an SUV over the Internet and steer it into a ditch. Certain vehicle models manufactured from 2013 onwards required a software update to stop them from being controlled remotely. The two well-known experts in the area, Charlie Miller and Chris Valasek, performed the hack by breaking into the Jeep's UConnect system, which is designed to allow motorists to start their car and unlock the doors through an app.

The second example related to Lidar used by autonomous vehicles. Jonathan Petit, Principal Scientist at the software security company Security Innovation, said he was able to take echoes of a fake car and put them at any location, and do the same with a pedestrian or a wall. Using such a system, with a cost of about £40, that uses a kind of Laser pointer, attackers could trick a self-driving car into thinking something is directly ahead of it, causing it to slow down. Or by using numerous false signals, the car would not move at all.

Endnotes

1 At 2015, but note range figures are changing as new technologies and improvements to existing ones are implemented.
2 At the time of writing (2015), the scandal of a manufacturer employing 'defeat' software to meet stringent standards of emission only during standardized test cycles was just hitting the news.
3 Notwithstanding 'cheating' of the figures, we should acknowledge that the emissions from modern vehicles are a fraction of what they were some years ago.
4 Tesla Motors chief Elon Musk called the news of the VW scandal 'obviously bad', but he did note that in clean electricity generation, Germany was ahead of many countries. He also said 'we've reached the limit of what's possible with diesel and gasoline. And so, the time, I think, has come to move to a new generation of technology'.
5 Or just 1p per mile when solar charging is used (see the case study at the end of Chapter 7).
6 Very much depends on the length of journey – an average value was used.
7 https://www.gov.uk/government/publications/driverless-cars-in-the-uk-a-regulatory-review

CHAPTER 2

Safe working, tools and hazard management

2.1 General safety precautions

2.1.1 Introduction

Safe working practices in relation to all automotive systems are essential, for your safety as well as that of others. When working on high-voltage systems, it is even more important to know what you are doing. However, you only have to follow two rules to be safe:

▶ Use your common sense – don't fool about.
▶ If in doubt, seek help.

The following section lists some particular risks when working with electricity or electrical systems, together with suggestions for reducing them. This is known as risk assessment.

> **Definition**
> Risk assessment: a systematic process of evaluating the potential risks that may be involved in an activity or undertaking.

2.1.2 Safety

Electric vehicles (pure or hybrid) use high-voltage batteries so that energy can be delivered to a drive motor or returned to a battery pack in a very short time. The Honda Insight system, for example, uses a 144-V battery module to store re-generated energy. The Toyota Prius originally used a 273.6-V battery pack but this was changed in 2004 to a 201.6-V pack. Voltages of 300 V are now common and some up to 700 V, so clearly there are electrical safety issues when working with these vehicles.

Figure 2.1 High-voltage battery pack (Source: Toyota Media)

EV batteries and motors have high electrical and magnetic potential that can severely injure or kill if not handled correctly. It is essential that you take note of all the warnings and recommended safety measures outlined by manufacturers and in this resource. Any person with a heart pacemaker or any other electronic medical devices should not work on an EV motor since the magnetic effects could be dangerous. In addition, other medical devices such as intravenous insulin injectors or meters can be affected.

Safety First

EV batteries and motors have high electrical and magnetic potential that can severely injure or kill if not handled correctly.

Most of the high-voltage components are combined in a power unit. This is often located behind the rear seats or under the luggage compartment floor (or the whole floor in a Tesla). The unit is a metal box that is completely closed with bolts. A battery module switch, if used, may be located under a small secure cover on the power unit. The electric motor is located between the engine and the transmission or as part of the transmission on a hybrid or on a pure-EV; it is the main driving component. A few vehicles use wheel motors too.

The electrical energy is conducted to or from the motor by thick orange wires. If these wires have to be disconnected, SWITCH OFF or DE-ENERGISE the high-voltage system. This will prevent the risk of electric shock or short circuit of the high-voltage system.

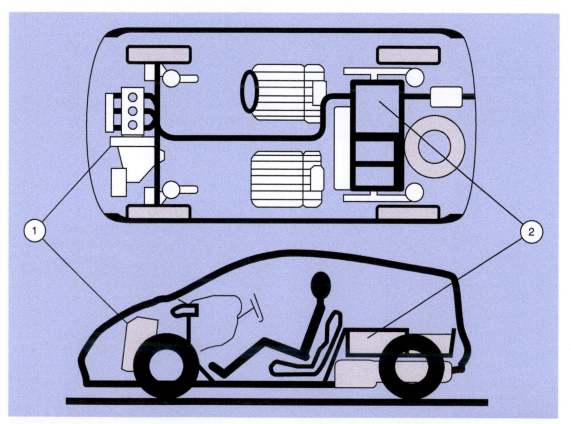

Figure 2.2 Motor and power pack locations on a typical hybrid: 1, integrated motor; 2, power pack

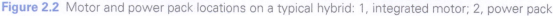

Safety First

High-voltage wires are always orange.

NOTE: Always follow the manufacturer's instructions – it is not possible to outline all variations here.

Figure 2.3 Honda battery pack (integrated power unit)

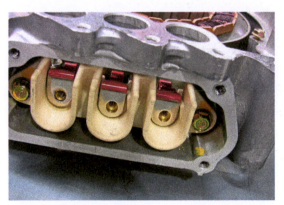

Figure 2.4 Motor power connections

2.1.3 General safety guidance

Before maintenance:

▶ Turn OFF the ignition switch and remove the key.
▶ Switch OFF the battery module switch or de-energize the system.
▶ Wait for 5 minutes before performing any maintenance procedures on the system. This allows any storage capacitors to be discharged.

Figure 2.5 High-voltage battery power switch

During maintenance:

▶ Always wear insulating gloves.
▶ Always use insulated tools when performing service procedures to the high-voltage system. This precaution will prevent accidental short-circuits.

Interruptions:

When maintenance procedures have to be interrupted while some high-voltage components are uncovered or disassembled, make sure that:

▶ The ignition is turned off and the key is removed.
▶ The battery module switch is switched off.
▶ No untrained persons have access to that area and prevent any unintended touching of the components.

After maintenance:

Before switching on or re-energizing the battery module after repairs have been completed, make sure that:

▶ All terminals have been tightened to the specified torque.
▶ No high-voltage wires or terminals have been damaged or shorted to the body.
▶ The insulation resistance between each high-voltage terminal of the part you disassembled and the vehicle's body has been checked.

17

Figure 2.6 High-voltage cables are always orange

Working on electric and hybrid vehicles is not dangerous **IF** the previous guidelines and **manufacturers' procedures** are followed. Before starting work, check the latest information – DON'T take chances. Dying from an electrical shock is not funny.

Crash safety: Electric vehicles are tested to the same high standards as other vehicles currently on UK roads. In February 2011 the first pure-electric car was assessed and passed the renowned Euro NCAP test.

> **Safety First**
> Electric vehicles are tested to the same high standards as other vehicles.

Pedestrian safety: The quietness of EVs is a benefit but can pose a threat to sight- and hearing-impaired people, particularly at low speeds. Having seen a vehicle, pedestrians are capable of reacting to avoid an accident at vehicle speeds up to 15 mph. However, research found that tyre noise will alert pedestrians to a vehicle's presence at speeds greater than 12.4 mph.

2.1.4 General risks and their reduction

Table 2.1 lists some identified risks involved with working on ALL vehicles. The table is by no means exhaustive but serves as a good guide.

2.2 High-voltage safety precautions

2.2.1 Introduction to high voltages

In this section we will consider the differences between AC and DC as well as high and low voltages. This can be confusing, so let's keep it very simple to start with:

The voltages (AC or DC) used on electric vehicles can kill, have killed and will kill again.

Follow all safety procedures and do not touch any electric circuit that is greater than the standard 12 V or 24 V that we are used to, and you will be fine!

> **Safety First**
> Do not touch any electric circuit that is greater than the standard 12 V or 24 V.

2.2.2 Low and high voltage

Low voltage is a relative term, the definition varying by context. Different definitions are used in electric power transmission and distribution, and in the electronics industry. Electrical safety codes define low-voltage circuits that are exempt from the protection required at higher voltages. These definitions vary by country and specific code. The International Electrotechnical Commission (IEC) define voltages as in Table 2.2.

> **Definition**
> IEC: International Electrotechnical Commission.

Table 2.1 Risks and their reduction

Identified risk	Reducing the risk
Electric shock 1	Voltages and the potential for electric shock when working on an EV mean a high risk level – see section 2.2 for more details.
Electric shock 2	Ignition HT is the most likely place to suffer a shock when working on an ICE vehicle; up to 40,000 V is quite normal. Use insulated tools if it is necessary to work on HT circuits with the engine running. Note that high voltages are also present on circuits containing windings due to back emf as they are switched off; a few hundred volts is common. Mains-supplied power tools and their leads should be in good condition and using an earth leakage trip is highly recommended. Only work on HEV and EVs if trained in the high-voltage systems.
Battery acid	Sulfuric acid is corrosive, so always use good personal protective equipment. In this case, overalls and if necessary rubber gloves. A rubber apron is ideal, as are goggles if working with batteries a lot.
Raising or lifting vehicles	Apply brakes and/or chock the wheels and when raising a vehicle on a jack or drive-on lift. Only jack under substantial chassis and suspension structures. Use axle stands in case the jack fails.
Running engines	Do not wear loose clothing; good overalls are ideal. Keep the keys in your possession when working on an engine to prevent others starting it. Take extra care if working near running drive belts.
Exhaust gases	Suitable extraction must be used if the engine is running indoors. Remember it is not just the carbon monoxide that might make you ill or even kill you; other exhaust components could cause asthma or even cancer.
Moving loads	Only lift what is comfortable for you; ask for help if necessary and/or use lifting equipment. As a general guide, do not lift on your own if it feels too heavy!
Short circuits	Use a jump lead with an in-line fuse to prevent damage due to a short when testing. Disconnect the battery (earth lead off first and back on last) if any danger of a short exists. A very high current can flow from a vehicle battery, it will burn you as well as the vehicle.
Fire	Do not smoke when working on a vehicle. Fuel leaks must be attended to immediately. Remember the triangle of fire: Heat–Fuel–Oxygen. Don't let the three sides come together.
Skin problems	Use a good barrier cream and/or latex gloves. Wash skin and clothes regularly.

Table 2.2 IEC voltages

IEC voltage range	AC	DC	Defining risk
High voltage (supply system)	>1000 Vrms*	>1500 V	Electrical arcing
Low voltage (supply system)	50–1000 Vrms	120–1500 V	Electrical shock
Extra-low voltage (supply system)	<50 Vrms	<120 V	Low risk

*The root mean square (rms) is a value characteristic of a continuously varying quantity, such as an AC electric current. This is the effective value in the sense of the value of the direct current that would produce the same power dissipation in a resistive load.

This is why it becomes confusing! For this reason allow me to repeat the obvious:

The voltages (AC or DC) used on electric vehicles can kill, have killed and will kill again.

For the purpose of the work we do on vehicles, low voltage means the 12- or 24-V systems and high voltage refers to the drive battery, motor and other associated components.

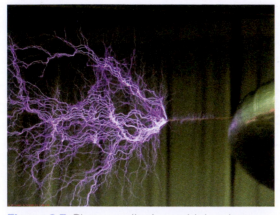

Figure 2.7 Plasma trails due to high voltage

Safety First

For EVs, DC voltages between 60 V and 1500 V are referred to as 'high voltage'.

2.2.3 Personal protective equipment (PPE)

In addition to the normal automotive-related PPE, the following are also recommended for work on high-voltage systems:

▶ overalls with non-conductive fasteners
▶ electrical protection gloves
▶ protective footwear; rubberized soles; non-metallic protective toe caps
▶ goggles (when necessary).

Safety First

Electrical safety gloves are NOT the same as general working gloves.

Figure 2.8 Insulated gloves

2.2.4 High-energy cables and components

Electric vehicles use high-voltage batteries so that energy can be delivered to a drive motor or returned to a battery pack efficiently in a very short time. It is important to be able to correctly identify high-energy cabling and associated components. This is done by:

▶ colouring
▶ warning symbols
▶ warning signs.

The following pictures show the location of high-voltage components and wires (orange) together with some warning stickers:

Figure 2.9 Orange high-voltage cables

Figure 2.10 Danger sticker

Figure 2.11 Warning labels

Figure 2.12 General warning sticker

2.2.5 AC electric shock

When an AC current exceeding 30 mA passes through a part of a human body, the person concerned is in serious danger if the current is not interrupted in a very short time. The protection of persons against electric shock must be provided in conformity with appropriate national standards, statutory regulations, codes of practice, official guides and circulars.

> **Safety First**
>
> When an AC current exceeding 30 mA passes through a part of a human body, the person concerned is in serious danger.

An electric shock is the physical effect of an electric current through the human body. It

affects the muscular, circulatory and respiratory functions and sometimes results in serious burns. The degree of danger for the victim is a function of the size of the current, the parts of the body through which the current passes and the duration of current flow.

IEC publication 60479-1 defines four zones of current-magnitude/time-duration, in each of which the pathophysiological effects are described. Any person coming into contact with live metal risks an electric shock.

Curve C_1 in Figure 2.13 shows that when a current greater than 30 mA passes through a human body from one hand to their feet, the person concerned is likely to be killed, unless the current is interrupted in a relatively short time. This is the real benefit of modern residual current circuit breakers, because they can trip before serious injury or death!

Here are the abstracts from some appropriate international standards:

IEC 60479-1 Abstract: For a given current path through the human body, the danger to persons depends mainly on the magnitude and duration of the current flow. However, the time/current zones specified in this publication are, in many cases, not directly applicable in practice for designing measures of protection against electrical shock. The necessary criterion is the admissible limit of touch voltage (i.e. the product of the current through the body called touch current and the body impedance) as a function of time. The relationship between current and voltage is not linear because the impedance of the human body varies with the touch voltage, and data on this relationship is therefore required. The different parts of the human body (such as the skin, blood, muscles, other tissues and joints) present to the electric current a certain impedance composed of resistive and capacitive components. The values of body impedance depend on a number of factors and, in particular, on current path, on touch voltage, duration of current flow, frequency, degree of moisture of the skin,

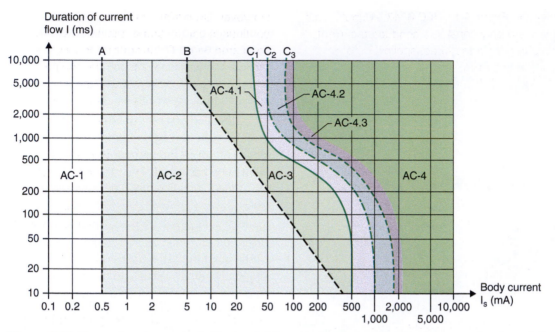

Figure 2.13 Zones time/current of effects of AC current on human body when passing from left hand to feet

AC-1 zone: imperceptible; AC-2 zone: perceptible, AC-3 zone: reversible effects, muscular contraction; AC-4 zone: possibility of irreversible effects; AC-4.1 zone: up to 5% probability of heart fibrillation; AC-4.2 zone: up to 50% probability of heart fibrillation; AC-4.3 zone: more than 50% probability of heart fibrillation. A curve: threshold of perception of current; B curve: threshold of muscular reactions; C_1 curve: threshold of 0% probability of ventricular fibrillation; C_2 curve: threshold of 5% probability of ventricular fibrillation; C_3 curve: threshold of 50% probability of ventricular fibrillation. (Source: http://www.electrical-installation.org/enwiki/Electric_shock)

surface area of contact, pressure exerted and temperature. The impedance values indicated in this technical specification result from a close examination of the experimental results available from measurements carried out principally on corpses and on some living persons. This technical specification has the status of a basic safety publication in accordance with IEC Guide 104. (Source https://webstore.iec.ch/home)

IEC 60479-2 Abstract: [This] technical specification describes the effects on the human body when a sinusoidal alternating current in the frequency range above 100 Hz passes through it. The effects of current passing through the human body for

▶ alternating sinusoidal current with d.c. components
▶ alternating sinusoidal current with phase control
▶ alternating sinusoidal current with multicycle control, are given but are only deemed applicable for alternating current frequencies from 15 Hz up to 100 Hz.

This standard furthermore describes the effects of current passing through the human body in the form of single unidirectional rectangular impulses, sinusoidal impulses and impulses resulting from capacitor discharges. The values specified are deemed to be applicable for impulse durations from 0.1 ms up to and including 10 ms. For impulse durations greater than 10 ms, the values given in Figure 20 of IEC 60479-1 apply. This standard only considers conducted current resulting from the direct application of a source of current to the body, as does IEC 60479-1 and IEC 60479-3. It does not consider current induced within the body caused by its exposure to an external electromagnetic field. This third edition cancels and replaces the second edition, published in 1987, and constitutes a technical revision. The major changes with regard to the previous edition are as follows:

▶ the report has been completed with additional information on effects of current passing through the human body for alternating sinusoidal current with d.c. components, alternating sinusoidal current with phase control, alternating sinusoidal current with multicycle control in the frequency range from 15 Hz up to 100 Hz
▶ an estimation of the equivalent current threshold for mixed frequencies
▶ the effect of repeated pulses (bursts) of current on the threshold of ventricular fibrillation
▶ effects of electric current through the immersed human body. (Source https://webstore.iec.ch/home)

2.2.6 DC electric shock

The three basic factors that determine what kind of shock you experience when current passes through the body are:

▶ size of the current
▶ duration
▶ frequency.

Direct currents actually have zero frequency, as the current is constant. However, there are physical effects during electrocution no matter what type of current. The factor deciding the effects of the AC and DC current is the path the current takes through the body. If it is from the hand to the foot, but it does not pass through the heart, then the effects might not be lethal.

However, DC current causes a single continuous contraction of the muscles compared with AC current, which will make a series of contractions depending on the frequency. In terms of fatalities, both kill but more milliamps are required of DC current than AC current at the same voltage.

If the current takes the path from hand to hand, thus passing through the heart, it can result in fibrillation of the heart. It affects the ability of the heart to pump blood, resulting in brain damage and eventual cardiac arrest.

Definition
Fibrillation: a condition when all the heart muscles start moving independently in a disorganized manner.

Either AC or DC currents can cause fibrillation of the heart at high enough levels. This typically takes place at 30 mA of AC (rms, 50–60 Hz) or 300–500 mA of DC.

Facts about electric shock

▶ It is the magnitude of current and the duration that produces effect. That means a low-value current for a long duration can also be fatal. The current/time limit for a victim to survive at 500 mA is 0.2 seconds and at 50 mA is 2 seconds.
▶ The voltage of the electric supply is only important because it ascertains the magnitude of the current. As Voltage = Current × Resistance, the bodily resistance is an important factor. Sweaty or wet persons have a lower body resistance and so they can be fatally electrocuted at lower voltages.
▶ Let-go current is the highest current at which the subject can release a conductor. Above this limit, involuntary clasping of the

conductor occurs: it is 22 mA in AC and 88 mA in DC.

▶ Severity of electric shock depends on body resistance, voltage, current, path of the current, area of contact and duration of contact.

Heating due to resistance can cause extensive and deep burns; damaging temperatures are reached in a few seconds.

An arc flash is the light and heat produced from an electric arc supplied with sufficient electrical energy to cause substantial damage, harm, fire or injury. Note that welding arcs can turn steel into a liquid with an average of only 24 V DC. When an uncontrolled arc forms at very high voltages, arc flashes can produce deafening noises, supersonic concussive-forces, super-heated shrapnel, temperatures far greater than the Sun's surface, and intense, high-energy radiation capable of vaporizing nearby materials.

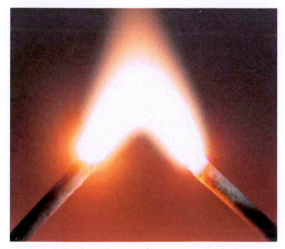

Figure 2.14 Electrical arc

In summary and in addition to the potential for electric shock, careless work on electrical systems (at any voltage) can result in:

▶ fire
▶ explosion

▶ chemical release
▶ gases/fumes.

2.2.7 Protection devices

The first-line protection against high voltages includes direct methods such as:

▶ enclosure (keeping things covered)
▶ insulation (always orange-coloured)
▶ location (positions to prevent accidental tampering).

The four main indirect methods to protect against high voltages and excess current flow are:

▶ fuses
▶ miniature circuit breakers (MCBs)
▶ residual current devices (RCDs)
▶ residual current breaker with overcurrents (RCBOs).

These four methods will now be outlined in more detail.

A fuse is a deliberate weak link in an electrical circuit that acts as a sacrificial device to provide overcurrent protection. It is a metal wire or strip that melts when too much current flows through it and therefore it breaks the circuit. Short circuits, overloading, mismatched loads or device failure are the main reasons for excessive current.

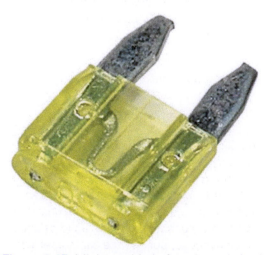

Figure 2.15 Miniature blade fuse (actual size is about 15 mm)

An MCB (miniature circuit breaker) does the same job as a fuse in that it automatically switches off the electrical circuit during an overload condition. MCBs are more sensitive to overcurrent than fuses. They are quick and easy to reset by simply switching them back on. Most MCBs work by either the thermal or electromagnetic effect of overcurrent. The thermal operation is achieved with a bimetallic strip. The deflection of the bimetallic strip as it is heated by excess current releases a mechanical latch and opens the circuit. The electromagnetic type uses magnetism to operate the contacts. During short-circuit condition, the sudden increase in current causes a plunger to move and open the contacts.

Figure 2.16 RCD circuit breaker

Definition

MCB: miniature circuit breaker.

An RCD (residual current device) is designed to prevent fatal electric shock if a live connection is touched. RCDs offer a level of personal protection that ordinary fuses and circuit breakers cannot provide. If it detects electricity flowing down an unintended path, such as through a person who has touched a live part, the device will switch the circuit off very quickly, significantly reducing the risk of death or serious injury.

Definition

RCD: residual current device.

An RCBO (residual current breaker with overcurrent) is a type of circuit breaker designed to protect life in the same way as the RCD, but it also protects against an overload on a circuit. An RCBO will normally have two circuits for detecting an imbalance and an overload, but use the same interrupt method.

2.3 Safe work process

2.3.1 Risks of working with EVs

EVs introduce hazards into the workplace in addition to those normally associated with the repair and maintenance of vehicles, roadside recovery and other vehicle-related activities. These include:

▶ the presence of high-voltage components and cabling capable of delivering a fatal electric shock
▶ the storage of electrical energy with the potential to cause explosion or fire
▶ components that may retain a dangerous voltage even when a vehicle is switched off
▶ electric motors or the vehicle itself that may move unexpectedly due to magnetic forces within the motors
▶ manual handling risks associated with battery replacement
▶ the potential for the release of explosive gases and harmful liquids if batteries are damaged or incorrectly modified
▶ the possibility of people being unaware of vehicles moving, because when electrically driven they are silent in operation

▶ the potential for the electrical systems on the vehicle to affect medical devices such as pacemakers and insulin controllers.

Control of substances hazardous to health (COSHH) regulations with regard to hazardous battery chemicals and compounds exist to assist with how to deal with leakage from battery packs.

However, batteries are in protective cases and even if the case is damaged, batteries will not leak a significant amount of electrolyte. NiMH and Li-ion are dry-cell batteries, and will only produce a few drops per cell if crushed. Some models may leak coolant and this should not be confused with electrolyte.

2.3.2 Work categories

Four categories of work have been identified. These are:

▶ Valeting, sales and other lower risk activities.
▶ Incident response, including emergency services and vehicle recovery.
▶ Maintenance and repair, excluding high-voltage electrical systems.
▶ Working on high-voltage electrical systems.

Based on information from HSE,[1] these categories are outlined below with the suggested primary controls.

Valeting, sales and other lower risk activities

Remote operation keys that only need to be close to the vehicle for the vehicle to be powered up should be kept away from vehicles. This is to prevent the vehicle from accidentally moving. People who move these vehicles around the workplace should be aware that others may not hear it approaching them. Similarly, people who work around EVs should be aware that they may move without warning. Pressure washing has the potential to damage high-voltage electrical components

and cables. High-voltage cables are usually coloured orange. Refer to guidance from manufacturers before valeting any under body areas, including the engine bay.

Incident response, including emergency services and vehicle recovery

Vehicles should be visually checked for signs of damage to high-voltage electrical components or cabling (usually coloured orange). Consider whether the integrity of the battery is likely to have been compromised. Shorting or loss of coolant may present ignition sources in the event of fuel spillage. If the vehicle is damaged or faulty, and if safe to do so, isolate the high-voltage battery system using the isolation device on the vehicle. Refer to the manufacturer's instructions for guidance. During any recovery onto a recovery vehicle, the remote operation key should be removed to a suitable distance and the standard 12/24 V battery disconnected to prevent the vehicle from being activated/started. Have access to reliable sources of information for specific vehicle types. For example, mobile data terminals used by fire and rescue services or by reference to manufacturer's data. Avoid towing EV vehicles unless it can be determined that it is safe to do so. Dangerous voltages can be generated by movement of the drive wheels.

Maintenance and repair, excluding high-voltage electrical systems

Refer to vehicle-specific sources of information from the manufacturer and trade bodies to identify precautions necessary to prevent danger. Remote operation keys should be kept away from the vehicle to prevent any accidental operation of electrical systems and accidental movement of the vehicle. Keys should be locked away with access controlled by the person working on the vehicle. If the key is required during the work, the person working on the vehicle should check that the vehicle is in a safe condition before the key is retrieved. Visually check the vehicle for signs of damage to high-voltage cabling (usually coloured orange) or electrical components before starting any work on the vehicle. Unless a specific task requires the vehicle to be energized, always isolate or disconnect the high-voltage battery in accordance with the manufacturer's instructions. Determine the locations of high-voltage cables before carrying out tasks such as panel replacement, cutting or welding. Take appropriate precautions to prevent them from being damaged.

Working on high-voltage electrical systems

Refer to vehicle-specific sources of information from the manufacturer (and trade bodies) to identify precautions you need to implement that are necessary to prevent danger. Remote operation keys should always be kept away from the vehicle to prevent any accidental operation of electrical systems and accidental movement of the vehicle. Keys should be locked away with access controlled by the person working on the vehicle. If the key is required during the work, the person working on the vehicle should check that the vehicle is in a safe condition before the key is retrieved. Visually check the vehicle for signs of damage to high-voltage electrical components or cabling (usually coloured orange). High-voltage systems should be isolated (that is, the power disconnected and secured such that it cannot be inadvertently switched back on) and proven dead by testing before any work is undertaken. Always isolate and lock off the source of electricity, and in accordance with manufacturer's instructions. You must always test and prove that any high-voltage cable or electrical component is dead before carrying out any work on it.

Even when isolated, vehicle batteries and other components may still contain large amounts of energy and retain a high voltage. Only suitable tools and test equipment should be used. These may include electrically insulated tools and test equipment compliant with GS38.

Some electronic components may store dangerous amounts of electricity even when the vehicle is off and the battery isolated. Refer to manufacturers data on how to discharge stored energy.

> **Safety First**
> Some electronic components may store dangerous amounts of electricity even when the vehicle is off and the battery isolated.

There may be circumstances (e.g. after collision damage) where it has not been possible to fully isolate the high-voltage electrical systems and to discharge the stored energy in the system. Refer to the manufacturer's instructions about what control measures should be implemented before attempting to carry out further remedial work.

Battery packs are susceptible to high temperatures. The vehicle will typically be labelled advising of its maximum temperature and this should be considered when carrying operations such as painting, where booth temperatures may exceed this limit. Measures should be implemented to alleviate any potential risks, e.g. by removing the batteries or by providing insulation to limit any temperature increase in the batteries.

Working on live electrical equipment should **only** be considered when there is no other way for work to be undertaken. Even then, it should only be considered if it is both reasonable and safe to do so. You should consider the risks for working on this live equipment and implement suitable precautions, including, as a final measure, the use of personal protective equipment (PPE). Refer to the manufacturer's instructions for precautions when working live, including their PPE requirements.

It may be necessary to locate the vehicle within an area that can be secured such that people who could be put at risk are not able to approach the vehicle. Warning signs should be used to make people aware of the dangers.

The following section will outline some further practical advice relating to this level of work.

2.3.3 Before work starts

Electrical work should not start until protective measures have been taken against electric shock, short-circuits and arcs. Work should not be performed on live parts of electrical systems and equipment. For this purpose, these systems and equipment must be placed in the non-live state before and for the duration of the work. This is achieved by following these three steps:

1 Isolate

▶ Switch off the ignition.
▶ Remove service plug or switch off main battery switch.
▶ Remove fuses where appropriate.
▶ Disconnect charging plug.

2 Safeguard against reconnection

▶ Remove the ignition key and prevent unauthorized access to it.
▶ Store the service plug against unauthorized access/safeguard the main battery switch against reconnection, for example by means of a lock of some sort.
▶ Observe any additional manufacturer or company instructions.

3 Verify the non-live state

▶ The provisions of the vehicle manufacturer must be observed for verification of the non-live state.
▶ Suitable voltage testers or test apparatus specific to the manufacturer must be used.
▶ Until the non-live state has been verified, the system is to be assumed to be live.
▶ Wait an additional 5 minutes before performing any maintenance procedures on

the system. This allows storage capacitors to be discharged.

▶ Make sure that the junction board terminal voltage is nearly 0 V.

> **Safety First**
> A non-live state is achieved by following three steps:
> 1. Isolate.
> 2. Safeguard against reconnection.
> 3. Verify the non-live state.

Figure 2.17 High-voltage cable

2.3.4 During the work

During work it is important to prevent shorts to earth and short circuits between components – even though they are disconnected. Remember a battery that has been disconnected is still live! If necessary, you should shroud or cover adjacent live parts.

▶ Always wear insulating gloves.

Always use insulated tools when performing service procedures to the high-voltage system. This precaution will prevent accidental short-circuits.

2.3.5 Interruption to work

When maintenance procedures have to be interrupted while some high-voltage

Figure 2.18 Insulated gloves

components are uncovered or disassembled, make sure that:

▶ The ignition is turned off and the key is removed.
▶ The battery module switch is switched off.
▶ No untrained persons have access to that area.
▶ Any unintended touching of the components is prevented.

2.3.6 Completion of work

Once the work has been completed, the safety process can be lifted. All tools, materials and other equipment must first be removed from the site of the work and the hazard area. Guards removed before the start of work must be properly replaced and warning signs removed.

Before switching on the battery module switch after repairs have been completed, make sure that:

▶ All terminals have been tightened to the specified torque.
▶ No high-voltage wires or terminals have been damaged or shorted to the body.
▶ The insulation resistance between each high-voltage terminal of the part you disassembled and the vehicle's body has been checked.

Safety First
Working on electric vehicles is not dangerous IF the previous guidelines and

manufacturers' procedures are followed. Before starting work, check the latest information – DON'T take chances. Dying from an electrical shock is not funny.

2.4 Hazard management

To manage hazards you should also be able to identify vehicles and components and be aware of high voltages as covered in other sections of this book.

2.4.1 Initial assessment

First responders should carry out an initial visual risk assessment. Personal protection should be worn. Steps should then be taken to secure the safety of themselves and others at incident scenes involving EVs. For example, people who may be at risk are:

▶ occupants
▶ on-lookers
▶ recovery personnel
▶ emergency service personnel.

Vehicles damaged by fire or impact can result in these risks:

▶ electric shock
▶ burns
▶ arc flash
▶ arc blast
▶ fire
▶ explosion
▶ chemicals
▶ gases/fumes.

It may therefore be necessary to implement evacuation procedures and site protection.

Safety First
First responders should carry out an initial visual risk assessment.

2.4.2 Fire

There are substantial differences in the designs of EVs and their component parts from different manufacturers. Having information specific to the manufacturer and the vehicle being worked on is important in identifying what actions are necessary to work safely.

As well as the obvious need to take personal precautions, incorrect maintenance operations when dealing with EV high-voltage systems can result in damage to the vehicle, other people and property.

When working on EVs, normal protection should be used such as wing covers, floor mats etc. Disposal of waste materials is no different from ICE vehicles, with the exception of the high-voltage battery. If high battery stacks/modules develop a fault, it is possible that thermal runaway can occur. Thermal runaway refers to a situation where an increase in temperature changes the conditions in a way that causes a further increase in temperature, often leading to a destructive result. It is a kind of uncontrolled positive feedback.

Fires may occur in an EV high-voltage battery, or a fire may extend to the battery. Most EV batteries currently on the road are Li-ion, but NiMH batteries are popular too. There is a range of guidance concerning the tactics for dealing with EVs in which the battery is burning. However, the general consensus is that the use of water or other standard agents does not present an electrical hazard to firefighting personnel.

If a high-voltage battery catches fire, it will require a large, sustained volume of water. If a Li-ion high-voltage battery is involved in fire, there is a possibility that it could reignite after extinguishment, so thermal imaging should be used to monitor the battery. If there is no immediate threat to life or property, it is recommended that a battery fire be allowed to burn out.

Another further consideration with an EV fire is that the automatic built-in measures to prevent electrocution from high voltages may be compromised. For example, the normally open relays for the high-voltage system could possibly fail in a closed position if they sustain damage due to heat, for example.

> **Safety First**
> If a battery fire occurs, it should be left to the Fire Brigade to deal with.

2.5 Tools and equipment

2.5.1 Introduction

By way of an introduction, Tables 2.3 and 2.4 lists some of the basic words and descriptions relating to tools and equipment.

2.5.2 Hand tools

Using hand tools is something you will learn by experience, but an important first step is to understand the purpose of the common types. This section therefore starts by listing some of the more popular tools, with examples of their use, and ends with some general advice and instructions.

Practise until you understand the use and purpose of the following tools when working on vehicles:

General advice and instructions for the use of hand tools (supplied by Snap-on):

▶ Only use a tool for its intended purpose.
▶ Always use the correct size tool for the job you are doing.
▶ Pull a spanner or wrench rather than pushing whenever possible.
▶ Do not use a file, or similar, without a handle.
▶ Keep all tools clean and replace them in a suitable box or cabinet.

Table 2.3 Tools and equipment

Hand tools	Spanners and hammers and screwdrivers, and all the other basic bits!
Special tools	A collective term for items not held as part of a normal tool kit. Or items required for just one specific job.
Test equipment	In general, this means measuring equipment. Most tests involve measuring something and comparing the result of that measurement with data. The devices can range from a simple ruler to an engine analyser.
Dedicated test equipment	Some equipment will only test one specific type of system. The large manufacturers supply equipment dedicated to their vehicles. For example, a diagnostic device that plugs in to a certain type of fuel injection engine control unit.
Accuracy	Careful and exact, free from mistakes or errors and adhering closely to a standard.
Calibration	Checking the accuracy of a measuring instrument.
Serial port	A connection to an electronic control unit, a diagnostic tester or computer for example. Serial means the information is passed in a 'digital' string, like pushing black and white balls through a pipe in a certain order.
Code reader or scanner	This device reads the 'black and white balls' mentioned above or the on–off electrical signals, and converts them into language we can understand.
Combined diagnostic and information system	Usually now PC-based, these systems can be used to carry out tests on vehicle systems and they also contain an electronic workshop manual. Test sequences guided by the computer can also be carried out.
Oscilloscope	The main part of the 'scope' is the display, which is like a TV or computer screen. A scope is a voltmeter, but instead of readings in numbers it shows the voltage levels by a trace or mark on the screen. The marks on the screen can move and change very quickly, allowing us to see the way voltages change.

Figure 2.19 Snap-on tool kit

Figure 2.20 Combination spanners (wrenches)

▶ Do not use a screwdriver as a pry bar.
▶ Look after your tools and they will look after you!

2.5.3 Test equipment

To remove, refit and adjust components to ensure the vehicle system operates within specification is a summary of almost all

the work you will be doing. The use, care, calibration and storage of test equipment are therefore very important. In this sense, 'test equipment' means:

▶ Measuring equipment – such as a micrometer.
▶ Hand instruments – such as a spring balance.

31

Table 2.4 Hand tools

Hand tool	Example uses and/or notes
Adjustable spanner (wrench)	An ideal standby tool, useful for holding one end of a nut and bolt.
Open-ended spanner	Use for nuts and bolts where access is limited or a ring spanner can't be used.
Ring spanner	The best tool for holding hexagon bolts or nuts. If fitted correctly it will not slip and damage both you and the bolt head.
Torque wrench	Essential for correct tightening of fixings. The wrench can be set in most cases to 'click' when the required torque has been reached. Many fitters think it is clever not to use a torque wrench. Good technicians realize the benefits.
Socket wrench	Often contains a ratchet to make operation far easier.
Hexagon socket spanner	Sockets are ideal for many jobs where a spanner can't be used. In many cases a socket is quicker and easier than a spanner. Extensions and swivel joints are also available to help reach that awkward bolt.
Air wrench	These are often referred to as wheel guns. Air-driven tools are great for speeding up your work, but it is easy to damage components because an air wrench is very powerful. Only special, extra strong, high-quality sockets should be used.
Blade (engineer's) screwdriver	Simple common screw heads. Use the correct size!
Pozidrive, Phillips and cross-head screwdrivers	Better grip is possible, particularly with the Pozidrive, but learn not to confuse the two very similar types. The wrong type will slip and damage will occur.
Torx®	Similar to a hexagon tool like an Allen key but with further flutes cut in the side. It can transmit good torque.
Special purpose wrenches	Many different types are available. As an example, mole grips are very useful tools because they hold like pliers but can lock in position.
Pliers	These are used for gripping and pulling or bending. They are available in a wide variety of sizes. These range from snipe nose, for electrical work, to engineers pliers for larger jobs such as fitting split pins.
Levers	Used to apply a very large force to a small area. If you remember this, you will realize how, if incorrectly applied, it is easy to damage a component.
Hammer	Anybody can hit something with a hammer, but exactly how hard and where is a great skill to learn!

► Electrical meters – such as a digital multimeter (DMM) or an oscilloscope.

The operation and care of this equipment will vary with different types. I suggest, therefore, that you should always read the manufacturer's instructions carefully before use or if you have a problem. The following list sets out good general guidelines:

► Follow the manufacturer's instructions at all times.
► Handle with care: do not drop, keep the instrument in its box.

Figure 2.21 Digital multimeter in use

- ▶ Ensure regular calibration: check for accuracy.
- ▶ Understand how to interpret results: if in doubt, ask!

One of my favourite pieces of test equipment is the PicoScope. This is an oscilloscope that works through a computer. It will test all engine management systems and other electrical and electronic devices. Check out https://www.picoauto.com for more information.

Figure 2.22 Automotive PicoScope (Source: PicoTech Media)

Key Fact

An oscilloscope draws a graph of voltage against time.

Figure 2.23 shows a signal from an inductive sensor taken using the PicoScope.

For EV work, electrical meters such as a voltmeter should be rated to a minimum 600 CAT. III or CAT. IV.

2.5.4 Workshop equipment

Safety First

For EV work, electrical meters such as a voltmeter should be rated to a minimum 600 CAT. III or CAT. IV.

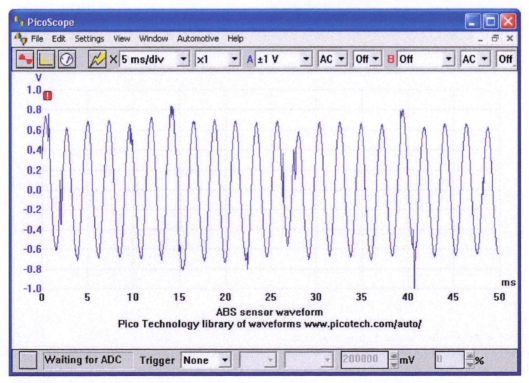

Figure 2.23 Waveform display from the PicoScope

Table 2.5 Examples of workshop equipment

Equipment	Common use
Ramp or hoist	Used for raising a vehicle off the floor. They can be a two-post wheel-free type, and other designs include four-post and scissor types where the mechanism is built in to the workshop floor.
Jack and axle stands	A trolley jack is used for raising part of a vehicle such as the front or one corner or side. It should always be positioned under suitable jacking points, axle or suspension mountings. When raised, stands must always be used in case the seals in the jack fail causing the vehicle to drop.
Air gun	A high-pressure air supply is common in most workshops. An air gun (or wheel gun) is used for removing wheel nuts or bolts. Note that when replacing wheel fixings it is essential to use a torque wrench.
Electric drill	The electric drill is just one example of electric power tools used for automotive repair. Note that it should never be used in wet or damp conditions.
Parts washer	There are a number of companies that supply a parts washer and change the fluid it contains at regular intervals.
Steam cleaner	Steam cleaners can be used to remove protective wax from new vehicles as well as to clean grease, oil and road deposits from cars in use. They are supplied with electricity, water and a fuel to run a heater, so caution is necessary.
Electric welder	There are a number of forms of welding used in repair shops. The two most common are metal inert gas (MIG) and manual metal arc (MMA).
Gas welder	Gas welders are popular in workshops because they can also be used as a general source of heat, for example, when heating a flywheel ring gear.
Engine crane	A crane of some type is essential for removing the engine on most vehicles. It usually consists of two legs with wheels that go under the front of the car and a jib that is operated by a hydraulic ram. Chains or straps are used to connect to or wrap around the engine.
Transmission jack	On many vehicles the transmission is removed from underneath. The car is supported on a lift and then the transmission jack is rolled underneath.

In addition to hand tools and test equipment, most workshops will also have a range of equipment for lifting and supporting as well as electrical or air-operated tools. Table 2.5 lists some examples of common workshop equipment together with typical uses.

2.5.5 High-voltage tools

Many manufacturers have designed ranges of tools that are designed to protect mechanics from the high-voltage systems in electric vehicles. The well-known company Facom was able to use its experience of manufacturing 1000 V insulated tools to produce a selection of products that comply with EN 60900. In fact, the tools were tested individually at 10,000 V for 10 seconds at a time.

Figure 2.24 Trolley jack and axle stands (Source: Snap–on Tools)

The range comprises a full complement of insulated tools, including ratchets, sockets, screwdrivers, spanners, T-wrenches, pliers and

Figure 2.25 Insulated tools are essential to reduce risk of harm to technicians and vehicles (Source: Facom Tools)

an insulated torque wrench. Latex insulation gloves, protective outer gloves and a secure roller cabinet are also available.

An important safety feature of the EV tool range is the two-step colour-code system. If any of the orange-coloured outer insulation material is missing, a bright yellow interior is exposed, clearly indicating to the technician that the tool is no longer safe for use.

2.5.6 On-board diagnostics

On-board diagnostics (OBD) is a generic term referring to a vehicle's self-diagnostic and reporting system. OBD systems give the vehicle owner or a technician access to information for various vehicle systems.

Definition
OBD: on-board diagnostics.

The amount of diagnostic information available via OBD has varied considerably since its introduction in the early 1980s. Early versions of OBD would simply illuminate a malfunction indicator light if a problem was detected, but did not provide any information about the problem. Modern OBD systems use a standardized digital communications port to provide real-time data in addition to a standardized series of diagnostic trouble codes, which allow a technician to identify and remedy faults on the vehicle. The current

versions are OBD2 and in Europe EOBD2. The standard OBD2 and EOBD2 are quite similar.

Figure 2.26 Diagnostic data link connector (DLC)

All OBD2 pin-outs use the same connector but different pins are utilized, with the exception of pin 4 (battery ground) and pin 16 (battery positive).

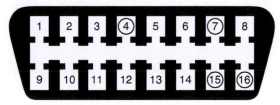

Figure 2.27 Connector pin-out: 4, battery ground/earth; 7, K line; 15, L line; t, battery positive

Author's Note: This section will outline the use and features of the Bosch KTS 650 diagnostic system. I have chosen this particular tool as a case study because it provides everything that a technician needs to diagnose faults, but at a professional price. The system is a combination of a scanner, multimeter, oscilloscope and information system (when used with Esitronic).

For more information, visit: http://www.bosch.com

Modern vehicles are being fitted with more and more electronics. That complicates diagnosis and repair, especially as the individual systems are often interlinked. The work of service and repair workshops is being fundamentally changed. Automotive engineers have to continually update their knowledge of vehicle electronics. But this is no longer sufficient on its own. The ever-growing number of electrical and electronic vehicle components is no longer manageable without modern diagnostic technology, such as the latest range of KTS control unit diagnostic testers from Bosch. In addition, more and more of the previously purely mechanical interventions on vehicles now require the use of electronic control units, for example, the oil change.

Figure 2.28 Diagnostic system in use (Source: Bosch Media)

Vehicle workshops operate in a very competitive environment and have to be able to carry out demanding repair work efficiently, to a high standard and at a competitive price on a wide range of vehicle makes and models. The Bosch KTS control-unit diagnostic testers, used in conjunction with the comprehensive Esitronic workshop software, offer the best possible basis for efficient diagnosis and repair of electrical and electronic components. The testers are available in different versions, suited to the individual requirements of the particular workshop:

The portable KTS 650 with built-in computer and touch-screen can be used anywhere. It has a 20-GB hard drive, a touch-screen and a DVD drive. When being used away from the workshop, the power supply of the KTS 650 comes from the vehicle battery or from rechargeable batteries with 1–2 hours' service life. For use in the workshop, there is a tough wheeled trolley with a built-in charger unit. As well as having all the necessary adapter cables, the trolley can also carry an inkjet printer and an external keyboard, which can be connected to the KTS 650 via the usual PC interfaces.

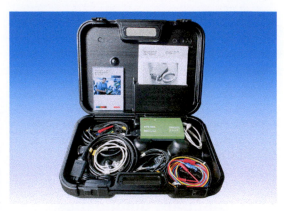

Figure 2.29 Adapter and cable kit (Source: Bosch Media)

The Esitronic software package accounts for the in-depth diagnostic capacity of the KTS diagnostic testers. With the new common rail diesel systems, for example, even special functions such as quantitative comparison and compression testing can be carried out. This allows for reliable diagnosis of the faulty part and avoids unnecessary dismantling and re-assembly or the removal and replacement of non-faulty parts.

Modern diagnostic equipment is also indispensable when workshops have to deal with braking systems with electronic control systems such as ABS, ASR and ESP. Nowadays, the diagnostic tester may even be needed for bleeding a brake system. EV de-energization procedures may also be included in due course.

In addition, KTS and Esitronic allow independent workshops to reset the service interval warning, for example after an oil change or a routine service, or perhaps find the correct default position for the headlamps after one or both of these have been replaced.

As well as ISO norms for European vehicles and SAE norms for American and Japanese vehicles, the KTS testers can also deal with CAN norms for checking modern CAN Bus systems, which are coming into use more and more frequently in new vehicles. The testers are connected directly to the diagnostics socket via a serial diagnostics interface by means of an adapter cable.

The system automatically detects the control unit and reads out the actual values, the error memory and other controller-specific data. Thanks to a built-in multiplexer, it is even easier for the user to diagnose the various systems in the vehicle. The multiplexer determines the connection in the diagnostics socket so that communication is established correctly with the selected control unit.

Endnote

1 http://www.hse.gov.uk

CHAPTER 3

Electrical and electronic principles

3.1 Basic electrical principles

3.1.1 Introduction

To understand electricity properly we must start by finding out what it really is. This means we must think very small. The molecule is the smallest part of matter that can be recognized as that particular matter. Sub-division of the molecule results in atoms, which are the smallest part of matter. An element is a substance that comprises atoms of one kind only.

The atom consists of a central nucleus made up of protons and neutrons. Around this nucleus orbit electrons, like planets around the sun. The neutron is a very small part of the nucleus. It has equal positive and negative charges and is therefore neutral and has no polarity. The proton is another small part of the nucleus, it is positively charged. The neutron is neutral and the proton is positively charged, which means that the nucleus of the atom is positively charged. The electron is an even smaller part of the atom, and is negatively charged. It orbits the nucleus and is held in orbit by the attraction of the positively charged

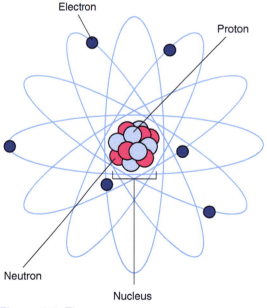

Figure 3.1 The atom

proton. All electrons are similar no matter what type of atom they come from.

When atoms are in a balanced state, the number of electrons orbiting the nucleus equals the number of protons. The atoms of some materials have electrons that are

Figure 3.2 Electronic components have made technology such as the 200+ km/h Tesla Roadster possible (Source: Tesla Motors)

easily detached from the parent atom and can therefore join an adjacent atom. In so doing, these atoms move an electron from the parent atom to another atom (like polarities repel) and so on through material. This is a random movement and the electrons involved are called free electrons.

Materials are called conductors if the electrons can move easily. In some materials it is extremely difficult to move electrons from their parent atoms. These materials are called insulators.

> **Definition**
> Materials are called insulators if the electrons are difficult to move.

> **Definition**
> Materials are called conductors if the electrons can move easily.

3.1.2 Electron and conventional flow

If an electrical pressure (electromotive force or voltage) is applied to a conductor, a directional movement of electrons will

take place (for example, when connecting a battery to a wire). This is because the electrons are attracted to the positive side and repelled from the negative side. Certain conditions are necessary to cause an electron flow:

▶ A pressure source, e.g. from a battery or generator.
▶ A complete conducting path in which the electrons can move (e.g. wires).

Figure 3.3 A simple electrical circuit

An electron flow is termed an electric current. Figure 3.3 shows a simple electric circuit where the battery positive terminal is connected, through a switch and lamp, to the battery negative terminal. With the switch open, the chemical energy of the battery will remove electrons from the positive terminal to the negative terminal via the battery. This leaves the positive terminal with fewer electrons and the negative terminal with a surplus of electrons. An electrical pressure therefore exists between the battery terminals.

> **Definition**
> An electron flow is termed an electric current.

With the switch closed, the surplus electrons at the negative terminal will flow through the lamp back to the electron-deficient positive terminal. The lamp will light and the chemical energy of the battery will keep the electrons moving in this circuit from negative to positive. This movement from negative to positive is called the electron flow and will continue while the battery supplies the pressure – in other words, while it remains charged.

▶ Electron flow is from negative to positive.

It was once thought, however, that current flowed from positive to negative and this convention is still followed for most practical purposes. Therefore, although this current flow is not correct, the most important point is that we all follow the same convention.

▶ Conventional current flow is said to be from positive to negative.

Key Fact

Conventional current flow is said to be from positive to negative.

3.1.3 Effects of current flow

When a current flows in a circuit, it can produce only three effects:

▶ Heating.
▶ Magnetic.
▶ Chemical.

The heating effect is the basis of electrical components such as lights and heater plugs. The magnetic effect is the basis of relays and motors and generators. The chemical effect is the basis for electroplating and battery charging.

In the circuit shown in Figure 3.4, the chemical energy of the battery is first converted to electrical energy, and then into heat energy in the lamp filament.

The three electrical effects are reversible. Heat applied to a thermocouple will cause a small electromotive force and therefore a small current to flow. Practical use of this is mainly in instruments. A coil of wire rotated in the

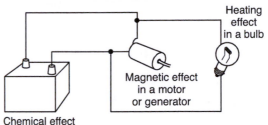

Figure 3.4 A bulb, motor and battery – heating, magnetic and chemical effects

field of a magnet will produce an electromotive force and can cause current to flow. This is the basis of a generator. Chemical action, such as in a battery, produces an electromotive force, which can cause current to flow.

Key Fact

The three electrical effects are reversible.

3.1.4 Fundamental quantities

In Figure 3.5, the number of electrons through the lamp every second is described as the rate of flow. The cause of the electron flow is the electrical pressure. The lamp produces an opposition to the rate of flow set up by the electrical pressure. Power is the rate of doing work, or changing energy from one form to another. These quantities, as well as several others, are given names, as shown in Table 3.1.

If the voltage pressure applied to the circuit was increased but the lamp resistance stayed the same, then the current would also increase. If the voltage was maintained constant but the lamp was changed for one with a higher resistance, the current would decrease. Ohm's Law describes this relationship.

Ohm's Law states that in a closed circuit 'current is proportional to the voltage and inversely proportional to the resistance'. When 1 V causes 1 A to flow, the power used (P) is 1 W.

Using symbols this means:

Voltage = Current × Resistance

($V = IR$) or ($R = V/I$) or ($I = V/R$)

Power = Voltage − Current

($P = VI$) or ($I = P/V$) or ($V = P/I$)

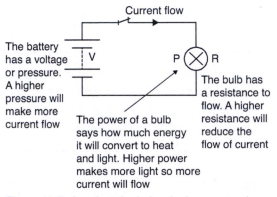

The battery has a voltage or pressure. A higher pressure will make more current flow

The power of a bulb says how much energy it will convert to heat and light. Higher power makes more light so more current will flow

The bulb has a resistance to flow. A higher resistance will reduce the flow of current

Current flow

Figure 3.5 An electrical circuit demonstrating links between voltage, current, resistance and power

3.1.5 Describing electrical circuits

Three descriptive terms are useful when discussing electrical circuits.

▶ **Open circuit**. This means the circuit is broken, therefore no current can flow.
▶ **Short circuit**. This means that a fault has caused a wire to touch another conductor and the current uses this as an easier way to complete the circuit.
▶ **High resistance**. This means a part of the circuit has developed a high resistance (such as a dirty connection), which will reduce the amount of current that can flow.

3.1.6 Conductors, insulators and semiconductors

All metals are conductors. Gold, silver, copper and aluminium are among the best and are frequently used. Liquids that will conduct an electric current are called electrolytes. Insulators are generally non-metallic and

include rubber, porcelain, glass, plastics, cotton, silk, wax paper and some liquids. Some materials can act as either insulators or conductors, depending on conditions. These are called semiconductors and are used to make transistors and diodes.

> **Key Fact**
> Gold, silver, copper and aluminium are among the best conductors.

3.1.7 Factors affecting the resistance of a conductor

In an insulator, a large voltage applied will produce a very small electron movement. In a conductor, a small voltage applied will produce a large electron flow or current. The amount of resistance offered by the conductor is determined by a number of factors.

▶ Length – the greater the length of a conductor, the greater is the resistance.
▶ Cross-sectional area – the larger the cross-sectional area, the smaller the resistance.
▶ The material from which the conductor is made – the resistance offered by a conductor will vary according to the material from which it is made. This is known as the resistivity or specific resistance of the material.
▶ Temperature – most metals increase in resistance as temperature increases

3.1.8 Resistors and circuit networks

Good conductors are used to carry the current with minimum voltage loss due to their low resistance. Resistors are used to control the current flow in a circuit or to set voltage levels. They are made of materials that have a high resistance. Resistors intended to carry low currents are often made of carbon. Resistors for high currents are usually wire wound.

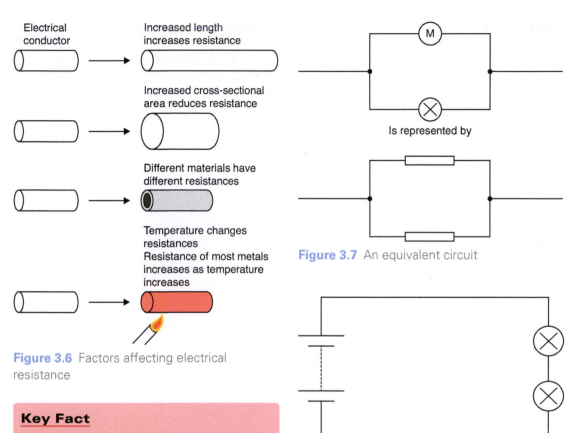

Electrical conductor

Increased length increases resistance

Increased cross-sectional area reduces resistance

Different materials have different resistances

Temperature changes resistances
Resistance of most metals increases as temperature increases

Figure 3.6 Factors affecting electrical resistance

Is represented by

Figure 3.7 An equivalent circuit

Key Fact

Resistors are used to control the current flow in a circuit or to set voltage levels.

Figure 3.8 Series circuit

Resistors are often shown as part of basic electrical circuits to explain the principles involved. The circuits shown below are equivalent. In other words, the circuit just showing resistors is used to represent the other circuit.

When resistors are connected so that there is only one path (Figure 3.8), for the same current to flow through each bulb they are connected in series and the following rules apply.

▶ Current is the same in all parts of the circuit.
▶ The applied voltage equals the sum of the volt drops around the circuit.
▶ Total resistance of the circuit (RT) equals the sum of the individual resistance values ($R_1 + R_2$ etc.).

When resistors or bulbs are connected such that they provide more than one path (Figure 3.9 shows two paths) for the current to flow through and have the same voltage across each component they are connected in parallel and the following rules apply.

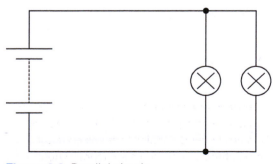

Figure 3.9 Parallel circuit

- The voltage across all components of a parallel circuit is the same.
- The total current equals the sum of the current flowing in each branch.
- The current splits up depending on each component resistance.
- The total resistance of the circuit (RT) can be calculated by:

$$1/R_T = 1/R_1 + 1/R_2 \text{ or}$$
$$R_T = (R_1 \times R_2)/(R_1 + R_4)$$

3.1.9 Magnetism and electromagnetism

Magnetism can be created by a permanent magnet or by an electromagnet (it is one of the three effects of electricity remember). The space around a magnet in which the magnetic effect can be detected is called the magneticfield. The shape of magnetic fields in diagrams is represented by flux lines or lines of force.

Some rules about magnetism:

- Unlike poles attract. Like poles repel.
- Lines of force in the same direction repel sideways; in the opposite direction they attract.
- Current flowing in a conductor will set up a magnetic field around the conductor. The strength of the magnetic field is determined by how much current is flowing.
- If a conductor is wound into a coil or solenoid, the resulting magnetism is the same as that of a permanent bar magnet.

Electromagnets are used in motors, relays and fuel injectors, to name just a few applications. Force on a current-carrying conductor in a magnetic field is caused because of two magnetic fields interacting. This is the basic principle of how a motor works. Figure 3.10 shows a representation of these magnetic fields.

Key Fact

Force on a current-carrying conductor in a magnetic field is caused because of two magnetic fields interacting.

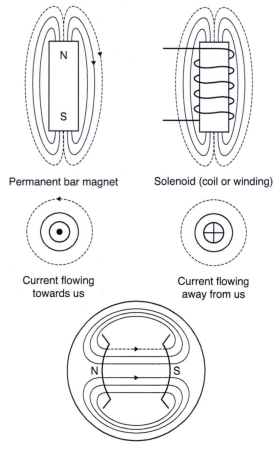

Permanent bar magnet Solenoid (coil or winding)

Current flowing towards us Current flowing away from us

Section of a motor

Figure 3.10 Magnetic fields

3.1.10 Electromagnetic induction

Basic laws:

- When a conductor cuts or is cut by magnetism, a voltage is induced in the conductor.
- The direction of the induced voltage depends on the direction of the magnetic field and the direction in

which the field moves relative to the conductor.

▶ The voltage level is proportional to the rate at which the conductor cuts or is cut by the magnetism.

This effect of induction, meaning that voltage is made in the wire, is the basic principle of how generators such as the alternator on a car work. A generator is a machine that converts mechanical energy into electrical energy. Figure 3.11 shows a wire moving in a magnetic field.

Definition

A generator is a machine that converts mechanical energy into electrical energy.

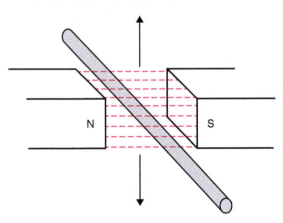

Figure 3.11 Induction

3.1.11 **Mutual induction**

If two coils (known as the primary and secondary) are wound onto the same iron core, then any change in magnetism of one coil will induce a voltage into the other. This happens when a current to the primary coil is switched on and off. If the number of turns of wire on the secondary coil is more than the primary, a higher voltage can be produced. If the number of turns of wire on the secondary coil is less than the primary, a lower voltage is obtained. This is called 'transformer action' and is the principle of the ignition coil. Figure 3.12 shows

the principle of mutual induction. The value of this 'mutually induced' voltage depends on:

▶ The primary current.
▶ The turns ratio between primary and secondary coils.
▶ The speed at which the magnetism changes.

Key Fact

Transformer action is the principle of the ignition coil. It is also used in a DC–DC converter.

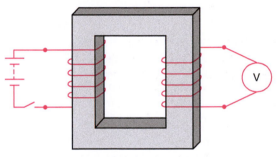

Figure 3.12 Mutual induction

3.1.12 **Definitions and laws**

Ohm's law

▶ For most conductors, the current that will flow through them is directly proportional to the voltage applied to them.

The ratio of voltage to current is referred to as resistance. If this ratio remains constant over a wide range of voltages, the material is said to be 'ohmic'.

Key Fact

The ratio of voltage to current is referred to as resistance.

$V = I/R$

where I = current in amps, V = voltage in volts, R = resistance in ohms.

Georg Simon Ohm was a German physicist, well known for his work on electrical currents.

Lenz's law

▶ The emf induced in an electric circuit always acts in a direction so that the current it creates around the circuit will oppose the change in magnetic flux which caused it.

Lenz's law gives the direction of the induced emf resulting from electromagnetic induction. The 'opposing emf' is often described as a 'back emf'.

The law is named after the Estonian physicist Heinrich Lenz.

Kirchhoff's laws

Kirchhoff's 1st law:

▶ The current flowing into a junction in a circuit must equal the current flowing out of the junction.

This law is a direct result of the conservation of charge; no charge can be lost in the junction, so any charge that flows in must also flow out.

Kirchhoff's 2nd law:

▶ For any closed loop path around a circuit, the sum of the voltage gains and drops always equals zero.

This is effectively the same as the series circuit statement that the sum of all the voltage drops will always equal the supply voltage.

Gustav Robert Kirchhoff was a German physicist; he also discovered caesium and rubidium.

Faraday's law

▶ Any change in the magnetic field around a coil of wire will cause an emf (voltage) to be induced in the coil.

It is important to note here that no matter how the change is produced, the voltage will be generated. In other words, the change could be produced by changing the magnetic field

strength, moving the magnetic field towards or away from the coil, moving the coil in or out of the magnetic field, rotating the coil relative to the magnetic field and so on!

Michael Faraday was a British physicist and chemist, well known for his discoveries of electromagnetic induction and of the laws of electrolysis.

Fleming's rules

▶ In an electrical machine, the first finger lines up with the magnetic Field, the second finger lines up with the Current and the thumb lines up with the Motion.

Fleming's rules relate to the direction of the magnetic field, motion and current in electrical machines. The left hand is used for motors, and the right hand for generators (remember gener-righters).

The English physicist John Fleming devised these rules.

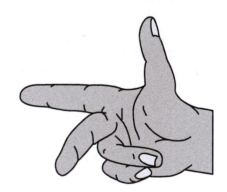

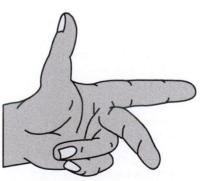

Figure 3.13 Fleming's rules

Ampere's law

▶ For any closed loop path, the sum of the length elements × the magnetic field in the direction of the elements = the permeability × the electric current enclosed in the loop.

In other words, the magnetic field around an electric current is proportional to the electric current which creates it and the electric field is proportional to the charge which creates it.

André Marie Ampère was a French scientist, known for his significant contributions to the study of electrodynamics.

Summary

It was tempting to conclude this section by stating some of Murphy's laws, for example:

▶ If anything can go wrong, it will go wrong.
▶ You will always find something in the last place you look.
▶ In a traffic jam, the lane on the motorway that you are not in always goes faster.

… but I decided against it!

Definition

Murphy's law: if anything can go wrong, it will go wrong.

Table 3.1 Quantities, symbols and units

Name	Definition	Symbol	Common formula	Unit name	Abbreviation
Electrical charge	One coulomb is the quantity of electricity conveyed by a current of one ampere in one second.	Q	$Q = It$	Coulomb	C
Electrical flow or current	The number of electrons past a fixed point in one second	I	$I = V/R$	Ampere	A
Electrical pressure	A pressure of 1 volt applied to a circuit will produce a current flow of 1 amp if the circuit resistance is 1 ohm.	V	$V = IR$	Volt	V
Electrical resistance	This is the opposition to current flow in a material or circuit when a voltage is applied across it.	R	$R = V/I$	Ohm	Ω
Electrical conductance	Ability of a material to carry an electrical current. One Siemens equals 1 amp per volt. It was formerly called the mho or reciprocal ohm.	G	$G = 1/R$	Siemens	S
Current density	The current per unit area. This is useful for calculating the required conductor cross-sectional areas.	J	$J = I/A$ (A = area)		A m^{-2}
Resistivity	A measure of the ability of a material to resist the flow of an electric current. It is numerically equal to the resistance of a sample of unit length and unit cross-sectional area, and its unit is the ohm metre. A good conductor has a low resistivity (1.7×10^{-8}Ω m copper); an insulator has a high resistivity (10^{15} Ω m polyethane).	ρ (rho)	$R = \rho L/A$ (L = length; A = area)	Ohm metre	Ω m

Table 3.1 (Continued)

Name	Definition	Symbol	Common formula	Unit name	Abbreviation
Conductivity	The reciprocal of resistivity.	σ (sigma)	$\sigma = 1/\rho$	Ohm^{-1} metre^{-1}	$\Omega^{-1}\,m^{-1}$
Electrical power	When a voltage of 1 volt causes a current of 1 amp to flow the power developed is 1 watt.	P	$P = IV$ $P = I^2R$ $P = V^2/R$	Watt	W
Capacitance	Property of a capacitor that determines how much charge can be stored in it for a given potential difference between its terminals.	C	$C = Q/V$ $C = \varepsilon A/d$ (A = plate area, d = distance between, ε = permittivity of dielectric)	Farad	F
Inductance	Where a changing current in a circuit builds up a magnetic field, which induces an electromotive force either in the same circuit and opposing the current (self-inductance) or in another circuit (mutual inductance).	L	$i = \dfrac{V}{R}(1 - e^{-Rt/L})$ (i = instantaneous current, R = resistance, L = inductance, t = time, e = base of natural logs)	Henry	H
Magnetic field strength or intensity	Magnetic field strength is one of two ways that the intensity of a magnetic field can be expressed. A distinction is made between magnetic field strength H and magnetic flux density B.	H	$H = B/\mu_0$ (μ_0 being the magnetic permeability of space)	Amperes per metre	A/m (An older unit for magnetic field strength is the oersted: 1 A/m = 0.01257 oersted)
Magnetic flux	A measure of the strength of a magnetic field over a given area.	Φ (phi)	$\Phi = \mu HA$ (μ = magnetic permeability, H = magnetic field intensity, A = area)	Weber	Wb
Magnetic flux density	The density of magnetic flux, 1 tesla is equal to 1 weber per square metre. Also measured in Newton-metres per ampere (Nm/A).	B	$B = H/A$ $B = H \times \mu$ (μ = magnetic permeability of the substance, A = area)	Tesla	T

3.2 Electronic components

3.2.1 Introduction

This section, describing the principles and applications of various electronic circuits, is not intended to explain their detailed operation. The intention is to describe briefly how the circuits work and, more importantly, how and where they may be utilized in vehicle applications.

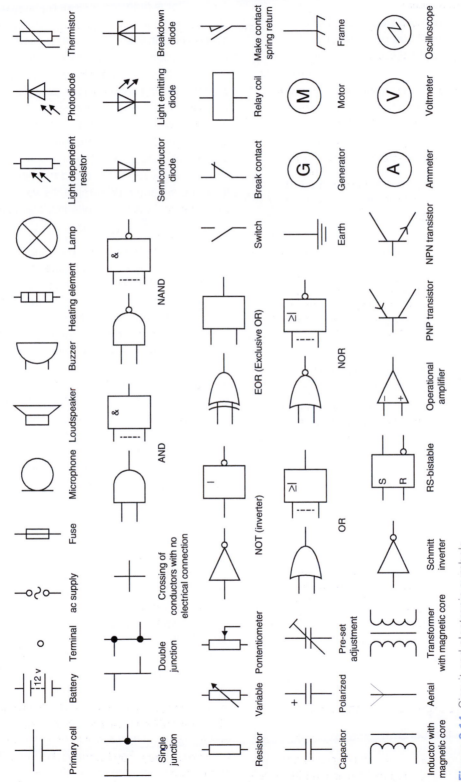

Figure 3.14 Circuit and electronic symbols

The circuits described are examples of those used and many pure electronics books are available for further details. Overall, an understanding of basic electronic principles will help to show how electronic control units work, ranging from a simple interior light delay unit to the most complicated engine management system.

3.2.2 Components

The main devices described here are often known as discrete components. Figure 3.14 shows the symbols used for constructing the circuits shown later in this section. A simple and brief description follows for many of the components.

Resistors are probably the most widely used component in electronic circuits. Two factors must be considered when choosing a suitable resistor, namely the ohms value and the power rating. Resistors are used to limit current flow and provide fixed voltage drops. Most resistors used in electronic circuits are made from small carbon rods, and the size of the rod determines the resistance. Carbon resistors have a negative temperature coefficient (NTC) and this must be considered for some applications. Thin film resistors have more stable temperature properties and are constructed by depositing a layer of carbon onto an insulated former such as glass. The resistance value can be manufactured very accurately by spiral grooves cut into the carbon film. For higher power applications, resistors are usually wire wound. This can, however, introduce inductance into a circuit. Variable forms of most resistors are available in either linear or logarithmic forms. The resistance of a circuit is its opposition to current flow.

Definition

Negative temperature coefficient (NTC): as temperature increases, resistance decreases.

A capacitor is a device for storing an electric charge. In its simple form, it consists of two plates separated by an insulating material. One plate can have excess electrons compared with the other. On vehicles, its main uses are for reducing arcing across contacts and for radio interference suppression circuits as well as in electronic control units. Capacitors are described as two plates separated by a dielectric. The area of the plates A, the distance between them d and the permittivity (ε) of the dielectric determine the value of capacitance. This is modelled by the equation:

$$C = \varepsilon A/d$$

Metal foil sheets insulated by a type of paper are often used to construct capacitors. The sheets are rolled up together inside a tin can. To achieve higher values of capacitance it is necessary to reduce the distance between the plates in order to keep the overall size of the device manageable. This is achieved by immersing one plate in an electrolyte to deposit a layer of oxide typically 104-mm thick, thus ensuring a higher capacitance value. The problem, however, is that this now makes the device polarity-conscious and only able to withstand low voltages. Variable capacitors are available that are varied by changing either of the variables given in the previous equation. The unit of capacitance is the farad (F). A circuit has a capacitance of one farad (1 F) when the charge stored is one coulomb and the potential difference is 1 V. Figure 3.15 shows a capacitor charged up from a battery.

Diodes are often described as one-way valves and, for most applications, this is an acceptable description. A diode is a simple PN junction allowing electron flow from the N-type material (negatively biased) to the P-type material (positively biased). The materials are usually constructed from doped silicon. Diodes are not perfect devices and a voltage of about 0.6 V is required to switch the diode on in its forward-biased direction. Zener diodes are very similar in operation, with the exception that they are

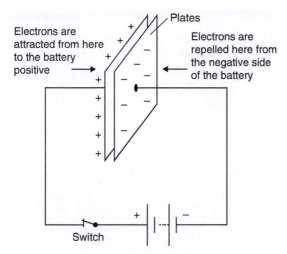

Electrons are attracted from here to the battery positive

Plates

Electrons are repelled here from the negative side of the battery

Switch

When the switch is opened, the plates stay as shown. This is simply called 'charged up'

Figure 3.15 A capacitor charged up

designed to break down and conduct in the reverse direction at a pre-determined voltage. They can be thought of as a type of pressure-relief valve.

Definition

Diodes are often described as one-way valves.

Transistors are the devices that have allowed the development of today's complex and small electronic systems. They replaced the thermal-type valves. The transistor is used as either a solid-state switch or as an amplifier. Transistors are constructed from the same P- and N-type semiconductor materials as the diodes, and can be either made in NPN or PNP format. The three terminals are known as the base, collector and emitter. When the base is supplied with the correct bias, the circuit between the collector and emitter will conduct. The base current can be of the order of 200 times less than the emitter current. The ratio of the current flowing through the base compared with the current through the emitter (I_e/I_b) is an indication of the amplification factor of the device and is often given the symbol β (beta).

Another type of transistor is the FET or field effect transistor. This device has higher input impedance than the bipolar type described above. FETs are constructed in their basic form as n-channel or p-channel devices. The three terminals are known as the gate, source and drain. The voltage on the gate terminal controls the conductance of the circuit between the drain and the source.

A further and important development in transistor technology is the insulated gate bipolar transistor (IGBT). The insulated gate bipolar transistor (Figure 3.16) is a three-terminal power semiconductor device, noted for high efficiency and fast switching. It switches electric power in many modern appliances: electric cars, trains, variable speed refrigerators, air-conditioners and even stereo systems with switching amplifiers. Since it is designed to rapidly turn on and off, amplifiers that use it often synthesize complex waveforms with pulse width modulation and low-pass filters.

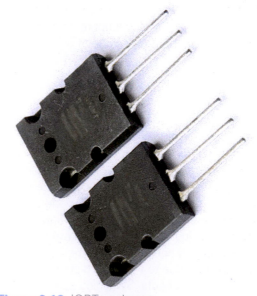

Figure 3.16 IGBT packages

Definition

IGBT: insulated gate bipolar transistor.

51

Inductors are most often used as part of an oscillator or amplifier circuit. In these applications, it is essential for the inductor to be stable and to be of reasonable size. The basic construction of an inductor is a coil of wire wound on a former. It is the magnetic effect of the changes in current flow that gives this device the properties of inductance. Inductance is a difficult property to control, particularly as the inductance value increases due to magnetic coupling with other devices. Enclosing the coil in a can will reduce this, but eddy currents are then induced in the can and this affects the overall inductance value. Iron cores are used to increase the inductance value as this changes the permeability of the core. However, this also allows for adjustable devices by moving the position of the core. This only allows the value to change by a few per cent but is useful for tuning a circuit. Inductors, particularly of higher values, are often known as chokes and may be used in DC circuits to smooth the voltage. The value of inductance is the henry (H). A circuit has an inductance of one henry (1 H) when a current, which is changing at one ampere per second, induces an electromotive force of one volt in it.

3.2.3 Integrated circuits

Integrated circuits are constructed on a single slice of silicon often known as a substrate. In an integrated circuit, some of the components mentioned previously can be combined to carry out various tasks such as switching, amplifying and logic functions. In fact, the components required for these circuits can be made directly on the slice of silicon. The great advantage of this is not just the size of the integrated circuits, but the speed at which they can be made to work due to the short distances between components. Switching speeds in excess of 1 MHz are typical.

There are four main stages in the construction of an integrated circuit. The first of these is oxidization by exposing the silicon slice to an oxygen stream at a high temperature. The

Figure 3.17 Integrated circuit components

oxide formed is an excellent insulator. The next process is photo-etching where part of the oxide is removed. The silicon slice is covered in a material called a photoresist, which, when exposed to light, becomes hard. It is now possible to imprint the oxidized silicon slice, which is covered with photoresist, by a pattern from a photographic transparency. The slice can now be washed in acid to etch back to the silicon those areas that were not protected by being exposed to light. The next stage is diffusion, where the slice is heated in an atmosphere of an impurity such as boron or phosphorus, which causes the exposed areas to become p- or n-type silicon. The final stage is epitaxy, which is the name given to crystal growth. New layers of silicon can be grown and doped to become n- or p-type as before. It is possible to form resistors in a similar way and small values of capacitance can be achieved. It is not possible to form any useful inductance on a chip. Figure 3.18 shows a representation of the 'packages' that integrated circuits are supplied in for use in electronic circuits.

The range and types of integrated circuits now available are so extensive that a chip is available for almost any application. The integration level of chips has now reached, and in many cases is exceeding, that of VLSI

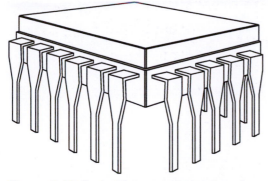

Figure 3.18 Typical integrated circuit package

(very large scale integration). This means there can be more than 100,000 active elements on one chip. Development in this area is moving so fast that often the science of electronics is now concerned mostly with choosing the correct combination of chips, and discreet components are only used as final switching or power output stages.

Key Fact

Today's microprocessors have many millions of gates and billions of individual transistors (well in excess of VLSI).

CHAPTER 4

Electric vehicle technology

4.1 Electric vehicle layouts

4.1.1 Identifying electric vehicles

There are several types of electric vehicle, but many look very similar to their none-electric counterparts so look out for the badging! The following pictures show some common types:

Figure 4.2 Plug-in hybrid car – VW Golf GTE (Source: Volkswagen)

Figure 4.1 Hybrid car – Toyota Prius (Source: Toyota Media)

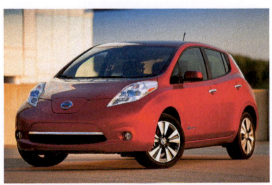

Figure 4.3 Pure electric car – Nissan Leaf (Source: Nissan)

Electric and Hybrid Vehicles. 978-1-138-84237-3 © Tom Denton.
Published by Taylor & Francis. All rights reserved.

Figure 4.4 Electric motorcycle (Yamaha)

Figure 4.5 Commercial hybrid truck

Figure 4.6 Passenger bus using electric power from a hydrogen fuel cell

Figure 4.7 shows the general layout in block diagram form of an electric vehicle (EV). Note that because the drive batteries are a few hundred volts, a lower 12/24 V system is still required for 'normal' lighting and other systems.

4.1.2 Single motor

The 'classic' pure-EV layout is to use a single motor driving either the front or rear wheels. Most EVs of this type do not have a transmission gearbox because the motor operates at suitable torque throughout the speed range of the vehicle.

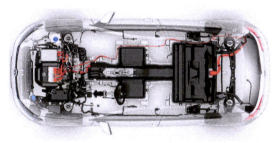

Figure 4.8 VW Golf-e layout with the motor at the front and the battery at the rear (Source: Volkswagen Media)

Figure 4.9 shows a sectioned view of a drive motor and the basic driveline consisting of a fixed ratio gear-set, the differential and driveshaft flanges.

Hybrid cars vary in layout and this is examined in detail later in this chapter. However, the basic design is similar to the pure-electric car mentioned above. The obvious difference being the addition of an ICE.

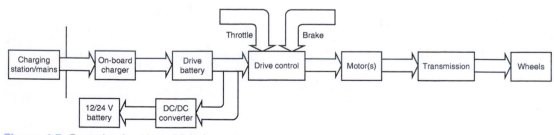

Figure 4.7 Generic electric vehicle layout

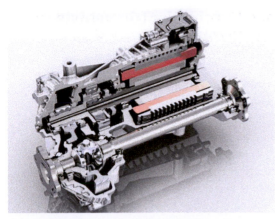

Figure 4.9 EV motor (Source: Volkswagen Media)

Figure 4.10 PHEV layout (Source: Volkswagen Media)

The motor for the plug-in hybrid is shown here where it forms part of the gearbox assembly. Motors used on light hybrids are sometimes described as integrated motor assist (IMA) because they form part of the flywheel. This type of motor is shown as Figures 4.11 and 4.12.

Figure 4.11 PHEV engine, motor and gearbox (Source: Volkswagen Media)

Figure 4.12 Motor integrated with the engine flywheel (Source: Bosch Media)

4.1.3 Wheel motors

Wheel motors integrate a motor into the wheel hub, creating a stator-rotor arrangement to generate torque when power is applied to the stationary coils. More sophisticated designs are liquid-cooled, and some even include suspension components. The three-phase permanent-magnet motors are typically

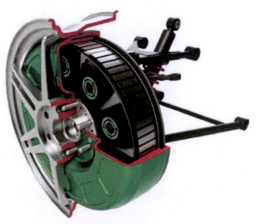

Figure 4.13 In-wheel motor (Source: Protean)

rated at 84 kW peak power for 20 seconds, and 54 kW continuous, depending on battery power. The design integrates the brake disc on the back of the motor's cast-aluminium rotor.

A disadvantage of wheel hub motors is that they add un-sprung weight. This adversely affects handling and steering. For example, GM used wheel hub motors that added 15 kg to each 18-inch wheel. However, this can be offset to some extent by tweaking suspension damping and spring rates.

Key Fact

A disadvantage of wheel hub motors is that they add un-sprung weight.

The integration of electric drive motors and various vehicle components into a vehicle's wheels has the potential to enable new vehicle designs by freeing up the space traditionally occupied by the powertrain and related accessories (Source: http://www.sae.org/mags/AEI/8458).

4.2 Hybrid electric vehicle layouts

4.2.1 Introduction

Hybrid vehicles use at least one electric drive motor in addition to the internal combustion engine (ICE). There are several different ways in which this can be combined and a number of different motors and engines. Note that for clarity we will generally refer to the ICE as an engine and the electric drive motor as a motor. Take care though in other parts of the world, the ICE can be referred to as a motor!

There are three main objectives in the design of a hybrid vehicle:

1 Reduction in fuel consumption (and CO_2).
2 Reduction in emissions.
3 Increased torque and power.

A hybrid vehicle needs a battery to supply the motor; this is sometimes called an accumulator. The most common types are nickel–metal hydride (Ni–MH) or lithium-ion (Li-ion) and usually work at voltages between 200 and 400 V.

The motors are generally permanent magnet synchronous types and work in conjunction

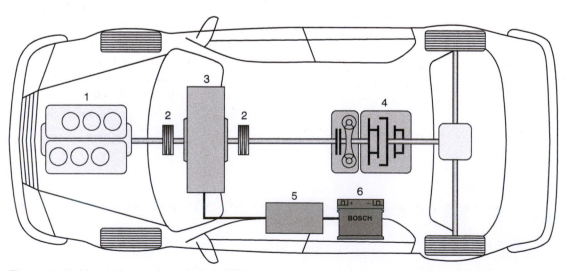

Figure 4.14 Hybrid layout (parallel): 1, ICE; 2, clutch; 3, motor; 4, transmission; 5, inverter; 6, battery

with an inverter (converts DC to AC, but more on this later). The key benefit of an electric drive is high torque at low speed, so it is an ideal supplement to an ICE where the torque is produced at higher speeds. The combination therefore offers good performance at all speeds. The following graph shows typical results – note also that the engine capacity is reduced in the hybrid, but the result is still an improvement.

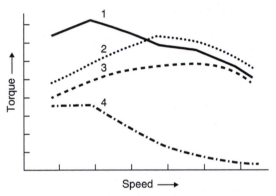

Figure 4.15 Comparing torque curves: 1, hybrid; 2, standard engine (1600cc); 3, downsized engine (1200cc); 4, motor (15 kW)

The result of the hybridization of a motor and an engine is that it can always be operated (with suitable electronic control) at its optimum speed for reducing emissions and consumption while still producing good torque. A smaller capacity engine can also be used (downsizing) in conjunction with a higher geared transmission so the engine runs a lower speed (downspeeding) but performance is maintained.

During braking the motor becomes a generator and the energy that would normally be wasted as heat from the brakes is converted into electrical energy and stored in the battery. This is used at a later stage and in some cases the vehicle can run on electric only with zero emissions. Plug-in hybrids take this option even further.

Key Fact

On all types of EV, during braking the motor becomes a generator and the energy that would normally be wasted as heat from the brakes is converted into electrical energy and stored in the battery – regenerative braking.

4.2.2 Classifications

Hybrids can be classified in different ways. There have been several different variations of this list, but the accepted classification is now that the vehicle fits in one of these four categories:

▶ Start/stop system.
▶ Mild hybrid.
▶ Strong hybrid.
▶ Plug-in hybrid.

The functions available from the different types are summarized in Table 4.1.

A stop/start system has the functions of stop/start as well as some regeneration. The control of the normal vehicle alternator is adapted to achieve this. During normal driving, the alternator operates with low output. During overrun the alternator output is increased in order to increase the braking effect to increase

Table 4.1 Hybrid functions

Classification/ function	Start/stop	Regeneration	Electrical assistance	Electric-only driving	Charging from a power socket
Start/stop system	√	√			
Mild hybrid	√	√	√		
Strong hybrid	√	√	√	√	
Plug-in hybrid	√	√	√	√	√

Figure 4.16 BMW 3-series plug-in hybrid

power generation. Stopping the engine when idling saves fuel and reduces emissions. An uprated starter motor is needed to cope with the increased use as the vehicle is auto-started as the driver presses the accelerator.

▶ Fuel savings in the NEDC[1] can be up to 5%

The mild hybrid is as above but also provides some assistance during acceleration, particularly at low speeds. Pure electric operation is not possible; the motor can propel the vehicle, but the engine is always running.

▶ Fuel savings in the NEDC can be up to 15%.

A strong hybrid takes all of the above functions further and over short distances the engine can be switched off to allow pure electric operation.

▶ Fuel savings in the NEDC can be up to 30%.[2]

The plug-in hybrid is a strong hybrid but with a larger high-voltage battery that can be charged from a suitable electrical power supply.

▶ Fuel savings in the NEDC can be up to 70%.[3]

4.2.3 Operation

In addition to a stop/start function and full electric operation, there are five main operating modes that a hybrid vehicle will use:

▶ Start up.
▶ Acceleration.
▶ Cruising.
▶ Deceleration.
▶ Idle.

These main modes and conditions are outlined in the following figure:

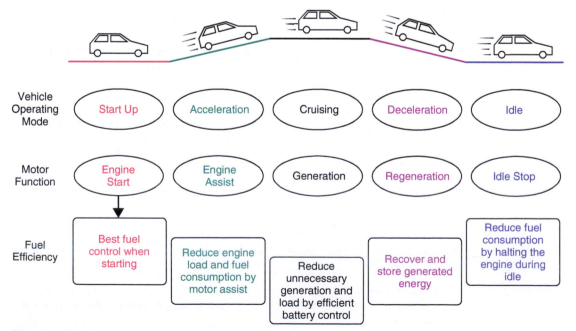

Figure 4.17 Hybrid vehicles operating modes

Further details of what is taking place during the different operating modes are outlined Figure 4.18.

The operating modes are explained in even more detail in Table 4.2.

These descriptions relate generally to a light-hybrid, sometimes described as integrated motor assist (IMA). This is a parallel configuration discussed further in the next section. The technique used by most hybrid

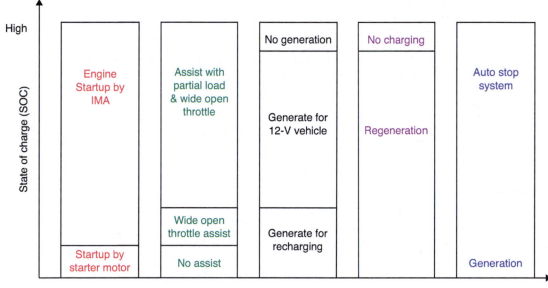

Figure 4.18 Operating mode details

Table 4.2 Detailed operating modes

Mode	Details
Start-up	Under normal conditions, the motor will immediately start the engine at a speed of 1000 rpm. When the state of charge (SOC) of the high-voltage battery module is too low, when the temperature is too low or if there is a failure of the motor system, the engine will be cranked by the normal 12 V starter.
Acceleration	During acceleration, current from the battery module is converted to AC by an inverter and supplied to the motor. The motor output is used to supplement the engine output so that power available for acceleration is maximized. Current from the battery module is also converted to 12 V DC for supply to the vehicle electrical system. This reduces the load that would have been caused by a normal alternator and so improves acceleration. When the remaining battery state of charge is too low, but not at the minimum level, assist will only be available during wide open throttle (WOT) acceleration. When the battery state of charge is reduced to the minimum level, no assist will be provided.
Cruising	When the vehicle is cruising and the battery requires charging, the engine drives the motor – which now acts as a generator. The resulting output current is used to charge the battery and is converted to supply the vehicle electrical system. When the vehicle is cruising and the high-voltage battery is sufficiently charged, the engine drives the motor. The generated current is converted to 12 V DC and only used to supply the vehicle electrical system.
Deceleration	During deceleration (during fuel cut), the motor is driven by the wheels such that regeneration takes place. The generated output is used to charge the high-voltage battery. Some vehicles cut the ICE completely.

(Continued)

Table 4.2 (Continued)

Mode	Details
	During braking (brake switch on), a higher amount of regeneration will be allowed. This will increase the deceleration force so the driver will automatically adjust the force on the brake pedal. In this mode, more charge is sent to the battery module. If the ABS system is controlling the locking of the wheels, an 'ABS-busy' signal is sent to the motor control module. This will immediately stop generation to prevent interference with the ABS system.
Idling	During idling, the flow of energy is similar to that for cruising. If the state of charge of the battery module is very low, the motor control system will signal the engine control module (ECM) to raise the idle speed to approximately 1100 rpm.
	On a stronger hybrid, the engine hardly ever idles as the motor will be used to move the vehicle and start the engine if necessary. Other vehicle functions such as AC can be run from the high-voltage battery if enough power is available.

cars can be thought of as a kinetic energy recovery system (KERS). This is because instead of wasting heat energy from the brakes as the vehicle is slowed down, a large proportion is converted to electrical energy and stored in the battery as chemical energy. This is then used to drive the wheels so reducing the use of chemical energy from the fuel.

Figure 4.19 Hybrid vehicles still need exhaust extraction!

4.2.4 Configurations

A hybrid power system for an automobile can have a series, parallel or power split configuration. With a series system, an engine drives a generator, which in turn powers a motor. The motor propels the vehicle. With a parallel system, the engine and motor can both

be used to propel the vehicle. Most hybrids in current use employ a parallel system. The power split has additional advantages but is also more complex.

Key Fact

A hybrid power system for an automobile can have a series, parallel or power split configuration.

There are numerous configurations as manufacturers have developed different systems and ideas. However, it is now generally accepted that HEVs fall into one of the following descriptions:

- ▶ Parallel hybrid with one clutch.
- ▶ Parallel hybrid with two clutches.
- ▶ Parallel hybrid with double-clutch transmission.
- ▶ Axle-split parallel hybrid.
- ▶ Series hybrid.
- ▶ Series-parallel hybrid.
- ▶ Power-split hybrid.

The 'parallel hybrid with one clutch' is shown in the following figure. This layout is a mild hybrid where the engine and motor can be used independently of each other but the power flows are in parallel and can be added together to get the total drive power. The engine will run all the time the vehicle is driving, at the same speed as the motor.

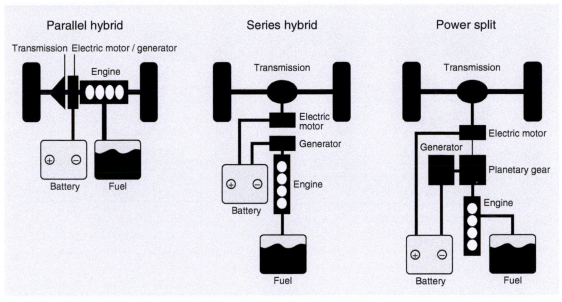

Figure 4.20 Three types of hybrid vehicles (parallel, series, power split)

The main advantage of this configuration is that the conventional drivetrain can be maintained. In most cases only one motor is used and fewer adaptations are needed when converting a conventional system. However, because the engine can be decoupled it produces drag on overrun and reduces the amount of regeneration. Pure electric driving is not possible.

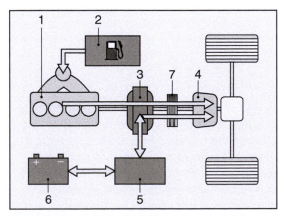

Figure 4.21 Parallel hybrid with one clutch (P1-HEV): 1, engine; 2, fuel tank; 3, motor (integrated motor generator – IMG); 4, transmission; 5, inverter; 6, battery; 7, clutch

A parallel hybrid with two clutches is a strong hybrid and is an extension of the mild hybrid outlined above, except that the additional clutch allows the engine to be disconnected. This means pure electric use is possible.

Electronic control systems are used to determine when the clutches are operated, for example the engine can be decoupled during deceleration to increase regenerative braking. It even allows the vehicle to go into 'sailing' mode, where it is slowed down only by rolling friction and aerodynamic drag.

If the engine-clutch is operated in such a way as to maintain torque, then the engine can be stopped and started using the clutch – a sophisticated bump start! Sensors and intelligent controls are needed to achieve this. In some cases a separate starter motor is used, which can normally be dispensed with.

Adding the extra clutch in the previous system increases the length of the transmission and this may be a problem, particularly in FWD cars. If a double-clutch transmission is used in the configuration shown in Figure 4.23 then this problem is overcome. The

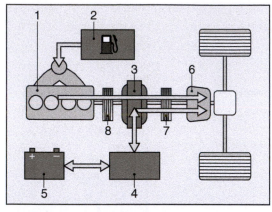

Figure 4.22 Parallel hybrid with two clutches (P2-HEV): 1, engine; 2, fuel tank; 3, motor (integrated motor generator – IMG); 4, inverter; 5, battery; 6, transmission; 7, clutch one; 8, clutch two

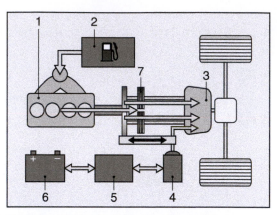

Figure 4.23 Parallel hybrid with double-clutch transmission: 1, engine; 2, fuel tank; 3, transmission; 4, motor; 5, inverter; 6, battery; 7, clutches

motor is connected to a sub unit of the transmission instead of the engine crankshaft or flywheel. These transmissions are also described as direct shift gearboxes or DSG. Pure electric driving is possible by opening the appropriate transmission clutch or both engine and motor can drive in parallel. The gear ratio between engine and motor can also be controlled in this system, allowing designers even greater freedom. Sophisticated electronic control, sensor and actuators are necessary.

Definition
DSG: direct shift gearbox.

The axle-split parallel hybrid is also a parallel drive even though the motor and engine are completely separated. As the name suggests, they drive an axle each. A semi-automatic transmission together with a stop/start system is needed with this layout. As the engine can be completely decoupled, this configuration is suitable for operation as a strong hybrid. It can effectively deliver all-wheel drive when the battery is charged and in some cases to ensure this an additional generator is fitted to the

engine to charge the high-voltage battery even when the vehicle is stationary.

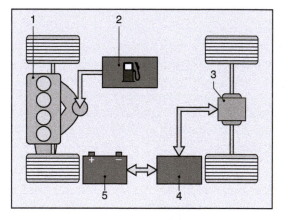

Figure 4.24 Axle-split parallel hybrid: 1, engine; 2, fuel tank; 3, motor; 4, inverter; 5, battery

A series hybrid configuration is a layout where the engine drives a generator (alternator) that charges the battery that powers a motor that drives the wheels! A series configuration is always a strong hybrid since all the previously stated functions are possible (Table 4.1). A conventional transmission is not needed, so this creates space for packaging the overall system – a larger battery for example. The engine can be optimized to only operate in a set range of rpm. Stopping and starting the engine has no effect on the vehicle drive, therefore the control systems are less sophisticated. The main disadvantage is that the energy has to be converted twice (mechanical to electrical, and electrical back to mechanical) and if the energy is also stored in the battery, three conversions are needed. The result is decreased efficiency, but this is made up for by operating the engine at its optimum point. There is a 'packaging advantage' in this layout because there is no mechanical connection between the engine and the wheels.

Definition

A series hybrid configuration is a layout where the engine drives a generator (alternator) that charges the battery that powers a motor that drives the wheels.

This configuration tended to be used in trains and large buses rather than cars. However, this layout is now used for range-extended electric vehicle (REVs). In this case the car is effectively pure electric, but a small engine is used to charge the battery and 'extend the range' or at least reduce range anxiety.

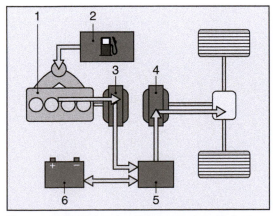

Figure 4.25 Series hybrid: 1, engine; 2, fuel tank; 3, alternator/generator; 4, motor; 5, inverter; 6, battery

Series-parallel hybrid systems are an extension of the series hybrid because of an additional clutch that can mechanically connect the generator and motor. This eliminates the double energy conversion except at certain speed ranges. However, the 'packaging advantage' of the series drive is lost because of the mechanical coupling. Further, two electric units are required compared with the parallel hybrid.

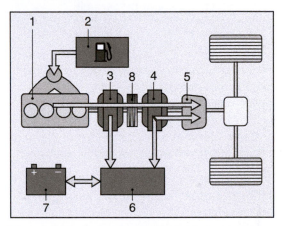

Figure 4.26 Series-parallel hybrid: 1, engine; 2, fuel tank; 3, alternator/generator; 4, motor; 5, transmission; 6, inverter; 7, battery; 8, clutch

The power-split hybrids combine the advantages of series and parallel layouts but at the expense of increased mechanical complexity. A proportion of the engine power is converted to electric power by the alternator and the remainder, together with the motor, drives the wheels. A power-split hybrid is a strong hybrid because it meets all the required functions.

The single mode concept shown in the following diagram uses one planetary gear set (a dual mode system uses two and can be more efficient, but even more complex mechanically). The gear set is connected to the engine, alternator and the motor. Because of the epicyclic gearing, the engine speed can be adjusted independently of the vehicle speed (think of a rear-wheel-drive differential action where the two halfshafts and propshaft all run at different speeds when the car is cornering). The system is effectively an electric constantly variable transmission (eCVT). A combination of mechanical and electrical power can be transmitted to the wheels. The electrical path can be used at low power requirements and the mechanical path for higher power needs.

Definition

eCVT: electric constantly variable transmission.

The system therefore achieves good savings at low and medium speeds, but none at high speeds where the engine only drives mostly via the mechanical path.

4.2.5 Hybrid with a 48-V system

Bosch has developed a hybrid powertrain that makes economic sense even in smaller vehicles. The system costs much less than normal hybrid systems, but could still reduce consumption by up to

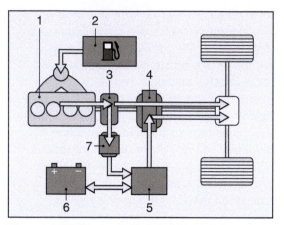

Figure 4.27 Power-split hybrid (single mode concept): 1, engine; 2, fuel tank; 3, planetary gear set; 4, motor; 5, inverter; 6, battery; 7, generator

15%. The electrical powertrain provides the combustion engine with an additional 150 Nm of torque during acceleration. That corresponds to the power of a sporty compact-car engine.

Unlike conventional high-voltage hybrids, the system is based on a lower voltage of 48 V and

Figure 4.28 Power-split hybrid (Source: Toyota)

can therefore make do with less expensive components. Instead of a large electric motor, the generator has been enhanced to output four times as much power. The motor generator uses a belt to support the combustion engine with up to 10 kW. The power electronics forms the link between the additional low-voltage battery and the motor generator. A DC/DC converter supplies the

Figure 4.29 Bosch expects some 4 million new vehicles worldwide to be equipped with a low-voltage hybrid powertrain in 2020 (Source: Bosch Media)

car's 12 V on-board network from the 48 V vehicle electrical system. The newly developed lithium-ion battery is also significantly smaller.

4.2.6 Hybrid control systems

The efficiency that can be achieved with the relevant hybrid drive is dependent on the hybrid configuration and the higher-level hybrid control. The following figure uses the example of a vehicle with a parallel hybrid drive. Shown are the networking of the individual components and control systems in the drivetrain. The higher-level hybrid control coordinates the entire system, the subsystems of which have their own control functions. These are:

- ▶ battery management
- ▶ engine management
- ▶ management of the electric drive
- ▶ transmission management
- ▶ management of the braking system.

In addition to control of the sub-systems, the hybrid control also includes an operating strategy that optimizes the way in which the

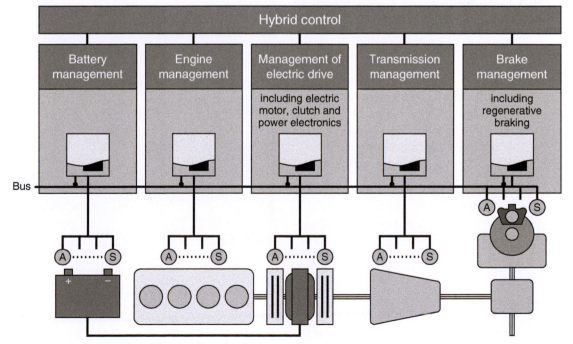

Figure 4.30 Parallel hybrid control system. A, actuator; S, sensor

drivetrain is operated. The operating strategy directly affects the consumption and emissions of the hybrid vehicle. This is during start–stop operation of the engine, regenerative braking, and hybrid and electric driving.

4.3 Cables and components

4.3.1 High-voltage cables

Any cable used on a vehicle should be insulated to prevent contact and short circuits. Most cables are made from many strands of copper wire as this offers low resistance and retains flexibility. The insulation is normally a form of PVC.

Figure 4.32 Orange cables and warning stickers on a Golf GTE

Figure 4.31 VW Golf-e showing some of the orange cables

High-voltage cables require greater insulation to prevent voltage leakage, but also because the risk of harm if touched is very high. Stickers with various symbols are used as a warning together with the bright orange colour.

Safety First

Stickers with various symbols are used as a warning together with the bright orange colour.

To deliver high power, they have to carry high current – even at high voltage! Remember, power equals voltage multiplied by current ($P = IV$). Current therefore

equals power divided by voltage ($I = P/V$). We will assume a voltage of 250 V to make the calculations easy! If a cable has to deliver, say, 20 kW (20,000 W) then 20,000/250 = 80 A. Under hard acceleration this figure is even higher: 80 kW for example would require a current of 320 A. For this reason the cables are quite thick as well as well insulated.

Definition

Power equals voltage multiplied by current ($P = IV$).

Figure 4.33 Toyota Prius under bonnet view

4.3.2 Components

It is important to be able to identify EV components. In many cases the manufacturer's information will be needed to assist with this task. Slightly different names are used by some manufacturers, but in general the main components are:

- ▶ battery
- ▶ motor
- ▶ relays (switching components)
- ▶ control units (power electronics)
- ▶ charger (on-board)
- ▶ charging points
- ▶ isolators (safety device)
- ▶ inverter (DC to DC converter)
- ▶ battery management controller
- ▶ ignition/key-on control switch
- ▶ driver display panel/interface.

Some of these components are also covered in other parts of this book. Possible additions to this list are other vehicle systems such as braking and steering or even air conditioning as they have to work in a different way on a pure EV.

The key components will now be described further.

Battery: The most common battery technology now is lithium-ion. The complete battery pack consists of a number of cell modules (the actual battery consisting of 200–300 cells), a cooling system, insulation, junction box, battery management and a suitable case or shell. These features combine so that the pack is able to withstand impacts and a wide range of temperatures.

Key Fact
The most common battery technology now is lithium-ion.

The battery is usually installed in the underbody of the car. On a pure-EV it can

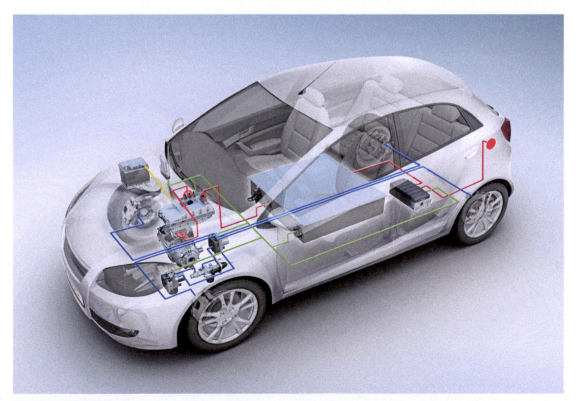

Figure 4.34 High-voltage components shown in red, braking components in blue, low voltage in yellow and sensor/date shown in green (Source: Bosch Media)

weigh in excess of 300 kg and for a PHEV in the region of 120 kg. Voltages vary and can be up to 650 V; however, typically this is around 300 V. The capacity of the battery is described in terms of kilowatt hours and will be in the region of 20–25 kWh.

> **Key Fact**
>
> The kilowatt hour (kWh) is a unit of energy equal to 1000 Wh or 3.6 MJ. It is used to describe the energy in batteries and as a billing unit for energy delivered by electricity suppliers. If you switch on a 1-kW electric fire and keep it on for 1 hour, you will consume 1 kWh of energy.

Battery management controller: This device monitors and controls the battery and determines, among other things, the state of charge of the cells. It regulates the temperature and protects the cells against overcharging and deep discharge. Electronically activated switches are included that disconnect the battery system when idle and in critical situations such as an accident or fire. The device is usually part of the battery pack – but not always, so check the manufacturer's data.

Motor: This is the component that converts electrical energy into kinetic energy or movement – in other words, it is what moves the vehicle. Most types used on EVs, HEVs and PHEVs are a type of AC synchronous motor supplied with pulses of DC. They are rated in the region of 85 kW on pure-EVs.

Inverter: The inverter is an electronic device or circuit that changes direct current (DC) from the battery to alternating current (AC) to drive the motor. It also does this in reverse for regenerative charging. It is often described as the power electronics or similar. Sometimes the same or a separate inverter is used to supply the 12-V system.

Control unit: Also called power control unit or motor control unit, this is the electronic device that controls the power electronics (inverter). It responds to signals from the driver (brake, acceleration etc.) and causes the power electronics to be switched accordingly.

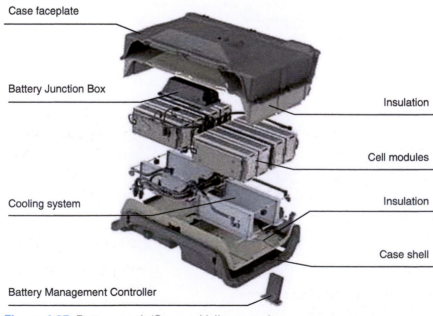

Figure 4.35 Battery pack (Source: Volkswagen)

The control makes the motor drive the car or become a generator and charge the battery. It can also be responsible for air conditioning, PAS and brakes.

Charging unit: This device is used on pure-EVs and PHEVs and is usually located near where the external power source is connected. It converts and controls the 'mains' voltage (typically 230/240 V AC in Europe and 120 V AC in the USA) to a suitable level for charging the battery cells (typically 300 V DC).

Driver interface: To keep the driver informed, a number of methods are used. Most common now is a touch screen interface where information can be delivered as well as allowing the driver to change settings such as the charge rate.

Figure 4.36 Setting the maximum charge current

4.3.3 ECE-R100

ECE-R100 is a standard developed by the UN to harmonize EV systems.[4] It is applicable for EVs, vehicle category M and N, capable of a top speed above 25 km/h. In this section I have highlighted some key aspects of the regulation. It is generally about safety of the high-voltage parts in an EV.

Definition
ECE-R100 is a standard developed by the UN to harmonize EV systems.

Key Fact
Category M: Motor vehicles with at least four wheels designed and constructed for the carriage of passengers.

Category N: Motor vehicles with at least four wheels designed and constructed for the carriage of goods.

Protection against electrical shock is a key aspect of the standard:

▶ It should not be possible that live high-voltage parts in passenger and luggage compartments can be touched with a standardized test-pin or test-finger.
▶ All covers and protection of live high-voltage parts should be marked with the official symbol (Figure 4.37) and access to live high-voltage parts should only be possible by using a tool, and on purpose.
▶ Traction battery and powertrain shall be protected by properly rated fuses or circuit breakers.
▶ The high-voltage powertrain must be isolated from the rest of the EV.

Figure 4.37 This warning symbol may be used with or without the text

Charging:

▶ The EV should not be able to move during charging.

▶ All parts that are used while charging should be protected from direct contact, under any circumstance.

▶ Plugging in the charging cable must shut the system off and make it impossible to drive.

General safety and driving points:

▶ Starting the EV should be enabled by a key or suitable keyless switch.

▶ Removing the key prevents the car being able to drive.

▶ It should be clearly visible if the EV is ready to drive (just by pushing the throttle).

▶ If the battery is discharged, the driver should get an early warning signal to leave the road safely.

▶ When leaving the EV, the driver should be warned by a visible or audible signal if the EV is still in driving mode.

▶ Changing the direction of the EV into reverse should only be possible by the combinations of two actuations or an electric switch that only operates when the speed is less than 5 km/h.

▶ If there is an event, like overheating, the driver should be warned by an active signal.

Search http://www.unece.org for 'ECE-R100' for a full copy of the latest standard.

4.4 Other systems

4.4.1 Heating and air conditioning

Most EVs now allow the operation of heating or cooling when the vehicle is plugged in and charging. Some also allow this function directly from the battery. The most important aspect is that this allows the vehicle cabin to be 'pre-conditioned' (heated or cooled) on mains power, therefore saving battery capacity and increasing range. The two most common systems allow:

▶ Cooling with an electrically driven air conditioner compressor.

▶ Heating with a high-voltage positive temperature coefficient (PTC) heater.

These cooling and heating functions using the high-voltage components are usually activated with a timer or a remote app.

Key Fact

Most EVs now allow the operation of heating or cooling when the vehicle is plugged in and charging.

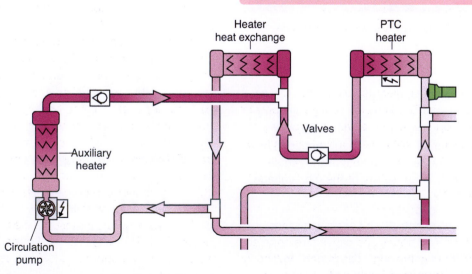

Figure 4.38 Heating circuit (Source: Volkswagen)

Hybrid car systems combine the heating circuit by running it in parallel to the coolant circuit. It consists of a heat exchanger, a heater unit and a feed pump.

Cooling systems operate in much the same way as on a conventional vehicle, except that the compressor is electrically driven. This can be by high-voltage or lower voltage systems such as 42 V (but not normally from 12 V).

When necessary, the battery control unit can request cooling of the battery when it is being charged, so for this reason the battery cooling circuit and in some case the motor cooling circuit are combined with the engine cooling system on a hybrid. The electric pump makes the coolant flow.

4.4.2 Brakes

Brakes are normally operated hydraulically, but with some sort of servo assistance. This can be from a hydraulic pump, but on most ICE-driven vehicles the vacuum (low pressure) from the inlet manifold is used to operate a servo. On a pure-EV or a hybrid running only on electricity, another method must be employed.

> **Key Fact**
> Brakes are normally operated hydraulically, but with some sort of servo assistance.

In most cases an electrically assisted master cylinder is used, which also senses the braking pressure applied by the driver. The reason for this is that as much braking effect as possible is achieved through regeneration because this is the most efficient method. The signals from the master cylinder sensor are sent to an electronic control system and this in turn switches the motor to regenerative mode, charging the batteries and causing retardation, or regenerative braking. If additional braking is needed, determined by driver foot pressure,

the traditional hydraulic brakes are operated, with electrical assistance if needed.

Figure 4.39 Electronically controlled brake master cylinder

Some braking systems have a feedback loop to the master cylinder to give the driver the appropriate feel from the brake pedal that is related to the amount of retardation overall (friction brakes and regenerative brakes).

Not yet in use but coming soon … A fully hydraulic actuation system (HAS) has been developed by Bosch for use on electric and hybrid vehicles. The system is suitable for all brake-circuit splits and drive concepts. It comprises a brake operation unit and a hydraulic actuation control module which supplement the ESP® hydraulic modulator. The brake pedal and wheel brakes are mechanically decoupled. The brake actuation unit processes the braking command, and an integrated pedal travel simulator ensures the familiar pedal feel. The braking pressure modulation system implements the braking command using the electric motor and wheel brakes. The aim is to achieve maximum recuperation while maintaining complete stability. Depending on the vehicle and system status, deceleration of up to $0.3g$ can be generated using only the electric motor. If this is not sufficient, the modulation system uses the pump and high-pressure accumulator.

Figure 4.40 Vacuum-independent braking system specially designed for plug-in hybrids and electric vehicles. It comprises a brake operation unit (left) and an actuation control module (right) which supplement the ESP® hydraulic modulator (Source: Bosch Media)

4.4.3 Power-assisted steering

When running on electric-only, or if there is no engine available to run a power steering pump, an alternative must be used. However, most modern ICE vehicles use one of two main ways to use electric power-assisted steering (ePAS); the second of these is now the most common by far:

1 An electric motor drives a hydraulic pump, which acts on a hydraulic ram/rack/servo cylinder.
2 A drive motor, which directly assists with the steering.

With the direct acting type, an electric motor works directly on the steering via an epicyclic gear train. This completely replaces the hydraulic pump and servo cylinder.

> **Key Fact**
>
> With a direct ePAS an electric motor works directly on the steering via an epicyclic gear train.

On many systems, an optical torque sensor is used to measure driver effort on the steering

Figure 4.41 Direct electric PAS (Source: Ford Media)

wheel (all systems use a sensor of some sort). The sensor works by measuring light from an LED, which is shining through holes. These are aligned in discs at either end of a torsion bar, fitted into the steering column. An optical sensor element identifies the twist of two discs on the steering axis with respect to each other, each disc being provided with appropriate codes. From this sensor information, the electronic control system calculates the torque as well as the absolute steering angle.

> **Key Fact**
>
> Electrical PAS occupies little under-bonnet space and typically a 400 W motor averages about 2 A even under urban driving conditions.

Endnotes

1 New European Driving Cycle.
2 Strong hybrids will be more economical over the NEDC so the fuel savings may not reflect normal use.
3 Plug-in hybrids do of course use electrical energy too, but that is much cheaper than fuel and arguably results in fewer emissions.
4 At the time of writing, the standard was on its third revision.

CHAPTER 5

Batteries

5.1 Overview

5.1.1 Battery range

The main thing that affects the range of an EV is your right foot! Smooth driving with gentle acceleration and minimal braking has the most impact on range – as it does in any vehicle.

However, the range is also affected by cold weather as well as the use of air conditioning (heating or cooling) and other items (such as lights). This is because these systems use battery energy. Vehicle manufacturers are using solutions such as LED exterior lights to reduce consumption. Control systems can also minimize the energy used by additional items. Mains powered pre-heating (or cooling) is now common, allowing the driver to start their journey with the interior at a comfortable temperature without draining the battery. One plus point is that EVs don't need a warm-up period like many conventional ICE vehicles in the winter.

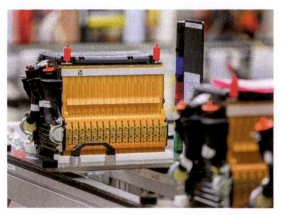

Figure 5.1 Battery pack for the Chevrolet Spark (Source: General Motors)

5.1.2 Battery life and recycling

Manufacturers usually consider the end of life for a battery to be when the battery capacity drops to 80% of its rated capacity. This means that if the original battery has a range of 100 km from a full charge, after 8–10 years of use the range may reduce to 80 km. However, batteries can still deliver usable power below 80% charge capacity. A number of vehicle manufacturers have designed the battery to last the lifetime of the car.

> **Key Fact**
> EV range is affected by cold weather and the use of air conditioning and lights.

The main sources of lithium for EV batteries are salt lakes and salt pans, which produce the soluble salt lithium chloride. The main producers of lithium are South America (Chile, Argentina and Bolivia), Australia, Canada and China. Lithium can also be extracted from sea water. It is expected that recycling will become a major source of lithium. Worldwide reserves are estimated to be about 30 million tons. Around 0.3 kg of lithium is required per kWh of battery storage. There is a range of opinion but many agree reserves will last over a thousand years!

The volume of lithium recycling at the time of writing is relatively small, but it is growing. Lithium-ion cells are considered non-hazardous and they contain useful elements that can be recycled. Lithium, metals (copper, aluminium, steel), plastic, cobalt and lithium salts can all be recovered.

Lithium-ion batteries have a lower environmental impact than other battery technologies, including lead–acid, nickel–cadmium and nickel–metal hydride. This is because the cells are composed of more environmentally benign materials. They do not contain heavy metals (cadmium for example) or compounds that are considered toxic, such as lead or nickel. Lithium iron phosphate is essentially a fertilizer. As more recycled materials are used, the overall environmental impact will be reduced.

All battery suppliers must comply with 'The Waste Batteries and Accumulators Regulations 2009'. This is a mandatory requirement, which means manufacturers take batteries back from customers to be reused, recycled or disposed of in an appropriate way.

5.2 Types of battery

5.2.1 Lead–acid batteries (Pb–PbO$_2$)

Even after about 150 years of development and much promising research into other techniques of energy storage, the lead–acid battery is still the best choice for low-voltage motor vehicle use. This is particularly so when cost and energy density are taken into account.

Incremental changes over the years have made the sealed and maintenance-free battery now in common use very reliable and long lasting. This may not always appear to be the case to some end-users, but note that quality is often related to the price the customer pays. Many bottom-of-the-range cheap batteries, with a 12-month guarantee, will last for 13 months!

The basic construction of a nominal 12 V lead–acid battery consists of six cells connected in series. Each cell, producing about 2 V, is housed in an individual compartment within a polypropylene, or similar, case. Figure 5.3 depicts a cut-away battery showing the main component parts. The active material is held in grids or baskets to form the positive and negative plates. Separators made from a micro-porous plastic insulate these plates from each other.

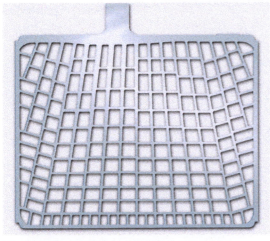

Figure 5.2 Battery grid before the active materials are added

However, even modern batteries described as sealed do still have a small vent to stop the pressure build-up due to the very small amount of gassing. A further requirement of sealed batteries is accurate control of charging voltage.

In use, a battery requires very little attention other than the following when necessary:

▶ Clean corrosion from terminals using hot water.
▶ Terminals should be smeared with petroleum jelly or Vaseline, not ordinary grease.
▶ Battery tops should be clean and dry.
▶ If not sealed, cells should be topped up with distilled water 3 mm above the plates.

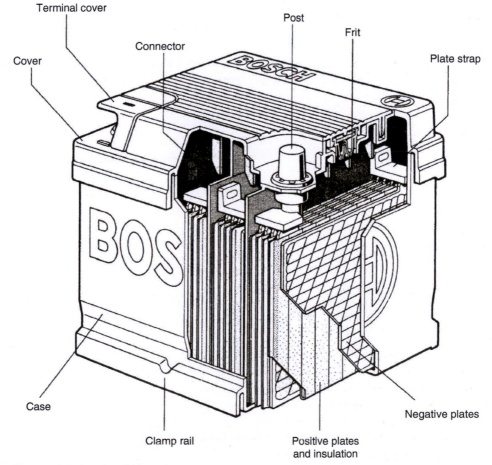

Figure 5.3 Lead–acid battery

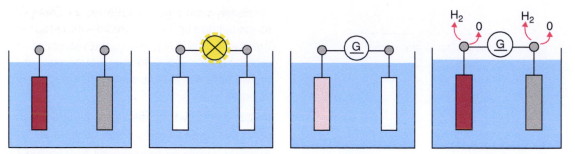

Figure 5.4 Battery discharge and charging process (left to right): Fully charged; discharging; charging; charging and gassing

Figure 5.5 Modern vehicle battery

▶ The battery should be securely clamped in position.

5.2.2 Alkaline (Ni–Cad, Ni–Fe and Ni–MH)

The main components of the nickel–cadmium (Ni–Cad or NiCad) cell for vehicle use are as follows:

▶ positive plate – nickel hydrate (NiOOH)
▶ negative plate – cadmium (Cd)
▶ electrolyte – potassium hydroxide (KOH) and water (H_2O).

The process of charging involves the oxygen moving from the negative plate to the positive plate, and the reverse when discharging. When fully charged, the negative plate becomes pure cadmium and the positive plate becomes nickel hydrate. A chemical equation to represent this reaction is given next, but

note that this is simplifying a more complex reaction.

$$2NiOOH + Cd + 2H_2O + KOH = 2Ni(OH)_2 + CdO_2 + KOH$$

The $2H_2O$ is actually given off as hydrogen (H) and oxygen (O_2) because gassing takes place all the time during charge. It is this use of water by the cells that indicates they are operating, as will have been noted from the equation. The electrolyte does not change during the reaction. This means that a relative density reading will not indicate the state of charge.

Key Fact
NiCad batteries do not suffer from over-charging because once the cadmium oxide has changed to cadmium, no further reaction can take place.

Nickel–metal hydride (Ni–MH or NiMH) batteries are used by some electric vehicles and have proved to be very effective. Toyota in particular has developed these batteries. The components of NiMH batteries include a cathode of nickel–hydroxide, an anode of hydrogen absorbing alloys and a potassium-hydroxide (KOH) electrolyte. The energy density of NiMH is more than double that of a lead–acid battery but less than lithium-ion batteries.

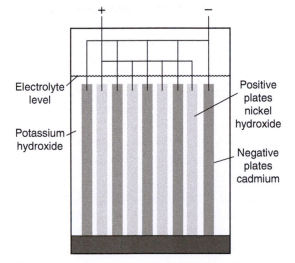

Figure 5.6 Simplified representation of a NiCad alkaline battery cell

Electrolyte level

Potassium hydroxide

Positive plates nickel hydroxide

Negative plates cadmium

Figure 5.7 Toyota NiMH battery and management components (Source: Toyota)

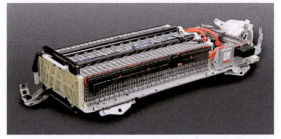

Figure 5.8 Third-generation NiMH battery (Source: Toyota)

Key Fact

NiMH batteries are used by some electric vehicles and have proved to be very effective.

Toyota developed a cylindrical NiMH battery in 1997 that powered the Rav4EV as well as the e-com electric vehicle. Since then, Toyota has continually improved its NiMH batteries by reducing size, improving power density, lowering weight, improving the battery pack/case and lowering costs. The current NiMH battery, which powers the third-generation Prius, costs 25% that of the battery used in the first generation.

Nickel–metal batteries are ideal for mass-producing affordable conventional hybrid vehicles because of their low cost, high reliability and high durability. There are first-generation Prius batteries still on the road with over 200,000 miles and counting. That is why NiMH remains the battery of choice for Toyota's conventional hybrid line up.

5.2.3 Sodium–nickel chloride (Na–NiCl$_2$)

Molten salt batteries (including liquid metal batteries) are a class of battery that uses molten salts as an electrolyte and offers both a high energy density and a high power density. Traditional 'use-once' thermal batteries can be stored in their solid state at room temperature for long periods of time before being activated by heating. Rechargeable liquid metal batteries are used for electric vehicles and potentially also for grid energy storage, to balance out intermittent renewable power sources such as solar panels and wind turbines.

Thermal batteries use an electrolyte that is solid and inactive at normal ambient temperatures. They can be stored indefinitely (over 50 years) yet provide full power in an instant when required. Once activated, they provide a burst of high power for a short period (a few tens of seconds) to 60 minutes or more, with output ranging from a few watts to several kilowatts. The high power capability is due to the very high ionic conductivity of the molten salt, which is three orders of magnitude (or more) greater than that of the sulfuric acid in a lead–acid car battery.

Key Fact

Thermal batteries use an electrolyte that is solid and inactive at normal ambient temperatures.

There has been significant development relating to rechargeable batteries using sodium (Na) for the negative electrodes. Sodium is attractive because of its high potential of 2.71 V, low weight, non-toxic nature, relative abundance and ready availability, and its low cost. In order to construct practical batteries, the sodium must be used in liquid form. The melting point of sodium is 98°C (208°F). This means that sodium-based batteries must operate at high temperatures between 400 and 700°C, with newer designs running at temperatures between 245 and 350°C.

Safety First

Sodium-based batteries must operate at high temperatures between 400 and 700°C, with newer designs running at temperatures between 245 and 350°C.

5.2.4 Sodium–sulphur (Na–S)

The sodium–sulphur or Na–S battery consists of a cathode of liquid sodium into which is placed a current collector. This is a solid electrode of alumina (a form of aluminium oxide). A metal can that is in contact with the anode (a sulphur electrode) surrounds the whole assembly. The major problem with this system is that the running temperature needs to be 300–350°C. A heater rated at a few hundred watts forms part of the charging circuit. This maintains the battery temperature when the vehicle is not running. Battery temperature is maintained when in use due to current flowing through the resistance of the battery (often described as I^2R power loss).

Each cell of this battery is very small, using only about 15 g of sodium. This is a safety feature because, if the cell is damaged, the sulphur on the outside will cause the potentially dangerous sodium to be converted into polysulphides, which are comparatively harmless. Small cells also have the advantage that they can be distributed around the car. The capacity of each cell is about 10 Ah. These cells fail in an open circuit condition and hence this must be taken into account, as the whole string of cells used to create the required voltage would be rendered inoperative. The output voltage of each cell is about 2 V.

5.2.5 Lithium-ion (Li-ion)

Lithium-ion technology is becoming the battery technology of choice, but it still has plenty of potential to offer. Today's batteries have an energy density of up to 140 Wh/kg or more in some cases, but have the potential to go as high as 280 Wh/kg. Much research in cell optimization is taking place to create a battery with a higher energy density and increased range. Lithium-ion technology is currently considered the safest.

Key Fact

Today's batteries have an energy density of approximately 140 Wh/kg or more in some cases, but have the potential to go as high as 280 Wh/kg.

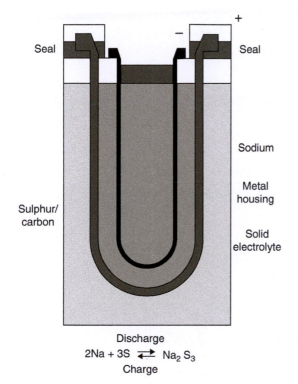

Seal

Seal

Sodium

Metal housing

Solid electrolyte

Sulphur/ carbon

Discharge
$$2Na + 3S \rightleftharpoons Na_2S_3$$
Charge

Figure 5.9 Sodium–sulphur battery

The cathode (marked +) half-reaction is:

$$Li_{1-x}CoO_2 + xLi^+ + xe^- \rightleftharpoons LiCoO_2$$

The anode (marked –) half-reaction is:

$$xLiC_6 \rightleftharpoons xLi^+ + xe^- + xC_6$$

One issue with this type of battery is that in cold conditions the lithium-ions' movement is slower during the charging process. This tends to make them reach the electrons on the surface of the anode rather than inside it. Also, using a charging current that is too high creates elemental lithium. This can be deposited on top of the anode covering the surface, which can seal the passage. This is known as lithium plating. Research is ongoing and one possible solution could be to warm up the battery before charging.

Key Fact

Lithium-ion movement is slower during the charging process if the battery is cold.

The Li-ion battery works as follows. A negative pole (anode) and a positive pole (cathode) are part of the individual cells of a lithium-ion battery together with the electrolyte and a separator. The anode is a graphite structure and the cathode is layered metal oxide. Lithium-ions are deposited between these layers. When the battery is charging, the lithium-ions move from the anode to the cathode and take on electrons. The number of ions therefore determines the energy density. When the battery is discharging, the lithium-ions release the electrons to the anode, and move back to the cathode.

Useful work is performed when electrons flow through a closed external circuit. The following equations show one example of the chemistry, in units of moles, making it possible to use coefficient X.

Bosch is working on post-lithium-ion batteries, such as those made using lithium–sulphur technology, which promises greater energy density and capacity. The company estimates that the earliest the lithium–sulphur battery will be ready for series production is the middle of the 2020s.

There are several ways to improve battery performance. For example, the material used for the anode and cathode plays a major role in the cell chemistry. Most of today's cathodes consist of nickel–cobalt–manganese (NCM) and nickel–carboxyanhydrides (NCA), whereas anodes are made of graphite, soft or hard carbon, or silicon carbon.

High-voltage electrolytes can further boost battery performance, raising the voltage within the cell from 4.5 to 5 volts. The technical

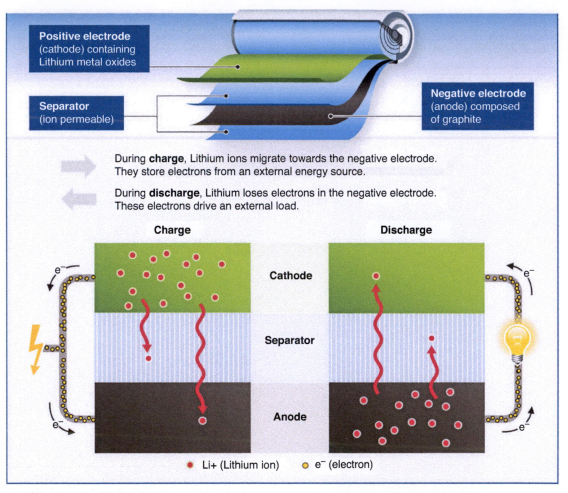

Positive electrode (cathode) containing Lithium metal oxides

Separator (ion permeable)

Negative electrode (anode) composed of graphite

During **charge**, Lithium ions migrate towards the negative electrode. They store electrons from an external energy source.

During **discharge**, Lithium loses electrons in the negative electrode. These electrons drive an external load.

Charge | Discharge

Cathode

Separator

Anode

● Li+ (Lithium ion)   ○ e⁻ (electron)

Figure 5.10 Basic operation of a lithium-ion battery (Source: Bosch Media)

challenge lies in guaranteeing safety and longevity while improving performance. Sophisticated battery management can further increase the range of a car by up to 10%, without altering the cell chemistry.

Key Fact

Sophisticated battery management can further increase the range of a car by up to 10%, without altering the cell chemistry.

5.2.6 Fuel cells

The energy of oxidation of conventional fuels, which is usually manifested as heat, can be

Figure 5.11 Battery developments are ongoing (Source: Bosch Media)

converted directly into electricity in a fuel cell. All oxidations involve a transfer of electrons between the fuel and oxidant, and this is employed in a fuel cell to convert the energy directly into electricity. All battery cells involve an oxide reduction at the positive pole and an oxidation at the negative during some part of their chemical process. To achieve the separation of these reactions in a fuel cell, an anode, a cathode and electrolyte are required. The electrolyte is fed directly with the fuel.

Key Fact

The energy of oxidation of conventional fuels can be converted directly into electricity in a fuel cell.

It has been found that a fuel of hydrogen when combined with oxygen proves to be a most efficient design. Fuel cells are very reliable and silent in operation, but are quite expensive to construct.

Operation of a fuel cell is such that as hydrogen is passed over an electrode (the anode), which is coated with a catalyst, the hydrogen diffuses into the electrolyte. This causes electrons to be stripped off the hydrogen atoms. These electrons then pass through the external circuit. Negatively charged hydrogen anions (OH) are formed at the electrode over which oxygen is passed such that it also diffuses into the solution. These anions move through the electrolyte to the anode. Water is formed as the by-product of a reaction involving the

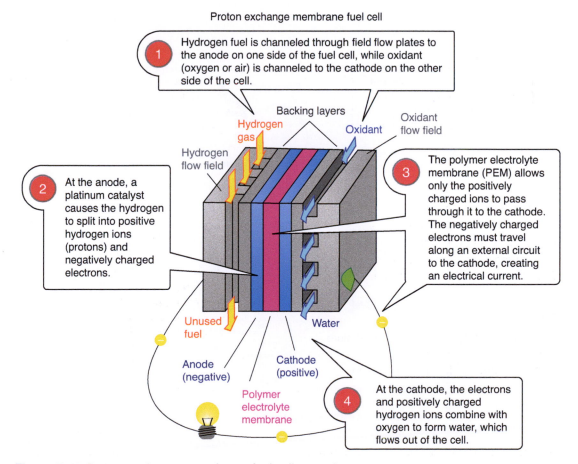

Proton exchange membrane fuel cell

1 Hydrogen fuel is channeled through field flow plates to the anode on one side of the fuel cell, while oxidant (oxygen or air) is channeled to the cathode on the other side of the cell.

Backing layers

Hydrogen gas

Oxidant

Oxidant flow field

Hydrogen flow field

2 At the anode, a platinum catalyst causes the hydrogen to split into positive hydrogen ions (protons) and negatively charged electrons.

3 The polymer electrolyte membrane (PEM) allows only the positively charged ions to pass through it to the cathode. The negatively charged electrons must travel along an external circuit to the cathode, creating an electrical current.

Unused fuel

Water

Anode (negative)

Cathode (positive)

Polymer electrolyte membrane

4 At the cathode, the electrons and positively charged hydrogen ions combine with oxygen to form water, which flows out of the cell.

Figure 5.12 Proton exchange membrane fuel cell operation

hydrogen ions, electrons and oxygen atoms. If the heat generated by the fuel cell is used, an efficiency of over 80% is possible, together with a very good energy density figure. A unit consisting of many individual fuel cells is often referred to as a stack.

Key Fact

A unit consisting of many individual fuel cells is often referred to as a stack.

The working temperature of these cells varies but about 200°C is typical. High pressure is also used and this can be of the order of 30 bar. It is the pressures and storage of hydrogen that are the main problems to be overcome before the fuel cell will be a realistic alternative to other forms of storage for the mass market.

Safety First

The working temperature of fuel cells varies but about 200°C is typical. High pressure is also used and this can be of the order of 30 bar.

Many combinations of fuel and oxidant are possible for fuel cells. Though hydrogen–oxygen is conceptually simple, hydrogen has some practical difficulties, including that it is a gas at standard temperature and pressure and that there does not currently exist an infrastructure for distributing hydrogen to domestic users. More readily usable, at least

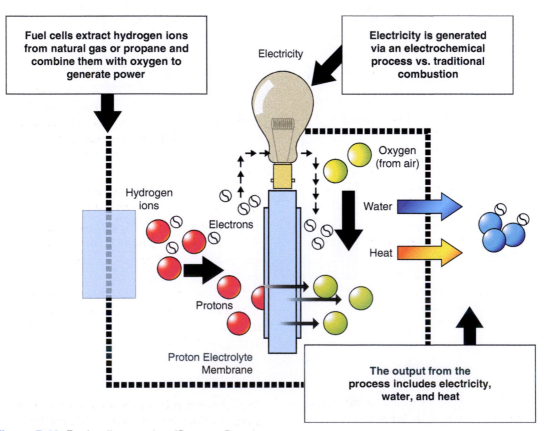

Figure 5.13 Fuel-cell operation (Source: Dana)

in the short term, would be a fuel cell powered by a more easily handled fuel. To this end, fuel cells have been developed that run on methanol. There are two types of fuel cell that use methanol:

▶ reformed methanol fuel cell (RMFC)
▶ direct methanol fuel cell (DMFC).

In the RMFC, a reaction is used to release hydrogen from the methanol, and then the fuel cell runs on hydrogen. The methanol is used as a carrier for hydrogen. The DMFC uses methanol directly. RMFCs can be made more efficient in the use of fuel than DMFCs, but are more complex.

DMFCs are a type of proton exchange membrane fuel cell (PEMFC). The membrane in a PEMFC fulfils the role of the electrolyte, and the protons (positively charged hydrogen ions) carry electrical charge between the electrodes.

Because the fuel in a DMFC is methanol, not hydrogen, other reactions take place at the anode. Methanol is a hydrocarbon (HC) fuel, which means that its molecules contain hydrogen and carbon (as well as oxygen in the case of methanol). When HCs burn, the hydrogen reacts with oxygen to create water and the carbon reacts with oxygen to create carbon dioxide. The same general process takes place in a DMFC, but in the process the hydrogen crosses the membrane as an ion, in just the same way as it does in a hydrogen-fuelled PEMFC.

The real benefit of methanol is that it can easily fit into the existing fuel infrastructure of filling stations and does not need highly specialized equipment or handling. It is easy to store on-board the vehicle, unlike hydrogen, which needs heavy and costly tanks.

5.2.7 Super-capacitors

Super- or ultra-capacitors are very high-capacity but (relatively) low-size capacitors. These two characteristics are achieved by employing several distinct electrode materials prepared using special processes. Some state-of-the-art ultra-capacitors are based on high surface area, ruthenium dioxide (RuO_2) and carbon electrodes. Ruthenium is extremely expensive and available only in very limited amounts.

> **Definition**
> Super- or ultra-capacitors are very high capacity but (relatively) low-size capacitors.

Electrochemical capacitors are used for high-power applications such as cellular electronics, power conditioning, industrial lasers, medical equipment and power electronics in conventional, electric and hybrid vehicles. In conventional vehicles, ultra-capacitors could be used to reduce the need for large alternators for meeting intermittent high-peak power demands related to power steering and braking. Ultra-capacitors recover braking energy dissipated as heat and can be used to reduce losses in electric power steering.

One system in use on a hybrid bus uses 30 ultra-capacitors to store 1600 kJ of electrical energy (20 farads at 400 V). The capacitor bank has a mass of 950 kg. Use of this technology allows recovery of energy when braking, which would otherwise have been lost because the capacitors can be charged in a very short space of time. The energy in the capacitors can also be used very quickly for rapid acceleration.

> **Key Fact**
> A benefit of methanol is that it can easily fit into the existing fuel infrastructure of filling stations.

> **Key Fact**
> Capacitors can be charged in a very short space of time (compared with batteries).

5.2.8 Flywheels

As discussed previously, recovering the energy that would otherwise be lost when a vehicle brakes is an extremely effective way to improve fuel economy and reduce emissions. However, there are some concerns about the environmental impact of widespread battery manufacture and end-of-life disposal. Flywheel technology is one possible answer. A company known as Flybrid produces a mechanically compact kinetic energy recovery system (KERS).

Flywheel technology itself is not new. Flywheel energy storage has been used in hybrid vehicles such as buses, trams and prototype cars before, but the installation tended to be heavy and the gyroscopic forces of the flywheel were significant. The new system overcomes these limitations with a compact and relatively lightweight carbon and steel flywheel.

Figure 5.14 Carbon fibre flywheel (Source: Flybrid)

KERS captures and stores energy that is otherwise lost during vehicle deceleration events. As the vehicle slows, kinetic energy is recovered through the KERS continuously variable transmission (CVT) or clutched transmission (CFT) and stored by accelerating a flywheel. As the vehicle gathers speed,

energy is released from the flywheel, via the CVT or CFT, back into the driveline. Using this stored energy to reaccelerate the vehicle in place of energy from the engine reduces engine fuel consumption and CO_2 emissions.

Figure 5.15 The Flybrid® hybrid system (Source: http://www.flybridsystems.com)

Flywheel systems offer an interesting alternative to batteries or super-capacitors. In a direct comparison they are less complex, more compact and lighter weight. However, the technology challenges involved in a flywheel that can rotate at speeds up to 64,000 rpm, extracting the energy and keeping it safe, should not be underestimated.

Key Fact

Flywheel systems offer an interesting alternative to batteries or super-capacitors.

5.2.9 Summary

As a summary to this section, the following table compares the potential energy density of several types of battery. Wh/kg means watt-hours per kilogram. This is a measure of the power it will supply, and for how long, per kilogram.[1]

Table 5.1 Voltages and energy densities of batteries and storage devices (Primary source: Larminie and Lowry 2012)

Battery type	Specific energy (Wh/kg)	Energy density (Wh/l)	Specific power (W/kg)	Nominal cell voltage (V)	Amp-hour efficiency	Internal resistance (Ohms)	Operating temperature (°C)	Self-discharge (%)	Life cycles to 80%	Recharge time (h)	Relative costs (2015)
Lead–acid	20–35	54–95	250	2.1	80%	0.022	Ambient	2%	800	8 (1 hour to 80%)	0.5
Nickel–cadmium (Ni–Cad)	40–55	70–90	125	1.35	Good	0.06	–40 to +80	0.5%	1,200	1 (20 min to 60%)	1.5
Nickel–metal hydride (Ni–MH)	65	150	200	1.2	Quite good	0.06	Ambient	5%	1,000	1 (20 min to 60%)	2.0
Sodium–nickel chloride (ZEBRA)	100	150	150	2.5	Very high	Very low (increasing at low charge level)	300–350	10%/day	>1,000	8	2.0
Lithium-ion (Li-ion)	140	250–620	300–1,500	3.5	Very good	Very low	Ambient	10%/month	>1,000	2–3 (1 hour to 80%)	3.0
Zinc–air	230	270	105	1.2	n/a	Medium	Ambient	High	>2,000	10 min	
Aluminium–air	225	195	10	1.4	n/a	High hence low power	Ambient	>10%/day but if air removed very low	1,000	10 min	
Sodium–sulphur	100	150	200	2	Very good	0.06	300–350	Quite low if kept warm	1,000	8	
Hydrogen fuel cell	400		650	0.3–0.9 (1.23 open circuit)							
Direct methanol fuel cell (DMFC)	1400		100–500	0.3–0.9 (1.23 open circuit)							
Super-capacitor[2]	1–10		1,000–10,000								
Flywheel	1–10		1,000–10,000								

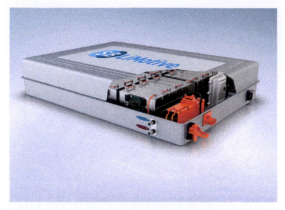

Figure 5.16 Lithium-ion battery
(Source: Bosch Media)

Endnotes

1 Note that figures vary, so use this table as a general guide.
2 Some super–capacitors can have an energy density of several kWh/kg and are used for short–term storage and rapid release.

CHAPTER 6

Motors and control systems

6.1 Introduction

6.1.1 Types of motor

There are several choices for the type of drive motor, the first being between an AC or DC motor. The AC motor offers many control advantages but requires the DC produced by the batteries to be converted using an inverter. A DC shunt wound motor rated at about 50 kW was a popular choice for smaller vehicles, but AC motors are now the most popular. Actually the distinction is blurred. The drive motors can be classed as AC or DC, but it becomes difficult to describe the distinctions between an AC motor and a brushless DC motor.

Key Fact

The AC motor offers many control advantages but requires the DC produced by the batteries to be converted using an inverter.

6.1.2 Trends

The three-phase AC motor with a permanent magnet rotor is now the main choice for most manufacturers. This is because of its efficiency, size and ease of control as well as its torque characteristics. It is powered by DC 'pulses'. This type is described as an electronically commutated motor (ECM).

6.2 Construction and function of electric motors

6.2.1 AC motors: basic principle

In general, all AC motors work on the same principle. A three-phase winding is distributed round a laminated stator and sets up a rotating magnetic field that the rotor 'follows'. The general term is an AC induction motor. The speed of this rotating field and hence the rotor can be calculated:

$$n = 60\frac{f}{p}$$

where n speed in rpm, f frequency of the supply and p number of pole pairs.

6.2.2 Asynchronous motor

The asynchronous motor is often used with a squirrel cage rotor made up of a number of pole pairs. The stator is usually three-phase and can be star or delta wound. The rotating magnetic field in the stator induces an EMF in the rotor which, because it is a complete circuit, causes current to flow. This creates magnetism, which reacts to the original field caused by the stator, and hence the rotor rotates. The amount of slip (difference in rotor and field speed) is about 5% when the motor is at its most efficient.

> **Key Fact**
>
> An asynchronous motor is often used with a squirrel cage rotor.

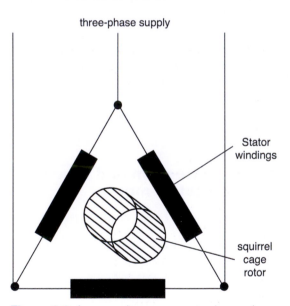

Figure 6.1 An asynchronous motor is used with a squirrel cage rotor made up of a number of pole pairs

6.2.3 Synchronous motor: permanent excitation

This motor has a wound rotor, known as the inductor. This winding is magnetized by a DC supply via two slip rings. The magnetism 'locks on' to the rotating magnetic field and produces a constant torque. If the speed is less than n (see above), fluctuating torque occurs and high current can flow. This motor needs

special arrangements for starting rotation. An advantage, however, is that it makes an ideal generator. The normal vehicle alternator is very similar.

> **Key Fact**
>
> A synchronous motor has a wound rotor known as the inductor.

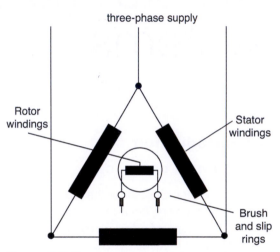

Figure 6.2 Representation of the synchronous motor

6.2.4 DC motor: series wound

The DC motor is a well-proven device and has been used for many years on electric vehicles such as milk floats and forklift trucks. Its main disadvantage is that the high current has to flow through the brushes and commutator.

The DC series wound motor has well-known properties of high torque at low speeds. The figure below shows how a series wound motor can be controlled using a thyristor and also provide simple regenerative braking.

> **Key Fact**
>
> The DC series wound motor has well-known properties of high torque at low speeds and is ideal as a starter motor.

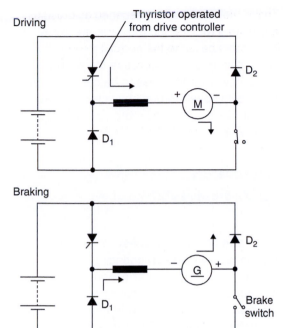

Driving

Thyristor operated from drive controller

D₂

D₁

M

Braking

D₂

D₁

G

Brake switch

Figure 6.3 A series wound motor can be controlled by using a thyristor and can also provide simple regenerative braking

6.2.5 DC motor: separately excited shunt wound

The fields on this motor can be controlled either by adding a resistance or using chopper control in order to vary the speed. Start-up torque can be a problem, but with a suitable controller this can be overcome. The motor is also suitable for regenerative braking by increasing field strength at the appropriate time. Some EV drive systems only vary the field power for normal driving and this can be a problem at slow speeds due to high current.

6.2.6 Motor torque and power characteristics

The torque and power characteristics of four types of drive motors are represented below. The four graphs show torque and power as functions of rotational speed.

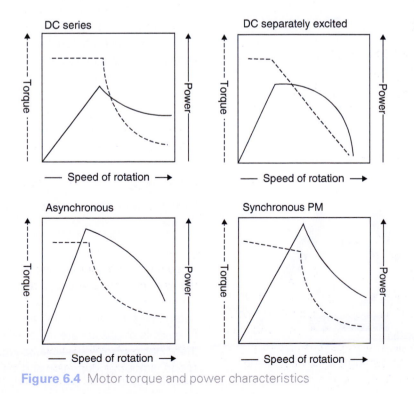

Figure 6.4 Motor torque and power characteristics

6.2.7 Electronically commutated motor

The electronically commutated motor (ECM) is, in effect, half way between an AC and a DC motor. The figure below shows a representation of this system. Its principle is very similar to the synchronous motor above, except the rotor contains permanent magnets and hence no slip rings. It is sometimes known as a brushless motor. The rotor operates a sensor, which provides feedback to the control and power electronics. This control system produces a rotating field, the frequency of which determines motor speed. When used as a drive motor, a gearbox is needed to ensure sufficient speed of the motor is maintained because of its particular torque characteristics. Some schools of thought suggest that if the motor is supplied with square-wave pulses it is DC, and if supplied with sine-wave pulses then it is AC.

Definition

ECM: electronically commutated motor.

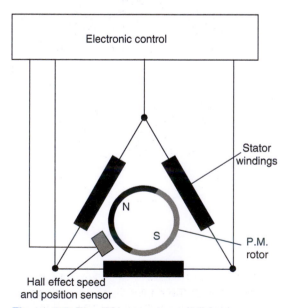

Figure 6.5 The EC motor is an AC motor

These motors are also described as brushless DC motors (BLDC) and they are effectively AC motors because the current through it alternates. However, because the supply frequency is variable, has to be derived from DC and its speed/torque characteristics are similar to a brushed DC motor, it is called a DC motor.

Definition

BLDC: brushless DC motor.

It can also be called a self-synchronous AC motor, a variable frequency synchronous motor, a permanent magnet synchronous motor, or an electronically commutated motor (ECM) – I hope that's clear and prevents any further confusion! However, it is now the motor used for the majority of EVs.

The operating principle is shown in more detail in the following figure. The rotor is a permanent magnet and the current flow through the coil determines the polarity of the stator. If switched in sequence and timed accordingly, the momentum of the rotor will keep it moving as the stator polarity is changed. Changing the switching timing can also make the rotor reverse. Overall therefore good control of the motor is possible.

Key Fact

The EC motor has a permanent magnet rotor.

The switching must be synchronized with the rotor position and this is done by using sensors, Hall Effect in many cases, to determine the rotor position and speed. If three coils or phases are used, as shown next, then finer control is possible as well as greater speed, smoother operation and increased

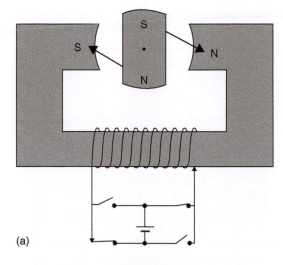

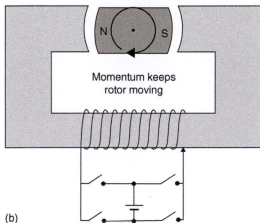

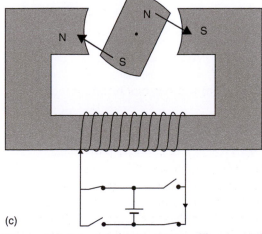

(a)

(b)

(c)

Figure 6.6 Principle of the DC brushless motor operation

torque. Torque reduces as speed increases because of back EMF. Maximum speed is limited to the point where the back EMF equals the supply voltage.

Key Fact

In any type of EC motor, supply switching must be synchronized with the rotor position. This is done by using position sensors.

Definition

Hall Effect: The production of a voltage difference across an electrical conductor, transverse to an electric current in the conductor and a magnetic field perpendicular to the current. This effect was discovered by Edwin Hall in 1879 and is used for sensing rotation speed and position.

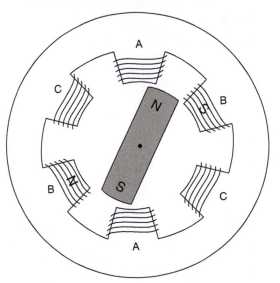

Figure 6.7 Three coils (three-phases) improve on the basic principle. Many more coils are used on real machines (see Figure 6.8)

Two typical motors are shown here, one is integrated with the engine flywheel and the other a separate unit. Both are DC brushless motors and are water cooled.

Figure 6.8 Bosch integrated motor generator (IMG) also called integrated motor assist (IMA) by some manufacturers

Figure 6.9 Separate motor unit showing the coolant connections on the side and the three main electrical connections on top

6.2.8 Switched reluctance motor

The switched reluctance motor (SRM) is similar to the brushless DC motor outlined above. However, the one major difference is that it does not use permanent magnets. The rotor is a form of soft iron and is attracted to the magnetized stator. The basic principle is shown in Figure 6.10 and an improved version in Figure 6.11.

Definition

SRM: switched reluctance motor.

Timing of the switching of the stator is again very important, but the key advantage is that no expensive rare earth magnets are needed. The raw materials for these are a source of

political discussion, with China being the main supplier. Overall the machine is very simple and therefore cheap. Early SRMs were noisy but this has been solved by more accurate switching control.

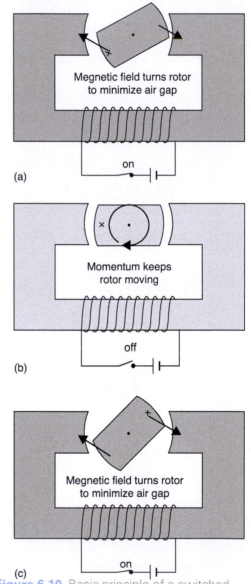

Figure 6.10 Basic principle of a switched reluctance motor

A company known as HEVT has developed a potentially game-changing alternative to induction and permanent magnet motors. These motors have a much reduced cost

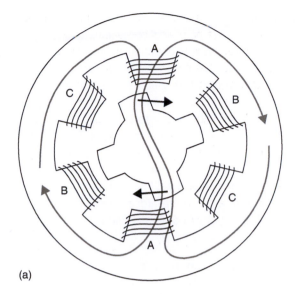

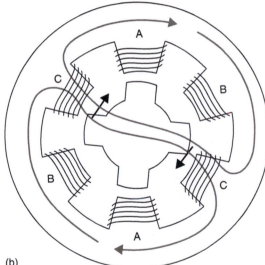

(a)

(b)

Figure 6.11 Improved SRM with additional poles (the rotor invariably has two fewer than the stator)

volatility due to the use of zero rare earth minerals.

The company's patented switched reluctance motors (SRMs) provide high-performance alternatives to induction and permanent magnet motor/generators. One product is being rolled out to provide electrical assist to eBikes, but current motor technology ranges from approximately 150 W scalable to 1 MW and it is expected they may appear

Figure 6.12 Switched reluctance motor stator (left) and rotor without windings on the stator (Source: HEVT)

in some EVs soon. However, they do not work well as generators because of the non-magnetic rotor.

> **Key Fact**
> Switched reluctance motors do not work well as generators because of a non-magnetic rotor.

The SRM control systems are similar to those for BLDC motors, but while they have slightly lower peak torque, their efficiency is maintained over a much wider speed and torque range. The SRM is effectively a powerful stepper motor.

6.2.9 Motor efficiency

Motor efficiency varies with type, size, number of poles, cooling and weight. The designers are always striving to get more out of smaller, lighter packages. In general the efficiency of a BLDC ranges from about 80% for a 1-kW motor to 95% for a 90-kW motor.

> **Key Fact**
> In general the efficiency of a BLDC ranges from about 80% for a 1-kW motor to 95% for a 90-kW motor.

Efficiency is the ratio between the shaft output power and the electrical input power. Power output is measured in watts (W), so efficiency can be calculated:

$$P_{out} / P_{in}$$

where P_{out} = shaft power out (W) and P_{in} = electric power in to the motor (W).

The electrical power lost in the primary rotor and secondary stator winding resistance are also called copper losses. The copper loss varies with the load in proportion to the current squared and can be calculated:

$$R I^2$$

where R = resistance (Ω) and I = current (amp).

Definition

Motor efficiency is the ratio between the shaft output power and the electrical input power.

Other losses include:

▶ Iron losses: the result of magnetic energy dissipated when the motor's magnetic field is applied to the stator core.

▶ Stray losses: the losses that remains after primary copper and secondary losses, iron losses and mechanical losses. The largest contribution to the stray losses is harmonic energies generated when the motor operates under load. These energies are dissipated as currents in the copper windings, harmonic flux components in the iron parts, or leakage in the laminate core.

▶ Mechanical losses: the friction in the motor bearings, in the fan for air cooling or a pump if water or oil cooling is used.

6.3 Control system

6.3.1 Introduction

The following figure shows a generic block diagram of a PHEV. Remove the AC mains block and it becomes an HEV or remove the internal combustion engine (ICE) and it becomes a pure-EV.

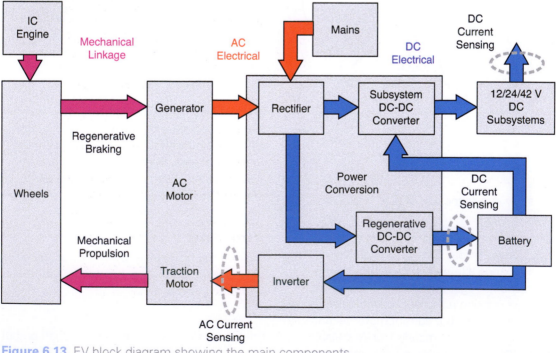

Figure 6.13 EV block diagram showing the main components

The control components are outlined in the next section. These are microprocessor control units that are programmed to react to inputs from sensors and from the driver.

6.3.2 Power control

Motor/generator control: The motor/generator control system mainly performs motor control to provide drive as well as regeneration when the motor is acting as a generator. The main MCU (microprocessor control unit) controls the inverter via a pre-driver circuit. The sequence in which the inverter (labelled IGBT in Figure 6.14) is switched and at what rate determines the torque and speed of the motor.

Key Fact
The main MCU (microprocessor control unit) controls the inverter.

The insulated-gate bipolar transistor (IGBT) is a three-terminal power semiconductor device primarily used as a fast-acting, high-efficiency electronic switch. It is used to switch electric power in many modern appliances as well as electric vehicles.

Inverter: The electronic circuit used to drive a motor is usually called an inverter because it effectively converts DC to AC. An important aspect of this type of motor and its associated control is that it works just as effectively as a generator for regenerative braking. It is controlled by the main MCU in the motor

Component	Purpose
Motor/generator	Provides drive to the wheels and generates electricity when the vehicle is slowing and braking
Inverter	A device to convert DC into AC
Rectifier	A device to convert AC into DC (the inverter and the rectifier are usually the same component)
DC–DC converter: regenerative	This converts the AC from the motor during braking after it has been rectified to DC. The conversion is necessary to ensure the correct voltage level for charging
DC–DC converter: subsystem	A device to convert high-voltage DC into low-voltage DC to run the general vehicle electrics
DC subsystems	The 12 V (or 24/42 V) systems of the vehicle such as lights and wipers – this may include a small 12-V battery
Battery (high voltage)	Usually lithium-ion or nickel–metal hydride cells that form the energy store to operate the drive motor
Battery control	A system to monitor and control battery charge and discharge to protect the battery as well as increasing efficiency
Motor control	Arguably the most important controller, this device responds to sensor signals and driver input to control the motor/generator during the various phases of operation (accelerating, cruising, braking etc.)
Internal combustion engine	Internal combustion engine used on HEVs and PHEVs only – it hybrids with the motor. On an REV the engine would drive a generator to charge the high-voltage battery only

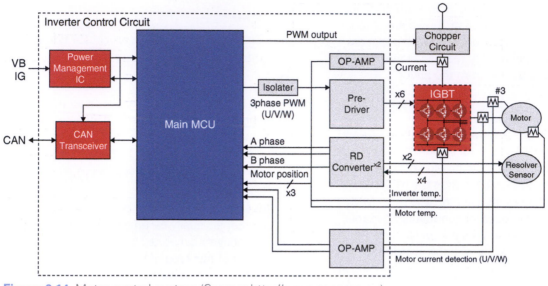

Figure 6.14 Motor control system (Source: http://www.renesas.eu)

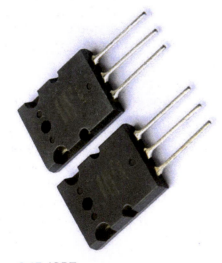

Figure 6.15 IGBTs

controller. The switches shown in Figure 6.16 will in reality be IGBTs. The IGBTs in turn are controlled by a pre-driver circuit that produces a signal that will switch the inverter in a suitable sequence.

Key Fact

An inverter converts DC to AC.

The output signal from the inverter when it is driving the motor is shown, in simplified format, in Figure 6.17.

(General source for this section: Larminie and Lowry, 2012.)

6.3.3 Sensors

In order to carry out motor/generator switching accurately, the power/control electronics need to know the condition and exact speed and position of the motor. The speed and position information is supplied by one or more sensors mounted on the casing in conjunction with a reluctor ring.

Key Fact

Power/control electronics need to know the condition and exact speed and position of the motor.

The system shown in Figure 6.18 uses 30 sensor coils and an eight-lobe reluctor ring. The output signal changes as a lobe approaches the

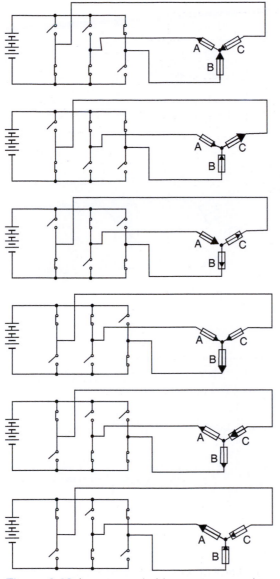

Figure 6.16 Inverter switching pattern used to generate three-phase AC from a DC supply

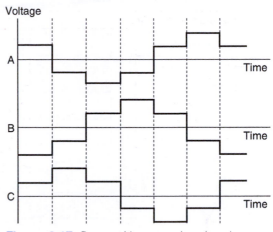

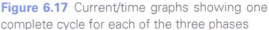

Figure 6.17 Current/time graphs showing one complete cycle for each of the three phases

The position of the rotor can therefore be determined with high accuracy using the amplitudes of the signals. The frequency of the signal gives the rotational speed. Some systems use a very simple sensor; see the Honda case study in Chapter 9.

A drive motor temperature sensor is usually used and it also sends signals to the electric drive control unit. Typically, the power of the drive motor is restricted at temperatures above about 150°C, and in some cases above 180°C it may even prevent the drive from being used to protect it against overheating. The sender is normally a negative temperature coefficient (NTC) thermistor.

6.3.4 **Battery**

Battery charger: A charger and DC–DC step-up system controls the AC input from a household power supply and boosts the voltage, using a DC–DC converter, to whatever is required by the battery. The MCU performs power factor correction and control of the DC–DC step-up circuit (Figure 6.20).

coils and this is recognized by the control unit. The coils are connected in series and consist of a primary and two secondary windings around an iron core. The separate windings produce different signals (Figure 6.19) because as the reluctor moves it causes the signal in each secondary winding to be amplified.

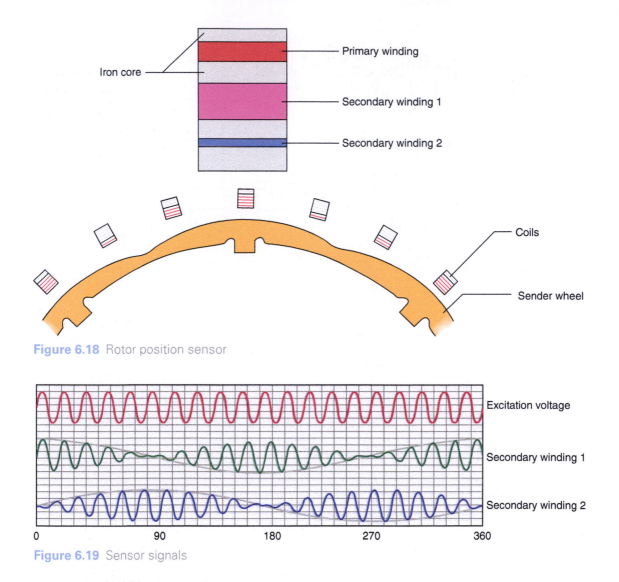

Figure 6.18 Rotor position sensor

- Iron core
- Primary winding
- Secondary winding 1
- Secondary winding 2
- Coils
- Sender wheel

Figure 6.19 Sensor signals

- Excitation voltage
- Secondary winding 1
- Secondary winding 2

0   90   180   270   360

and control of battery charging. Voltages of individual cells are monitored and the balance controlled by a battery cell monitor MCU and lithium-ion battery cell monitor integrated circuits (Figure 6.21).

Battery control: A battery control system is used for managing remaining battery voltage

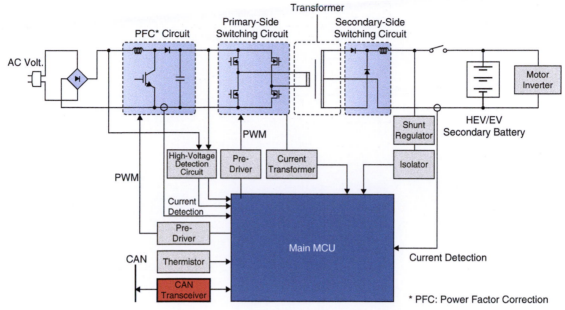

Figure 6.20 Battery charger circuit and control (Source: http://www.renesas.eu)

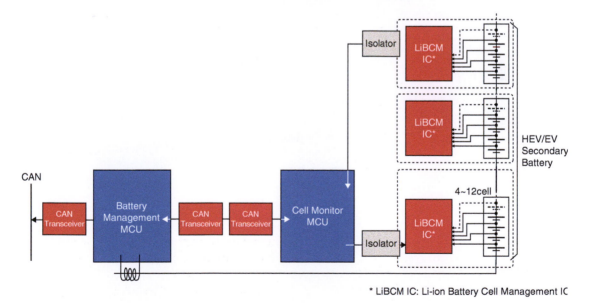

Figure 6.21 Battery control system (Source: http://www.renesas.eu)

CHAPTER 7

Charging

7.1 Charging, standards and infrastructure

7.1.1 Infrastructure

Most electric cars will be charged at home, but national infrastructures are developing. There are, however, competing organizations and commercial companies, so it is necessary to register with a few different organizations to access their charging points. Many businesses now also provide charging stations for staff and visitors. Some are pay in advance, some are pay as you go, and others require a monthly subscription. Many apps and websites are available for locating charge points. One of the best I have found is https://www.zap-map.com

Interestingly, having just completed a roundtrip UK journey in my PHEV of about 600 miles, I did not find any charging points on the main roads and would have had to search local towns for the facilities. I wonder why they are not available in service areas where fuel is sold by multinational oil companies…

Key Fact

There are competing organizations and commercial companies controlling charge points.

Safety note: Although the rechargeable electric vehicles and equipment can be recharged from a domestic wall socket, a charging station has additional current or connection-sensing mechanisms to disconnect the power when the EV is not charging. There are two main types of safety sensor:

1 Current sensors, which monitor the power consumed and only maintain the connection if the demand is within a predetermined range.
2 Additional sensor wires, which provide a feedback signal that requires special power plug fittings.

The majority of public charge points are lockable, meaning passers-by cannot unplug the cable. Some charge points can send a text message to the car owner if the vehicle is unexpectedly unplugged, or tell you when the vehicle is fully charged.

It is safe to charge in wet weather. When you plug in the charge lead, the connection to the supply is not made until the plug is completely in position. Circuit breaker devices are also used for additional safety. Clearly some common sense is necessary, but EV charging is very safe.

Figure 7.1 Charging point on the roadside (Source: Rod Allday, http://www.geograph.org.uk)

Domestic charge points: It is strongly recommended that home charging sockets and wiring are installed and approved by a qualified electrician. A home charge point with its own dedicated circuit is the best way of charging an EV safely. This will ensure the circuit can

Figure 7.2 Charging point (Source: Richard Webb, http://www.geograph.ie)

manage the electricity demand from the vehicle and that the circuit is activated only when the charger communicates with the vehicle, known as the 'handshake'. For rapid charging, special equipment and an upgraded electrical supply would be required and is therefore unlikely to be installed at home, where most consumers will charge overnight.

Figure 7.3 Charging at home

Figure 7.4 Domestic charging point

Key Fact

Most consumers will charge overnight, but charging from solar panels will also become popular.

7.1.2 Charging time

How long it takes to charge an EV depends on the type of vehicle, how discharged the battery is and the type of charge point used. Typically, pure-electric cars using standard charging will take between 6 and 8 hours to charge fully and can be 'opportunity charged' whenever possible to keep the battery topped up.

Key Fact

Charge time for an EV depends on the type of vehicle, how discharged the battery is and the type of charge point used.

Pure-EVs capable of using rapid charge points could be fully charged in around 30 minutes and can be topped up in around 20 minutes, depending on the type of charge point and available power. PHEVs take approximately 2 hours to charge from a standard electricity supply. E-REVs take approximately 4 hours to charge from a standard electricity supply. PHEVs and E-REVs require less time to charge because their batteries are smaller.

7.1.3 Cost

The cost of charging an EV depends on the size of the battery and how much charge is left in the battery before charging. As a guide, charging an electric car from flat to full will cost from as little as £1 to £4. This is for a typical pure-electric car with a 24 kWh battery that will offer around 100-mile range. This results in an average cost of a few pence per mile.

If you charge overnight you may be able to take advantage of cheaper electricity rates when there is surplus energy. The cost of charging from public points will vary; many will offer free electricity in the short term. It is also possible to register with supply companies who concentrate on energy from renewable sources.

Key Fact

The average cost of EV electrical use is a few pence per mile (2016).

Table 7.1 Estimated charging times

Charging time for 100-km range	Power supply	Power	Voltage	Max. current
6–8 hours	Single phase	3.3 kW	230 V AC	16 A
3–4 hours	Single phase	7.4 kW	230 V AC	32 A
2–3 hours	Three phase	10 kW	400 V AC	16 A
1–2 hours	Three phase	22 kW	400 V AC	32 A
20–30 minutes	Three phase	43 kW	400 V AC	63 A
20–30 minutes	Direct current	50 kW	400–500 V DC	100–125 A
10 minutes	Direct current	120 kW	300–500 V DC	300–350 A

7.1.4 Standardization

So that electric vehicles can be charged everywhere with no connection problems, it was necessary to standardize charging cables, sockets and methods. The IEC publishes the standards that are valid worldwide, in which the technical requirements have been defined. Table 7.2 below lists some of the most important standards associated with the charging of EVs:

Types of charging cables: IEC 61851-1 defines the different variants of the connection configuration:

Table 7.2 Charging standards

IEC 62196-1	IEC 62196-2	IEC 62196-3	IEC 61851-1	IEC 61851-21-1	IEC 61851-21-2	HD 60364-7-722
Plugs, socket-outlets, vehicle connectors and vehicle inlets. Conductive charging of electric vehicles	Dimensional compatibility and interchangeability requirements for AC pin and contact tube accessories. The permissible plug and socket types are described	Dimensional compatibility and interchangeability requirements for dedicated DC and combined AC/DC pin and contact-tube vehicle couplers	Electric vehicle conductive charging system. Different variants of the connection configuration, as well as the basic communication with the vehicle, are defined in this standard	Electric vehicle conductive charging systems. Electric vehicle on-board charger EMC requirements for conductive connection to an AC/DC supply	Electric vehicle conductive charging systems EMC requirements for off-board electric vehicle charging systems	Low-voltage electrical installations. Requirements for special installations supply of electric vehicles

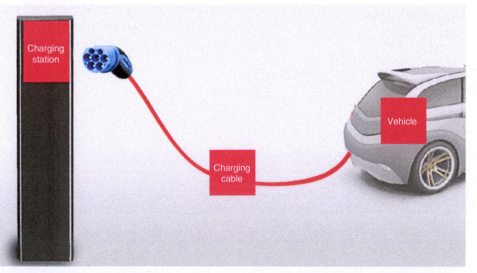

Figure 7.5 Case A: The charging cable is permanently connected to the vehicle (Source: Mennekes)

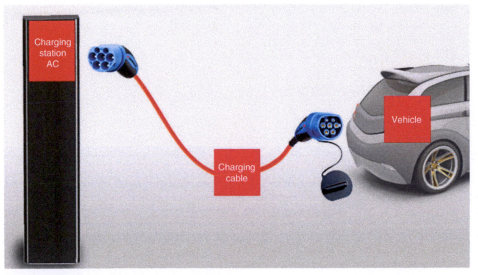

Figure 7.6 Case B: The charging cable is not permanently connected to the vehicle or the charging station (Source: Mennekes)

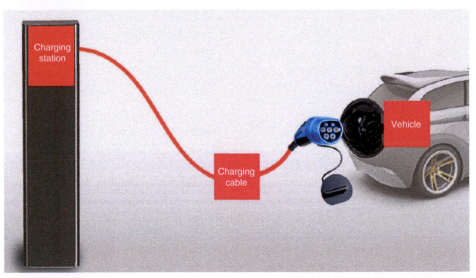

Figure 7.7 Case C: The charging cable is permanently connected to the charging station (Source: Mennekes)

7.1.5 Charging methods

AC charging: Alternating current charging has now established itself as the standard charging method. It is possible in the private sector, as well as at charging stations in the semi-public and public sector, with relatively low investments. Consequently, this charging method also has a long-term future. Standard charging occurs via an alternating current connection and is the most common and most flexible charging method. In charging modes 1 and 2, charging is possible on household sockets or on CEE sockets. On the household socket, charging can take up to several hours due to the power limited through the socket, depending on rechargeable battery capacity, fill level and charging current.

> **Key Fact**
> Alternating current charging has now established itself as the standard charging method.

In charging mode 3 a vehicle can be charged at a charging station where power of up to 43.5 kW is possible with a significantly reduced charging time. Particularly in the private sector, the usable power is limited by the fuse protection of the building connection. Charging powers to maximum 22 kW at 400 V AC are usually the high power limit for home charging stations.

The charging device is permanently installed in the vehicle. Its capacity is adjusted to the vehicle battery. Compared with other charging methods, the investment costs for AC charging are moderate

DC charging: With direct current charging there is a distinction between

▶ DC low charging: up to 38 kW with type 2 plugs
▶ DC high charging: up to 170 kW.

The charging device is part of the charging station, so DC charging stations are significantly more expensive as compared with AC charging stations. The prerequisite for DC charging is an appropriate network of charging stations, which due to the high power require high infrastructure investments. Fast charging with high currents requires appropriately dimensioned line cross-sections that make connecting the vehicles to the charging station more cumbersome. Standardization of the DC charging connection has not yet been concluded and market availability is still uncertain. In practice, vehicles with a DC charging connection have

an additional connection for standard charging so that the vehicle can also be charged at home.

> **Key Fact**
> DC charging stations are significantly more expensive compared with AC charging stations.

Inductive charging: Charging occurs without contacts via inductive loops. The technical complexity and thus the costs are considerable, for the charging station as well as the vehicle. This system is not yet ready for the market or for large-scale production.

> **Definition**
> Inductive charging: no physical connection is made, instead transformer action or mutual induction is used.

Battery replacement: The vehicle's rechargeable battery is replaced with a fully charged battery at the change station. In this case you can continue driving after a few minutes. The prerequisite for this concept would be that vehicle manufacturers would have to install standardized rechargeable batteries at standardized positions in the vehicle. However, such standardization would hardly be possible due to the different vehicle types and uses. The charge stations would have to keep battery types for the different vehicles on hand, which in practice would be equally difficult. Consequently, battery replacement could only be implemented today in closed fleets.

7.1.6 Charging modes

Four different charging modes have been defined for safe charging of electric vehicles

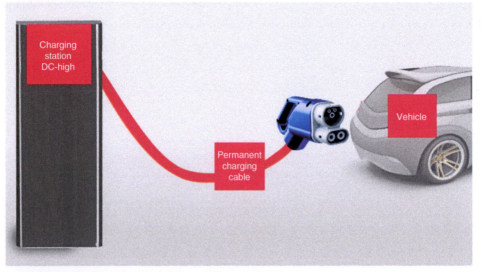

Figure 7.8 DC high charging (Source: Mennekes)

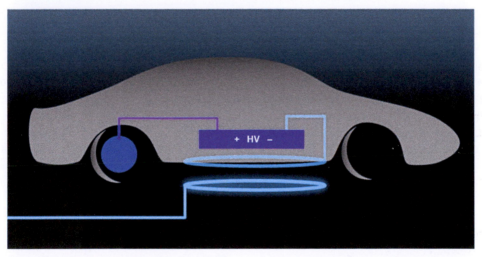

Figure 7.9 Inductive charging

in line with demand. These charging modes differ relative to the power source used (protective contact, CEE, AC or DC charging socket), and they differ relative to the maximum charging power and the communication possibilities.

Safety First
Four different charging modes have been defined for safe charging of electric vehicles.

Mode 1: Charging from a socket to max 16 A three-phase without communication with the vehicle. The charging device is integrated in the vehicle. Connection to the energy network occurs via an off-the-shelf, standardized plug and socket that must be fused via a residual current protective device. This method is not recommended because mode 2 offers greater safety thanks to communication with the vehicle.

Mode 2: Mode for charging from a socket to max. 32 A, three-phase with a control

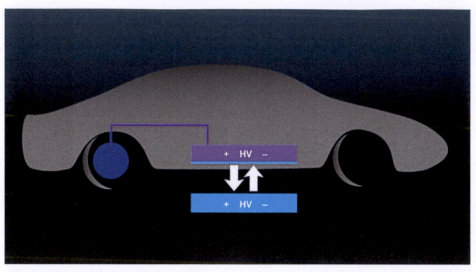

Figure 7.10 Replacement batteries

function and protective function integrated in the cable or the wall-side plug. The charging device is installed in the vehicle. Connection to the energy network occurs via an off-the-shelf, standardized plug and socket. For mode 2 the standard prescribes a mobile device to increase the level of protection. Moreover, for the power setting and to satisfy the safety requirements, a communication device is required with the vehicle. These two components are combined in the In-Cable Control Box (ICCB).

Mode 3: Mode for charging at AC charging stations. The charging device is a fixed component of the charging station and includes protection. In the charging station PWM communication, residual current device (RCD), overcurrent protection, shutdown, as well as a specific charging socket are prescribed. In mode 3 the vehicle can be charged three-phase with up to 63 A so a charging power of up to 43.5 kW is possible. Depending on rechargeable battery capacity and charge status, charges in less than 1 hour are possible.

> **Key Fact**
> Mode 3 for charging at AC charging stations is the most common now in use.

Mode 4: Mode for charging at DC charging stations. The charging device is a component of the charging station and includes protection. In mode 4 the vehicle can be charged with two plug-and-socket systems, both of which are based on the Type 2 plug geometry. The 'Combined Charging System' has two additional DC contacts to 200 A and up to

Figure 7.11 In-Cable Control Box (ICCB)

170 kW charging power. The other option is a plug and socket with lower capacity for a charge to 80 A and up to 38 kW in Type 2 design.

Standards continue to be reviewed and changed to improve safety and ease of use as well as compatibility.

7.1.7 Communication

Basic communication: Safety check and charging current limitation is determined. Even before the charging process starts, in charging modes 2, 3 and 4 PWM communication with the vehicle occurs via a connection known as the control pilot (CP) line. Several parameters are communicated and coordinated. The charging will only begin if all security queries clearly correspond to the specifications and the maximum permissible charging current has been communicated. These test steps are always executed:

> **Definition**
> PWM: pulse width modulation.

1 The charging station locks the infrastructure side charging coupler.
2 The vehicle locks the charging coupler and requests start of charging.
3 The charging station (in mode 2 the control unit in the charging cable) checks the connection of the protective conductor to the vehicle and communicates the available charging current.
4 The vehicle sets the charger accordingly.

If all other prerequisites are met, the charging station switches the charging socket on. For the duration of the charging process, the protective conductor is monitored via the PWM connection and the vehicle has the possibility of having the voltage supply switched off by the charging station. Charging is ended and the plugs and sockets are unlocked via a stop device (in the vehicle).

Limitation of the charging current: The vehicle's charging device determines the charging process. To prevent the vehicle charging device from overloading the capacity of the charging station or of the charging cable, the power data of the systems is identified and adjusted to match. The CP box reads the power data of the cable from the cable. Before the charging process is started, the box communicates the power data to the vehicle via PWM signal, the vehicle's charging device is adjusted accordingly and the charging process can begin, without the possibility of an overload situation occurring.

> **Key Fact**
> The vehicle's charging device determines the charging process.

The weakest link in the charging chain determines the maximum charging current: The charging current in the charger is limited depending on the power of the charging station and the resistance coding in the plug of the charging cable.

> **Key Fact**
> The weakest link in the charging chain determines the maximum charging current.

7.1.8 EU system

Due to the communication and safety devices used, charging couplers do not need a shutter. However, in some European countries national regulations for household couplers are applied to these charging couplers for charging of electric vehicles. Mennekes has developed an add-on for Type 2. Thus a modular system has been produced that enables the Type 2 socket to be equipped with a shutter. In countries that do not have these requirements, the shutter is simply omitted. Thus Type 2 is a solution for all of Europe.

7.1.9 Charging plugs

Worldwide, three different plug-and-socket systems are standardized in IEC 62196-2 for connection of electric vehicles; these three systems are not compatible. Basically, all three standardized systems meet the high safety requirements for the consumer. Voltage is only switched on when the system

has detected that the plugs on the vehicle side and infrastructure side are completely plugged in, that the plugs are locked, and that the protective conductor connection is correct. As long as one of these conditions is not satisfied, the contacts will remain de-energized.

Safety First

Voltage is only switched on when the system has detected that the plugs on the vehicle side and infrastructure side are completely plugged in, that the plugs are locked, and that the protective conductor connection is correct.

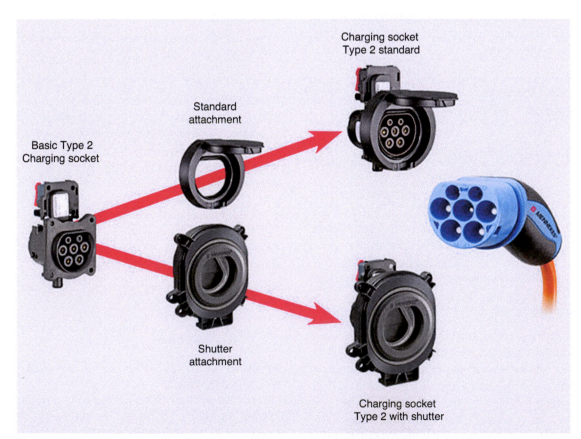

Charging socket
Type 2 standard

Standard
attachment

Basic Type 2
Charging socket

Shutter
attachment

Charging socket
Type 2 with shutter

Figure 7.12 Type 2 system with and without shutter (Source: Mennekes)

Type 1 is a single phase charging plug developed in Japan exclusively for the vehicle-side charging connection. The maximum charging power is 7.4 kW at 230 V AC. Type 1 offers insufficient possibilities for the three-phase European networks.

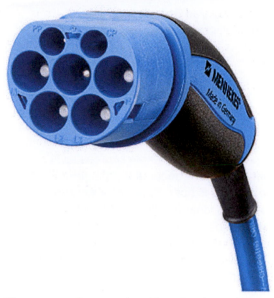

Figure 7.14 Type 2 plug. The pins from the top left and clockwise are: Proximity (PP), Control pilot (CP), Neutral (N), L3, L2, L1 and the Earth pin in the centre (Source: Mennekes)

Figure 7.13 Type 1 plug

Type 2 is the EU charging plug developed in Germany by Mennekes. This is appropriate to single phase alternating current in the private household to the powerful three-phase connection with 63 A. With the EU charging plug at a connection voltage of 230 V single phase, or 400 V three-phase, charging powers from 3.7 kW to 43.5 kW can be transmitted – with identical plug geometry. Type 2 is also the basis for the combined charging system for DC charging. Type 2 plugs and sockets can be used on the vehicle-side as well as on the infrastructure-side. Due to the extensive electronic safety architecture, there is no need for a mechanical touch guard in the charging plug or charging connector.

Type 3 variant was developed in Italy. It is suitable for a connection voltage of 230 V single phase or 400 V three-phase for charging powers from 3.7 kW to 43.5 kW. However, three different plug geometries that are not compatible with each other are required for the different power levels.

For the information in the previous sections I am most grateful to Mennekes (http://www. mennekes.de)

Key Fact

Type 2 is the EU charging plug developed in Germany by Mennekes and is now the most common system in use.

Figure 7.15 Type 3 plug

115

7.1.10 Vehicle-to-grid technology

Vehicle-to-grid (V2G) is a system that uses bidirectional power from the car to the grid as well as the normal charging routine of grid to car. If this system is employed the car battery can be used as a power back-up for the home or business. If the car is primarily charged from renewable sources such as PV panels or wind generation then returning this to the grid is not only ecologically beneficial, it is also an ideal way of stabilizing fluctuations of demand in the grid. The potential problem is managing inrush currents if lots of vehicles fast charge at the same time. This notion is a little way into the future at the time of writing (2015), but the concept of the 'smart grid' using techniques such as this is not far off.

7.1.11 Tesla Powerwall

While not an EV technology, the Tesla Powerwall is a spin-off and if combined with home solar charging it could have a significant impact on EV use. Powerwall is a home battery that charges using electricity generated from solar panels, or when utility rates are low, and powers your home in the evening. It also safeguards against power outages by providing a back-up electricity supply. Automated, compact and simple to install, Powerwall offers independence from the utility grid and the security of an emergency back-up.

> **Key Fact**
> Powerwall is a home battery that charges using electricity generated from solar panels, or when utility rates are low, and powers your home in the evening.

The average home uses more electricity in the morning and evening than during the day when solar energy is plentiful. Without a home battery, excess solar energy is often sold to the power company and purchased back in the evening. This mismatch adds demand on power plants and increases carbon emissions. Powerwall bridges this gap between renewable energy supply and demand by making your home's solar energy available to you when you need it. Home solar installations consist of a solar panel, an electrical inverter, and now a home battery to store surplus solar energy for later use.

- ▶ Solar panel: Installed in an array on your roof, solar panels convert sunlight into electricity.
- ▶ Home battery: Powerwall stores surplus electricity generated from solar panels during the day or from the utility grid when rates are low.
- ▶ Inverter: Converts direct current electricity from solar panels or a home battery into the alternating current used by your home's lights, appliances and devices.

Contained within Powerwall's outdoor-rated enclosure is a rechargeable lithium-ion battery, a liquid thermal management system, a battery management system and a smart DC–DC converter for controlling power flow. The batteries are 7 or 10 kW/h.

7.2 Wireless power transfer

7.2.1 Introduction

Range anxiety continues to be an issue to EV acceptance. Wireless power transfer (WPT) is a means to increase the range of an electric vehicle without substantial impact on the weight or cost. WPT is an innovative system for wirelessly charging the batteries in electric vehicles. There are three categories:

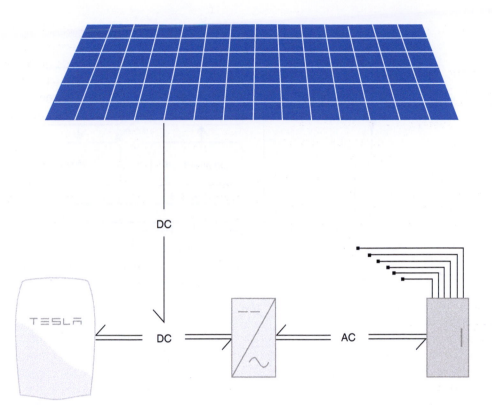

Figure 7.16 Tesla Powerwall System (Source: Tesla)

Figure 7.17 Powerwall (Source: Tesla)

▶ stationary WPT: vehicle is parked, no driver is in the vehicle
▶ quasi-dynamic WPT: vehicle stopped, driver is in the vehicle
▶ dynamic WPT: vehicle is in motion.

> **Definition**
> WPT: wireless power transfer.

There are also three WPT power classes (SAE J2954):

▶ Light Duty Home: 3.6 kW
▶ Light Duty Fast Charge: 19.2 kW
▶ High Duty: 200–250 kW.

With stationary charging, the electric energy is transferred to a parked vehicle (typically without passengers on board). It is important to keep the geometrical alignment of primary and secondary within certain tolerance values in order to ensure a sufficient efficiency rate of the energy transfer.

117

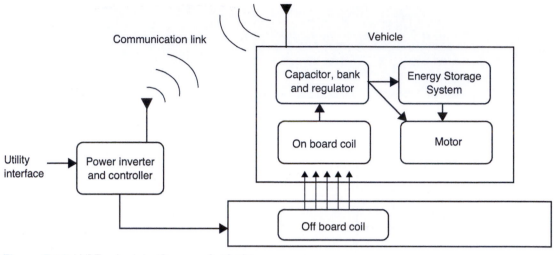

Figure 7.18 WPT principle (Source: CuiCAR)

With quasi-dynamic wireless charging the energy is transferred from the road-side primary coil system of limited length to the secondary coil of a slowly moving, or in stop-and-go mode moving, vehicle (with passengers).

With dynamic wireless charging the energy is transferred via a special driving lane equipped with a primary coil system at a high power level to a secondary coil of a vehicle moving with medium to high velocity.

7.2.2 Stationary WPT

Electric vehicles simply park over an induction pad and charging commences automatically. WPT requires no charging poles or associated cabling. It can accommodate differing rates of charge from a single on-board unit and the rate of charge or required tariff can be set from within the vehicle. It has no visible wires or connections and only requires a charging pad buried in the pavement and a pad integrated onto the vehicle.

Key Fact

Electric vehicles simply park over an induction pad and charging commences automatically.

The system works in a range of adverse environments including extremes of temperature, while submerged in water or covered in ice and snow. It will operate under asphalt or embedded in concrete and is also unaffected by dust or harsh chemicals. WPT systems can be configured to power all road-based vehicles from small city cars to heavy goods vehicles and buses.

A company called haloIPT (inductive power transfer) developed a technique where power at a frequency, usually in the range 20–100 kHz, can be magnetically coupled across IPT pads, which are galvanically isolated from the original source of power. A conceptual system is shown below. This comprises two separate elements. A primary-side power supply, with track and a secondary-side pick-up pad, with controller.

The power supply takes electrical power from the mains supply and energizes a lumped coil, with a current typically in the range 5–125 A. Since the coil is inductive, compensation using series or parallel capacitors may be required to reduce the working voltages and currents in the supply circuitry. These capacitors also ensure an appropriate power factor.

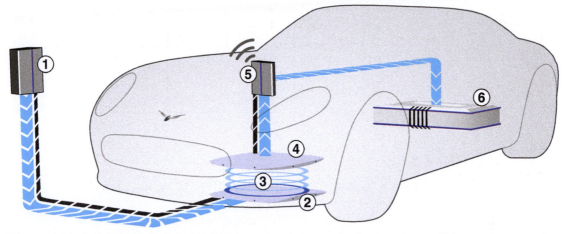

Figure 7.19 An inductive wireless charging system for statically charging an EV: 1, power supply; 2, transmitter pad; 3, wireless electricity and data transfer; 4, receiver pad; 5, system controller; 6, battery (Source: haloIPT)

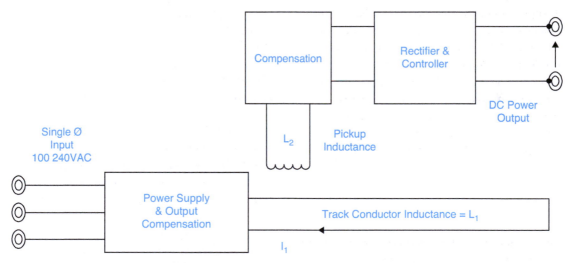

Figure 7.20 Conceptual wireless IPT charging system (Source: haloIPT)

Definition

Power factor: the ratio of the real power flowing to the load to the apparent power in the circuit, expressed as a percentage or a number between 0 and 1.

Real power: capacity of the circuit for performing work in a particular time.

Apparent power: the product of the current and voltage of the circuit.

Pick-up coils are magnetically coupled to the primary coil. Power transfer is achieved by tuning the pick-up coil to the operating frequency of the primary coil with a series or parallel capacitor. The power transfer is controllable with a switch-mode controller.

A block diagram for a single-phase wireless charger is shown as Figure 7.21. The mains supply is rectified with a full bridge rectifier

119

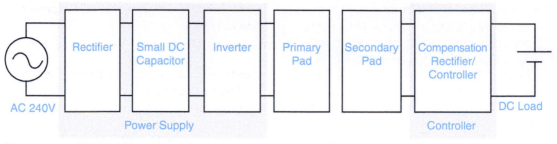

Figure 7.21 IPT (WPT) system components (Source: haloIPT)

followed by a small DC capacitor. Keeping this capacitor small helps the overall power factor and allows the system to have a fast start-up with a minimal current surge. The inverter consists of an H-bridge to energize the tuned primary pad with current at 20 kHz. The 20 kHz current also has a 100 Hz/120 Hz envelope as a result of the small DC bus capacitor. Power is coupled to the secondary tuned pad. This is then rectified and controlled to a DC output voltage appropriate to the vehicle and its batteries. The conversion from AC to DC and back to AC, in the power supply side, is necessary so the frequency can be changed.

> **Definition**
> Inverter: an electrical device that converts direct current into alternating current.

The system includes three distinct hardware components:

1 High-frequency generator or power supply.
2 Magnetic coupling system or transmitter/receiver pads.
3 Pick-up controller/compensation.

The high-frequency generator takes a mains voltage input (240 V AC at 50/60 Hz) and produces high-frequency current (>20 kHz). The output current is controlled and the generator may be operated without a load. The efficiency of the generator is high at over 94% at 2 kW. The generator comprises the following:

▶ mains filter (to reduce EMI)
▶ rectifier
▶ bridge (MOSFETs) converting DC to high-frequency
▶ combined isolating transformer/AC inductor
▶ tuning capacitors (specified for frequency and output current)
▶ control electronics (microcontroller, digital logic, feedback and protection circuits).

> **Definition**
> EMI: electromagnetic interference.

The design and construction of the transmitter and receiver pads gives important improvements over older pad topologies. This results in better coupling, lower weight and a smaller footprint, for a given power transfer and separation. The pads can couple power over gaps of up to 400 mm. The coupling circuits are tuned through the addition of compensation capacitors.

> **Safety First**
> All high voltages are completely isolated, but note that safe working methods are necessary.

A pick-up controller takes power from the receiver pad and provides a controlled output to the batteries, typically ranging from 250 V to 400 V DC. The controller is required to provide an output that remains independent of the load and the separation between pads. Without a controller, the voltage would rise as the gap decreased and fall as the load current increased.

For more information visit https://www.qualcomm.com/products/halo

7.2.3 Dynamic WPT

It seems illogical in many ways but the prospect of wirelessly charging an EV as it drives along a road is already possible and being trialled in a number of countries. The principle is fundamentally the same as static wireless charging but even more complex.

The technology is known as wireless power transfer (WPT).

The challenges with this technology are:

▶ synchronization of energizing coils (timing of power transfer)
▶ acceptable power levels
▶ vehicle alignment
▶ allowable speed profiles
▶ multiple vehicles on charging lane.

A number of feasibility studies and trials are ongoing (2015) and it is expected that this system will be available in the near future. The following image shows the principle of dynamic WPT.

Driver assistance systems may play a role in combination with wireless charging. With stationary wireless charging, a system could be developed where the vehicle is parked automatically and at the same time primary and secondary coils are brought into

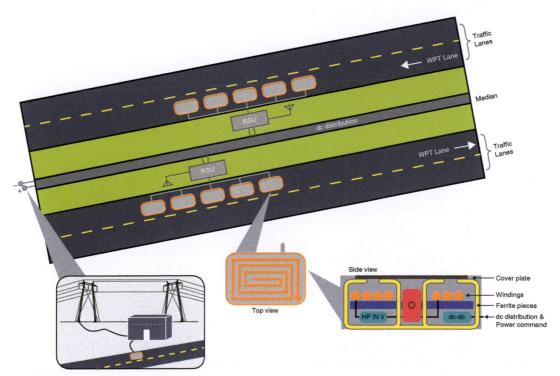

Figure 7.22 Principle of dynamic wireless charging – RSU is a road side unit (Source: Oakridge National Lab)

121

perfect alignment. With quasi-dynamic and dynamic charging the vehicle speed as well as horizontal and vertical alignment could be automatically adapted by dynamic cruise control and lane assist. This would increase the efficiency rate of the energy transfer because of the need to synchronize energy transfer via the coil systems.

> **Key Fact**
> Driver assistance systems may play a role in combination with wireless charging.

Communication will be essential to exchange standardized control commands in real time between the grid and the vehicle control systems. For safety reasons, vehicles in other lanes and other users of the main coil system in the charging lane need to be monitored in real time.

Dedicated short-range communication (IEEE 802.11p) is a likely technology that will be used for low-latency wireless communication in this context.

Finally, powerful electromagnetic fields are used in the active charging zone between primary and secondary coils. For human safety in this respect, compliance with international standards needs to be achieved.

7.3 Solar charging case study

7.3.1 Introduction

In January 2015 I started running an experiment using domestic solar panels, energy saving and monitoring systems, and a plug-in hybrid car. The key part of the plan was to see if I could run the car for free – or at least at very low cost. The 4-kW array of panels was fitted and commissioned on 16 January 2015.

The following charts will show how much electricity (in kilowatt hours; kWh) my panels generated each week compared with my electricity use from the grid, and in due course,

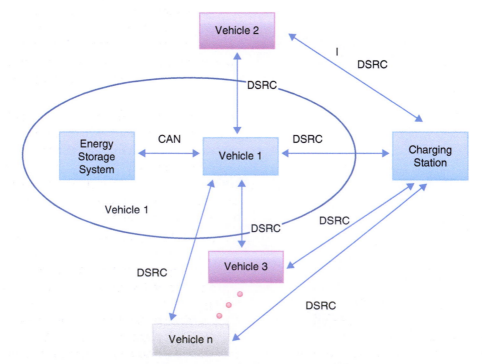

Figure 7.23 Communication is essential for dynamic WPT

Figure 7.24 DC panel connections

Figure 7.26 A 4kW array of PV panels (ten front and six more at the back)

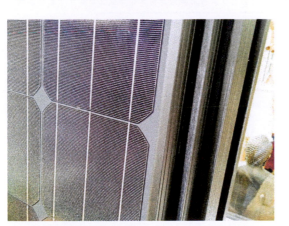

Figure 7.25 Photo voltaic (PV) cell arrangement

the amount used to charge the car. At the end of week 1, they generated 22 kWh; considering the snow and the time of year, I was reasonably impressed!

On 31 January I generated over 1 kW, even with snow, and was generating about 25 kWh a week.

The solar plot on Figure 7.27 is effectively a measure of the amount of weekly sunshine.

The other interesting issue is a matter of timing, because if you use electricity during the night it will come from the grid regardless of how much was generated by the panels during the day. This was something to consider when the car arrived.

My PV array has saved me buying a lot of electricity and has further resulted in an income. Over a period of six months I have received about £400 by selling the excess energy back to the grid (using what is known as a feed-in tariff). In addition, my electricity bill has reduced considerably.

As you would expect, we pay much more for the electricity we use than the price we get when selling it (something like 14p per unit when buying and 3p per unit – a kWh –when selling). The way the feed-in tariff works is that the electricity generation company pays us for 50% of the amount generated by the PV panels. So the more we generate the more we get, but of course the other advantage is gained

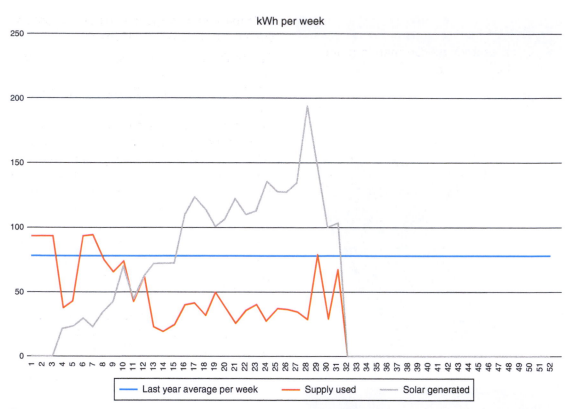

kWh per week

Figure 7.27 Over time it is clear how the solar generated increased and my use from the grid decreased

because the more of the PV energy we use, the less electricity we purchase.

On 7 August 2015 I took delivery of the final part of the puzzle that when put together will result in further savings. Here is my new Golf GTE taking its first charge on my drive – during the day so it uses power from the PV panels.

As well as the £5,000 grant towards the car, the government paid most of the cost of fitting a proper charging unit on the outside wall. This comes with a usage monitor and transmits data back to a central point so EV charging and electricity use can be monitored. This feels a bit 'Big Brother', but I could have paid the full amount! The reason for the monitoring is to look at the effect EVs will have on the grid as much as anything else.

The Golf GTE 1.4 TSI produces 204PS. It is a PHEV (plug-in hybrid electric vehicle) 5-door

Figure 7.28 Golf GTE – one of the first in my region

DSG boasting 0–62 mph in 7.6 seconds and up to 166.0 mpg. The electric range is 31 miles and when electric and petrol combine, the total range is 580 miles. The previous data are laboratory figures of course, but its performance is very impressive so far.

Definition

PS: pferdestärke, the German term for metric horsepower.

Figure 7.29 Domestic wall box mounted outside, with a permanent cable attached. It includes a residual current circuit breaker

The plan is that if doing a long journey all the available charge in the car's lithium-ion (Li-ion) traction batteries is used up when returning home. This can simply be done by switching the car to full e-mode when 35 miles from home. However, with practice it is better to use the electric-only drive under certain conditions and the hybrid on motorways for example. Shorter journeys of course don't require the ICE to run at all and this is where the biggest savings are.

The car has an 8.8 kWh lithium-ion battery (352 V) and this can be fully charged from empty in about 2.5 hours from a 3.6 kW domestic wall box or commercial charging post (9 kWh).[1] Ideally the car will only be charged at home when enough solar energy is available. The other important aspect, however, is to set the charge rate. This can be done in the car or by using a website or a phone app.

To give context for this, if the panels are generating about 1.5 kW on a typical day, that is about 6 A at 240 V, I will choose to set the

car's maximum charge rate to 5 A. The options are 5 A, 10 A, 13 A and Maximum.

At a setting of 5 A, this is about 1.2 kW. If we divide the battery capacity of 8.8 kWh by the 1.2 kW, the result is 7.33 hours. So allowing for some losses, it will take about 8 hours to charge. This is not a problem for say the 'summer half' of the year, but in the 'winter half' it could involve (on average) only having about 6 hours of solar – so I would have to buy about 2 kWh (2 units) from the grid – current cost total of 28 pence (2015). The bottom line therefore, for short journeys anyway, about 1 p per mile – I can live with that! Driving carefully, my previous car (almost identical to this one except it was a GTD) would do 60 mpg. At a cost of say £6 per gallon, 10 p a mile.

Only anecdotal and a one-off example, but I recently completed a journey, by pure coincidence, to the UK VW headquarters where they have a charge point (well they should have, shouldn't they!). This was about a 170-mile round trip for me. I set off with a fully charged battery and managed to add 20-miles worth of charge while I was there. The car trip computer showed an overall average 68 mpg so just under 2.5 gallons for the journey. My previous car would have done the same at an average of about 48 mpg (about 3.5 gallons). This journey was a good combination of country roads and motorway, so probably indicates a reasonably average real-world figure. I did not try to save fuel but equally I didn't accelerate/brake rapidly, so the figures are probably quite a good start for real-world use.

I win much more on the shorter local journeys we do, which will of course use no petrol. For other distances, as an example, my journey to the Institute of the Motor Industry (IMI), where I work, is 42 miles each way. We also have a free EV charging point. On this journey, without trying hard, I use up the battery fully both ways and achieve 80 mpg so only use about half a gallon of petrol. I could improve on this with a little more control of my right foot, I am sure!

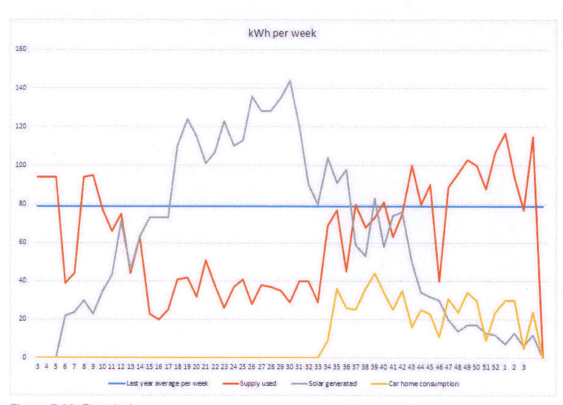

Figure 7.30 Electrical usage

7.3.2 **Latest results**

Figure 7.30 shows the latest plot of solar electricity generated, grid electricity purchased and how much was used to charge the car. The blue line shows last year's average use.

To learn more and see how this project progresses, please visit my blog at http://www. automotive-technology.co.uk

Endnote

1   3.6 kW × 2.5 h = 9 kWh.

CHAPTER 8

Maintenance, repairs and replacement

8.1 Before work commences

8.1.1 Introduction

Before carrying out any practical work on an EV, you should be trained or supervised by a qualified person. Refer to Chapter 1 for procedures on safe working and PPE and making the system safe for work. Key aspects of practical work on EVs (and any other vehicles for that matter) are as follows:

▶ observation of health and safety
▶ correct use of PPE
▶ correct use of tools and equipment
▶ following repair procedures
▶ following workplace procedures
▶ referral to manufacturer-specific information.

> **Safety First**
> Before carrying out any practical work on an EV, you should be trained or supervised by a qualified person.

Note: Before starting work on any high-voltage system you should have been suitably trained and have access to appropriate information – do not guess when it comes to your life!

8.1.2 Technical information

There are many sources of technical and other information, but in the case of EVs it is essential to refer to the manufacturer's data, safety data sheets and workshop manuals. You should also be aware of the appropriate technique for gathering information from drivers/customers. For example, asking questions politely about when, where or how a problem developed can often start you on the road to the solution. General sources of information include the following:

▶ paper-based, electronic
▶ on vehicle data/warnings
▶ wiring diagrams
▶ repair instructions
▶ bulletins
▶ verbal instruction.

An example of a manufacturer's data about component location is shown in the following figure.

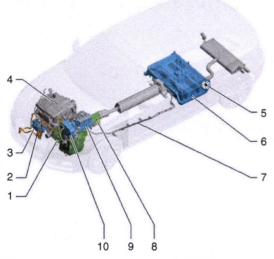

Figure 8.1 Components on a Golf GTE:
1, three-phase current drive (electric drive motor, drive motor temperature sender); 2, high-voltage battery charging socket; 3, electrical air conditioner compressor; 4, combustion engine; 5, battery regulation control unit; 6, high-voltage battery; 7, high-voltage cables; 8, high-voltage heater (PTC); 9, power and control electronics for electric drive (control unit for electric drive, intermediate circuit capacitor, voltage converter, DC/AC converter for drive motor); 10, charging unit 1 for high-voltage battery (Source: Volkswagen Group)

8.1.3 De-energizing

Different manufacturers have different ways to de-energize the high-voltage system – you **must** refer to specific data for this operation. Below I have presented a typical example of a de-energization process on a VW vehicle with model year 2015:

> **Safety First**
>
> Different manufacturers have different ways to de-energize the high-voltage

system – you **must** refer to specific data for this operation.

1. Park the vehicle securely.
2. Connect diagnostic tester.
3. Select Diagnosis mode, and start diagnosis.
4. Select Test plan tab.
5. Push Select own test button, and select the following menu items one after the other:

▶ Body/Electrical system.
▶ Self-diagnosis compatible systems.
▶ Electric drive control unit.
▶ Electric drive control unit, Functions.
▶ De-energize high-voltage system.

Figure 8.2 Maintenance connector (green) and warning label on a Golf GTE

You will be requested to pull off the maintenance connector for the high-voltage system during the program sequence. The maintenance connector for the high-voltage system is an electrical coupling point between the contactors and the high-voltage battery. It must always be removed if the high-voltage system is to be worked on. Final actions are to:

▶ ascertain that the system is de-energized, and secure it to prevent reactivation using a padlock

- lock the high-voltage system, the ignition key and the key for the padlock must then be stored at a safe location
- attach appropriate warning signs.

It may also be appropriate to check:

- fault codes
- driver display module warning information
- warning signs are in place.

Figure 8.3 Warning signs used when work is being carried out on a vehicle after de-energization

In some cases a technician qualified in high voltage may carry out the de-energization process for others to then do specific work.

8.2 Maintenance

8.2.1 Repairs affecting other vehicle systems

If care is not taken, work on any one system can affect another. For example, removing and replacing something as simple as an oil filter can affect other systems if you disconnect the oil pressure switch accidently or break it by slipping with a strap wrench.

For this reason, and of course it is even more important when dealing with a high-energy system, you should always consider connections to other systems. A good example would be if disconnecting a 12-V battery on an HEV, the system could still be powered by the high-voltage battery and DC–DC converter. Manufacturer's information is therefore essential.

Electro-magnetic radiation (or interference) can affect delicate electronics. Most engine control units are shielded in some way, but

the very high-strength magnets in the rotor of some EV motors could cause damage. From a different perspective, an interesting news article recently noted how lots of drivers in a specific car park could not unlock their vehicles remotely. This is still under investigation but it sounds like an electromagnetic radiation (EMR) issue to me – power lines nearby perhaps!

> **Definition**
> EMR: electro-magnetic radiation.

8.2.2 Inspect high-voltage components

During any service or repair operation it is important to inspect high-voltage components. This includes the charging cables shown as Figure 8.4.

Figure 8.4 Domestic mains and charge point cables

Cables

Two key aspects when inspecting high-voltage components to be aware of are the:

- current draw capability of the vehicle
- potential for short circuits and the subsequent vehicle component damage.

In addition you must be able to identify components and the connection methods used. High-voltage components and

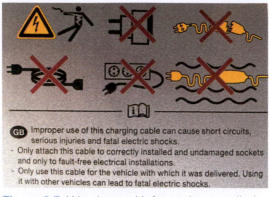

Figure 8.5 Warning and information supplied as part of the charging cables

high-voltage cables should undergo a visual check for damage and correct routing as well as security. Pay attention to the following during the visual check:

▶ any external damage to the high-voltage components
▶ defective or damaged insulation of high-voltage cables
▶ any unusual deformations of high-voltage cables.

Figure 8.6 High-voltage cables

Battery

Check high-voltage batteries for:

▶ cracks in upper part of battery housing or battery tray

▶ deformation of upper part of battery housing or battery tray
▶ colour changes due to temperature and tarnishing of housing
▶ escaping electrolyte
▶ damage to high-voltage contacts
▶ fitted and legible information stickers
▶ fitted potential equalization line
▶ corrosion damage.

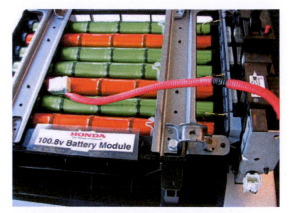

Figure 8.7 Honda battery pack

Other components

Engine compartment area: check the condition of the power and control electronics for electric drive, high-voltage cables for battery and air conditioning compressor, high-voltage cable for electric drive as well as high-voltage charging socket in radiator grille or in tank cap as appropriate.

Underbody: check high-voltage battery as well as high-voltage cables for battery.

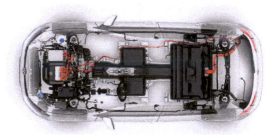

Figure 8.8 High-voltage and other components (Source: Volkswagen Media)

PHEV maintenance issue

An interesting issue that has the potential for causing maintenance problems for a PHEV is if the driver completes journeys that are always less than the full electric range. This could result in the ICE not being used for very long periods of time. The fuel could go stale and mechanical parts could seize in extreme cases.

The solution is that most cars of this type now have a maintenance mode that can either be activated by the driver or will, more likely, operate automatically from time to time.

8.3 Remove and replace

8.3.1 High-voltage components

The main high-voltage (also described as high-energy) components are generally classified as:

- cables (orange!)
- drive motor/generator
- battery management unit
- power and control unit (includes inverter)
- charging unit
- power steering motor
- electric heater
- air conditioning pump.

Figure 8.9 The AC compressor on this car is driven by a high-voltage motor but still deep down on the side of the engine. You can just make out the orange supply cable here! (Source: Volkswagen Group)

General safety points to note with this type of work (see also Chapter 2, Safe Working):

- Poisonous dust and fluids pose a health hazard.
- Never work on high-voltage batteries that have short-circuited.
- Danger of burns from hot high-voltage battery.
- Hands may sustain burns.
- Wear protective gloves.
- Cooling system is under pressure when the engine is hot.
- Risk of scalding to skin and body parts.
- Wear protective gloves.
- Wear eye protection.
- Risk of severe or fatal injury due to electric shock.

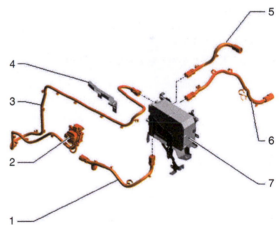

Figure 8.10 High-voltage cables: 1, AC compressor cable; 2, charging socket; 3, charging socket cable; 4, guide; 5, battery charger cable; 6, high-voltage heater cable; 7, charging unit

All high-voltage remove-and-replace jobs will start with the de-energizing process and, after completion, the re-energizing process.

Manufacturer's information is essential for any remove-and-replace job that involves high voltage. Generic instructions for any

131

Figure 8.11 Toyota Prius engine bay

Figure 8.12 Golf GTE engine bay

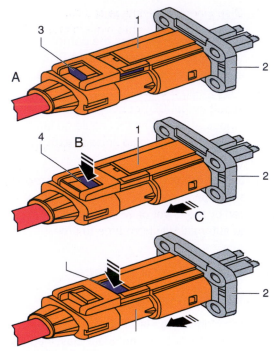

Figure 8.13 Locking connectors: Pull out lock 3 in direction A, Push mechanism 4 in direction B and pull off connector 1 until it is against the second lock, Push mechanism 5 in direction D and the connector can now be removed completely

component would be something like the following, but more detailed:

1 De-energize the system.
2 Drain coolant if appropriate (many high-voltage components require cooling).
3 Remove any covers or cowling.
4 Remove high-voltage cable connections (for safety reasons, some connectors are double locked, Figure 8.13 shows an example).
5 Remove securing bolts/nuts as necessary.
6 Remove the main component.

Safety First

Manufacturer's information is essential for any remove-and-replace job that involves high voltage.

8.3.2 Battery pack

For most battery-removal jobs, special tools and workshop equipment may be necessary, for example:

▶ hose clamps
▶ scissor-type lift platform
▶ drip tray
▶ protective cap for power plug.

Typical removal process:

1 De-energize high-voltage system.
2 Remove underbody covers.
3 Remove silencer.
4 Remove heat shield for high-voltage battery.
5 Open filler cap on coolant expansion tank.
6 Set drip tray underneath.
7 Remove potential equalization line.

8 Disconnect high-voltage cables.
9 Fit protective cap onto high-voltage connection.
10 Clamp off coolant hoses with hose clamps.
11 Lift retaining clips, remove coolant hoses from high-voltage battery, and drain coolant.
12 Prepare scissor-type lift assembly platform with supports.
13 Raise lift assembly platform to support the high-voltage battery.
14 Remove mounting bolts.
15 Lower high-voltage battery using lift assembly platform.

Installation is carried out in the reverse order; note the following:

▶ Tighten all bolts to specified torque.
▶ Before connecting high-voltage cable, pull protective cap off high-voltage connection.
▶ Refill coolant.
▶ Re-energize high-voltage system.

8.3.3 Low-voltage components

As well as high voltage, a large part of our work on EVs will be working on the low-voltage systems. Sometimes these are described as 'low-energy' to distinguish them from the 'high-energy' components such as the drive motor – but do remember that components such as a starter motor are low voltage but not low energy! Low-voltage systems will include:

▶ control units/fuse boxes
▶ low-energy components associated with interior heating
▶ wiring harness/cabling
▶ battery
▶ starter motor
▶ alternator
▶ switches
▶ lighting
▶ low-energy components associated with air conditioning
▶ alarm/immobilizer
▶ central locking
▶ electric windows/wipers/washers
▶ central locking.

For full details on these systems, please refer to *Automobile Electrical and Electronic Systems* (Denton 2013) – a new edition will be available in 2016.

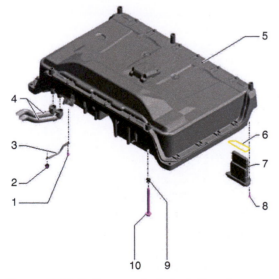

Figure 8.14 Battery pack: 1, bolt; 2, nut; 3, potential equalization line; 4, coolant hoses; 5, high-voltage battery; 6, gasket; 7, battery regulation control unit; 8, bolt; 9, captive nut; 10, bolt (Source: Volkswagen Group)

Figure 8.15 Standard 12 V starter motor (Source: Bosch Media)

8.4 Completion of work

8.4.1 Re-energizing

Different manufacturers have different ways to re-energize the high-voltage system – you **must** refer to specific data for this operation. Below I have presented a typical example of a re-energization process on a VW vehicle with model year 2015:

> **Safety First**
>
> Different manufacturers have different ways to re-energize the high-voltage system – you **must** refer to specific data for this operation.

1. Connect diagnostic tester.
2. Select Diagnosis mode, and start diagnosis.
3. Select Test plan tab.
4. Push Select own test button, and select the following menu items one after the other:

▶ Body/Electrical system.
▶ Self-diagnosis compatible systems.
▶ Electric drive control unit.
▶ Electric drive control unit, Functions.
▶ Re-energize high-voltage system.

You will be requested to replace the maintenance connector for high-voltage system during the program sequence. It may also be necessary to:

▶ clear fault codes
▶ check and update the driver display module
▶ reset warning information.

8.4.2 Results, records and recommendations

This alliterative section is often overlooked, but it is very important to make a final check of any test results, keep a record of them and then, when appropriate, make recommendations to the customer. To interpret results, good sources of information are essential, for example:

▶ wiring diagrams
▶ repair instructions
▶ bulletins
▶ torque settings
▶ technical data
▶ research and development data.

All manufacturers now have online access to this type of information. It is essential that proper documentation is used and that records are kept of the work carried out. For example:

▶ job cards
▶ stores and parts records
▶ manufacturers' warranty systems.

These are needed to ensure the customer's bill is accurate and also so that information is kept on file in case future work is required or warranty claims are made. Recommendations may also be made to the customer, such as the need for:

▶ further investigation and repairs
▶ replacement of parts.

Or, of course, the message that the customer will like to hear, that no further action is required!

Figure 8.16 Electronic data source

Recommendations to your company are also useful, for example to improve working methods or processes to make future work easier or quicker.

Results of any tests carried out will be recorded in a number of different ways. The actual method will depend on what test equipment was used. Some equipment will produce a printout, for example. However, results of all other tests should be recorded on the job card. In most cases this will be done electronically but it is the same principle.

Key Fact

Always make sure that the records are clear and easy to understand.

8.5 Roadside assistance

8.5.1 Introduction

Some EVs require special handling when it comes to roadside assistance and recovery operations. EV manufacturers provide detailed

information and a number of other sources are becoming available such as phone apps.

Safety First

Some EVs require special handling when it comes to roadside assistance and recovery operations.

Much of the information in these sections is freely available to first responders and is provided by Tesla Motors on their website (https://www.teslamotors.com/firstresponders).

8.5.2 Roadside repairs

Roadside repairs should only be carried out by qualified personnel and by following all the safety and repair procedures outlined previously in this book. General information as well as more specific details are available.

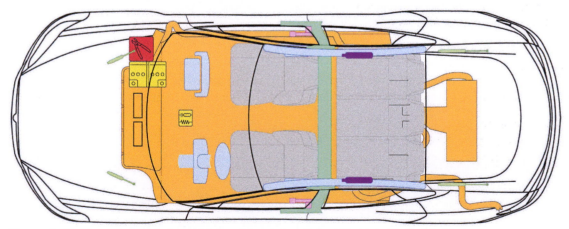

Figure 8.17 Key component and high-voltage information (Source: Tesla Motors)

(Continued)

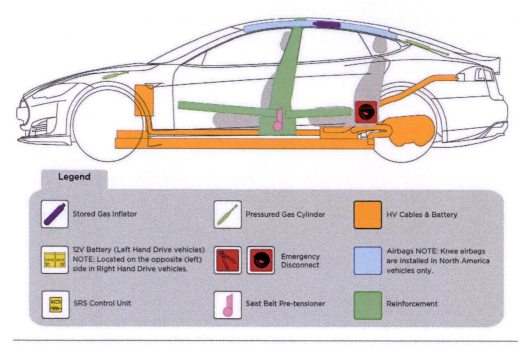

Figure 8.17 (Continued)

MODEL S 2014

GENERAL INSTRUCTIONS

- Always assume the vehicle is powered, even if it is silent!
- Never touch, cut, or open any orange high voltage cable or high voltage component.
- Do not damage the battery pack, even if the propulsion system is deactivated.
- In the event of a collision with pre-tensioner or airbag deployment, the high voltage system should automatically disable.

⚠ WARNING: After deactivation, the high voltage circuit requires two minutes to deplete.

⚠ WARNING: The SRS control unit has a backup power supply with a discharge time of approximately ten seconds.

IMMOBILIZE THE VEHICLE

STEP 1: Chock the wheels.

STEP 2: Set the Parking Brake by pushing in the button on the end of the gearshift stalk.

Figure 8.18 General instructions and deactivation information (Source: Tesla Motors)

(Continued)

DEACTIVATE THE VEHICLE

The cut loop is located under the hood on the right side of the vehicle.

STEP 1: Open the hood using one of these methods:

- Double-click the Front Trunk (hood) button on the key.

- Touch Front Trunk on the touchscreen.

- Pull the release handle located under the glove box, then push down on the secondary catch lever. To release the pressure against the secondary catch, you may need to push the hood down slightly.

STEP 2: Remove the access panel (cowl screen) by pulling its rear edge upward to release the five clips that hold it in place.

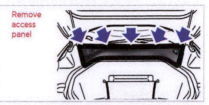

Remove access panel

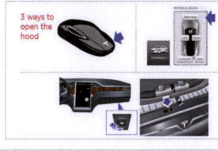

3 ways to open the hood

STEP 3: Double cut a section out of the loop so that the ends cannot reconnect.

Double cut the loop

- If you cannot access the front cut loop, disable the high voltage by cutting into the second-row door pillar nearest the charge port.

- Use a 12" circular saw to cut 6 in (152 mm) through the label (right) and into the pillar.

P/N: SC-14-94-002 R1

Figure 8.18 (Continued)

8.5.3 Recovery

For roadside recovery, many manufacturers provide roadside assistance numbers for the driver to call. In addition, detailed data sheets are provided that give information similar to the following instructions for transporters (provided by Tesla in relation to the Model S):

Use a flatbed only

Use a flatbed trailer only, unless otherwise specified by Tesla. Do not transport Model S with the tyres directly on the ground. To transport Model S, follow the instructions exactly as described. Damage caused by transporting Model S is not covered by the warranty.

Disable self-levelling (air suspension vehicles only)

If Model S is equipped with Active Air Suspension, It automatically self-levels, even when power is off. To prevent damage, you must use the touchscreen to activate Jack mode, which disables self-levelling:

1. Touch CONTROLS on the bottom left of the touchscreen.
2. Press the brake pedal, then touch **Controls > Driving > Very High** to maximize height.
3. Touch Jack

When jack mode is active, Model S displays this indicator light on the instrument panel, along with a message telling you that active suspension is disabled. NOTE: Jack mode cancels when model S is driven over 4.5 mph (7 km/h).

CAUTION: Failure to activate Jack mode on a Model S equipped with active suspension can result in the vehicle becoming loose during transport, which may cause significant damage.

Activate tow mode

Model S may automatically shift into Park when it detects the driver leaving the vehicle, even if it has previously been shifted into Neutral. To keep Model S in Neutral (which disengages the parking brakes), you must use the touchscreen to activate Tow Mode:

1. Shift into Park.
2. Press the brake pedal, then on the touchscreen, touch **Controls > E-Brakes & Power Off > Tow Mode.**

When Tow mode is active, Model S displays this indicator light on the instrument panel along with a message telling you that Model S is free-rolling.

NOTE: Tow mode cancels when Model S is shifted into Park.

CAUTION: If the electrical system is not working, and you therefore cannot release the electric parking brake, attempt to quick start the 12-V battery. For instructions, call the number noted on the previous page. If a situation occurs where you cannot disengage the parking brakes, use tyre skids or transport Model S for the shortest possible distance using wheeled dollies. Before doing so, always check the dolly manufacturer's specifications and recommended load capacity.

Connect the tow chain

The method used to connect the tow chain depends on whether Model S is equipped with a towing eye.

Lower suspension arms

Attach the tow chains using the large hold on each of the rearmost lower suspension arms. Place a 2" x 4" piece of wood between the tow chains and the underbody.
CAUTION: Before pulling, position the wood between the tow chain and the underbody to protect the underbody from any damage that could be caused by the tow chain.

Towing eye (if equipped)

Remove the nose cone by inserting a plastic pry tool into the top right corner, then gently pry the nose cone towards you. When the clip releases, pull the nose cone towards you, without twisting or bending it, to release the three remaining clips.

CAUTION: Do not use a metal object (such as a screwdriver). Doing so can damage the nose cone and the surrounding area.

Fully insert the towing eye (found in the front trunk) into the opening on the right side, then turn it counter-clockwise until securely fastened. When secure, attach the tow chain to the towing eye.

CAUTION: Before pulling, make sure the towing eye is securely tightened.

Pull onto the trailer and secure the wheels

▶ Secure wheels using chocks and tie-down straps.
▶ Ensure any metal parts on the tie-down straps do not contact painted surfaces or the face of the wheels.
▶ Do not place straps over body panels or through the wheels.

CAUTION: Attaching straps to the chassis, suspension or other parts of the vehicle body may cause damage.

CAUTION: To prevent damage, do not transport Model S with the tyres directly on the ground.

8.5.4 Emergency response

In an earlier section I outlined some general aspects that are important for emergency personnel. Most manufacturers supply detailed information that covers aspects such as:

▶ model identification
▶ high-voltage components
▶ low-voltage system
▶ disabling high voltage
▶ stabilizing the vehicle
▶ airbags and SRS
▶ reinforcements
▶ no-cut zones
▶ rescue operations
▶ lifting
▶ opening.

Key Fact

Most manufacturers supply detailed information.

A good example of this material is available from Tesla Motors on their website: https://www.teslamotors.com/firstresponders

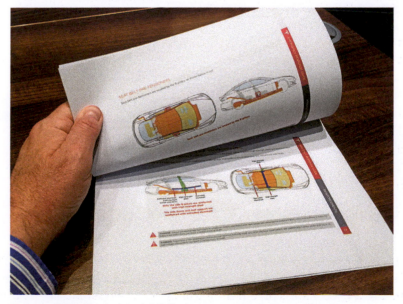

Figure 8.19 Tesla Model S Emergency response guide (showing information on seat belt tensioners and the location of reinforcements and high-strength steel)

8.5.5 Pro-Assist hybrid mobile app

Pro-moto are long-standing experts in the field of vehicle technical training, specializing in EVs, hybrids and hydrogen-propelled vehicle technologies. The company is committed to improving the effectiveness and experience of service professionals and businesses that provide rescue, recovery, recycling and repair services to the EV, HEV and hydrogen fuel cell industry. Safety is a key factor in this commitment. They are also focused on assisting any potential or active hybrid and EV owners to improve their education, insight, choice and options regarding their vehicles and in optimizing their experience of ownership and lifetime value. Pro-Assist is a subsidiary of Pro-moto.

The Pro-Assist hybrid app was commissioned to help first responders, recyclers and repairers understand the special and different requirements of hybrid vehicles. This is particularly important when dealing with emergency, critical, recovery, repair and routine maintenance situations. As well as continuing to develop the hybrid app, by adding more information and additional vehicles, further apps are planned for pure-electric and fuel cell vehicles. The apps are created in collaboration with the Society of Motor Manufacturers and Traders (SMMT) and the industry's leading hybrid and electric vehicle manufacturers. It is available through all major app stores.

Vehicle-specific information is accessed from the main menu and then by an alphabetical list of vehicles, as shown above. Generic information is also supplied in relation to hazard assessment, battery technology and some historical events. The following screenshot images are just a very small example of the detailed information supplied via this essential app.

Figure 8.20 Main menu of the Pro-Assist hybrid app

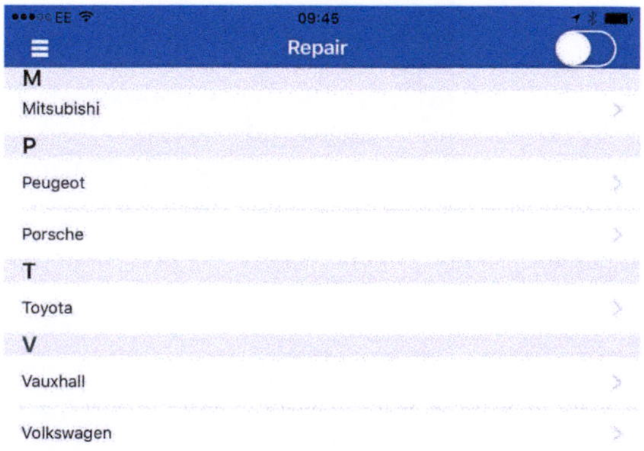

Figure 8.21 Alphabetical list showing just some of the manufacturers covered in the app

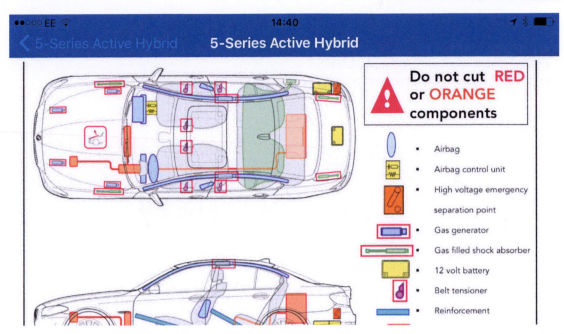

Figure 8.22 Information relating to locations and layouts on a BMW 5-series with the emphasis on safety critical and high-voltage component

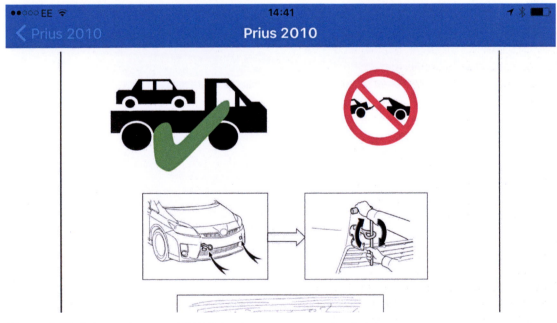

Figure 8.23 Information on a 2010 Prius for recovery professionals

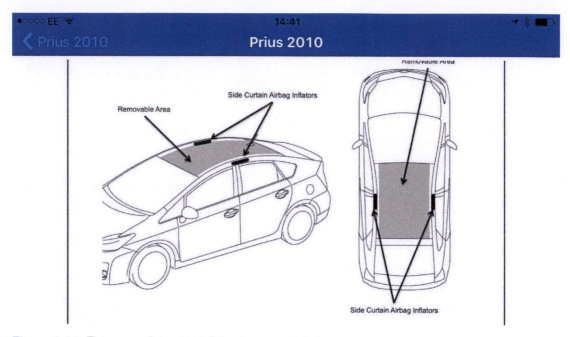

Figure 8.24 This area of the 2010 Prius is removable in an emergency rescue situation

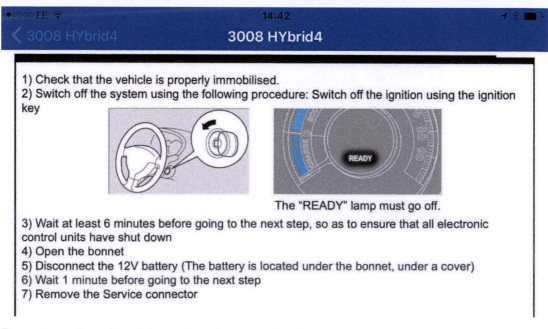

Figure 8.25 Part of the information relating to shut down and disconnection procedures on a selected vehicle

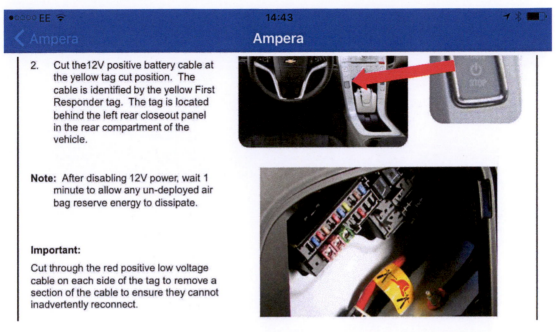

Figure 8.26 Like many vehicles, the Ampera has a dedicated cut-zone for emergency use when disconnecting the 12-V supply

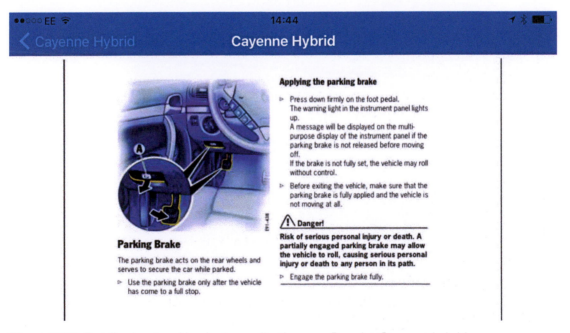

Figure 8.27 Details about parking brake application on a Porsche Cayenne hybrid

Content reproduced here by kind permission from the company. Find out more about

Pro-moto and the Pro-Assist hybrid app at http://www.pro-moto.co.uk

CHAPTER 9

Case studies

9.1 Introduction

This chapter serves to highlight some key developments and changes as well as innovative or different technologies used by EVs, HEVs and PHEVs. In many cases I have quoted manufacturers' figures, so remember to make allowances!

9.2 General motors EV-1

9.2.1 Overview

This is now an older type of EV, but as General Motors has been a leader in electric vehicle development since the 1960s it is an interesting case study. GM developed the EV-1 electric car as the world's first specifically designed production electric vehicle, and it became the first to go on sale (in the USA) in 1996.

9.2.2 EV-1 details

The EV-1 had a drag coefficient of just 0.19 and an aluminium spaceframe chassis (40% lighter than steel) with composite body panels. Weighing just 1350 kg in total, the car boasted an electronically regulated top speed of 128 km/h (80 mph) – although a prototype EV-1 actually held the world land-speed record for electric vehicles at 293 km/h (183 mph)! The current record is now over 300 mph, but in a car designed for record breaking not for normal use.

The EV-1 could reach 96 km/h (60 mph) from a standing start in less than 9 seconds. The key to the success of the EV-1 was its electrical powertrain, based on a 103 kW (137 hp) three-phase AC induction motor with an integral, single-speed, dual-reduction gear-set driving the front wheels. The unit required no routine maintenance for over 160,000 km (100,000 miles).

The battery pack used 26, 12 V maintenance-free lead–acid batteries, with a total voltage of 312 V. The range was 112 km (70 miles) per charge in urban conditions and 144 km (90 miles) on the open road. However, new nickel–metal hydride (NiMH) batteries were phased into production during 1998, almost doubling the range to 224 km (140 miles) in the city and 252 km (160 miles) on highways. An innovative

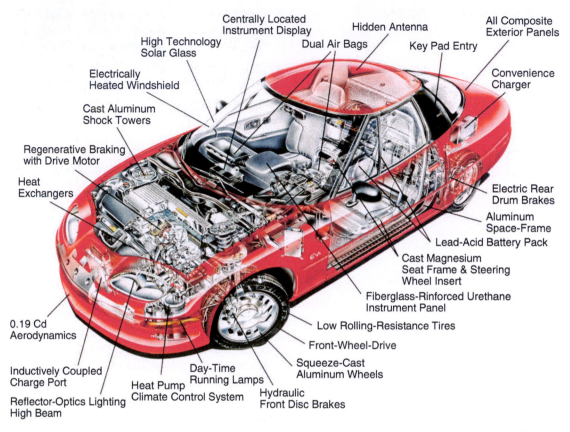

High Technology
Solar Glass

Centrally Located
Instrument Display

Hidden Antenna

Dual Air Bags

Key Pad Entry

All Composite
Exterior Panels

Electrically
Heated Windshield

Convenience
Charger

Cast Aluminum
Shock Towers

Regenerative Braking
with Drive Motor

Heat
Exchangers

Electric Rear
Drum Brakes

Aluminum
Space-Frame

Lead-Acid Battery Pack

Cast Magnesium
Seat Frame & Steering
Wheel Insert

Fiberglass-Rinforced Urethane
Instrument Panel

0.19 Cd
Aerodynamics

Low Rolling-Resistance Tires

Front-Wheel-Drive

Squeeze-Cast
Aluminum Wheels

Inductively Coupled
Charge Port

Day-Time
Running Lamps

Heat Pump
Climate Control System

Hydraulic
Front Disc Brakes

Reflector-Optics Lighting
High Beam

Figure 9.1 General Motors EV-1 (Source: GM Media)

regenerative braking system helped to extend that range still further by converting the energy used when braking back into electricity in order to partially recharge the battery pack.

Full recharging could be carried out safely in all weather conditions, taking 3–4 hours using a 220 V standard charger or 15 hours using the on-board 110 V convenience charger.

Regenerative braking was accomplished by using a blended combination of front hydraulic disc and rear electrically applied drum brakes and the electric propulsion motor. During braking, the electric motor generated electricity (regenerative) which was then used to partially recharge the battery pack.

The EV-1 came with traction control, cruise control, anti-lock brakes, dual airbags, power windows, door locks and outside mirrors, AM/FM CD/Cassette (whatever that is!), tyre inflation monitor system and numerous other features.

Figure 9.2 General motors EV (Source: GM Media)

146

9.3 Nissan LEAF 2016

9.3.1 Overview

One of the first mass market EVs, the LEAF continues to develop such that the 2016 LEAF 30 kWh now has a claimed range of up to 250 km. This 26% increase on the previous model is because of a 30 kWh battery with new technology.

Key Fact

The 2016 LEAF 30 kWh now has a claimed range of up to 250 km.

The new battery delivers a longer range with no compromise on internal packaging. It has exactly the same exterior dimensions as previous 24 kWh units and only a modest 21 kg increase in weight. The result is a car that goes significantly further while offering the same practicality and usability as previous versions.

Key to the new battery's higher performance is an update to its internal design and chemistry. The introduction of a high-capacity cathode improves performance, while the change to the cell layout also contributes to the gain. Indeed, Nissan is so confident about the performance and reliability of the new battery that the capacity of the new 30 kWh battery will be covered by an 8-year, 160,000-km warranty.

Quick charging time remains at just 30 minutes to charge the LEAF from zero to 80% – exactly the same period of time it takes the 24 kWh battery to achieve the same level of charge.

9.3.2 Remote control

One of the LEAF's most celebrated and useful features is its ability to interact with and be controlled remotely by its owner via NissanConnect EV. From being able to check charge status to pre-heating the cabin on cold winter days, owners across the world have used this advanced smartphone-enabled telematics facility to make life even easier.

Figure 9.3 Nissan LEAF charging socket (Source: Nissan Media)

NissanConnect EV not only brings greater comfort but also improves driving range, thanks to the ability to pre-heat or pre-cool the cabin without using battery energy.

One of the many advances of the new NissanConnect EV system is the new charging map that is capable of showing which charging points are available and which are being used. Production of the LEAF 30 kWh will continue at Nissan's Sunderland UK factory, with European sales starting in January 2016.

Figure 9.4 Nissan LEAF dashboard (Source: Nissan Media)

9.4 GM Volt 2016 (USA version)

9.4.1 Overview

The GM Volt is an REV, a range-extended EV. The second-generation model has a range of

147

53 miles, with greater efficiency and stronger acceleration than the previous model. It has a new two-motor drive unit, is up to 12% more efficient and 100 lb (about 50 kg) lighter than the first-generation unit. The total driving range is achieved using the on-board generator and is stated as 420 miles. The car has a new sleek design and seats up to five passengers. Enhanced Chevrolet MyLink is available with smartphone projection technology, featuring Apple CarPlay capability.

Figure 9.5 GM Volt (Source: GM Media)

The new 192-cell/18.4 kWh lithium-ion battery pack and new 111 kW two-motor drive unit mean it will go from 0 to 60 in 8.4 seconds.

The Volt remains the only electrically driven vehicle with range capability similar to traditional engine or hybrid cars of its size. It can be driven across town strictly on electricity or across the country with the assist of its range extender.

> **Key Fact**
> The Volt remains the only electrically driven vehicle with range capability similar to traditional engine or hybrid cars of its size.

9.4.2 Battery

General Motors' battery technology includes revised cell chemistry, developed in conjunction with LG Chem. Storage capacity is 20% higher on a volume basis when compared with the original cell, while the number of cells decreases from 288 to 192.

The new Volt's battery pack stores more energy, 18.4 kWh compared with 17.1 kWh, with fewer cells, because there is more energy capacity per cell. It also has a more powerful discharge rate of 120 kW compared with the previous 110 kW, which contributes to greater performance.

The battery pack retains the familiar T-shape of the first-generation Volt, but with revised dimensions. The new cells are layered in pairs in each cell group rather than the previous three-layer configuration. They are also positioned lower in the pack for improved (lower) centre of gravity in the vehicle, and the overall mass of the pack decreases too. The improved battery system continues to use the Volt's industry-leading active thermal control system that helps maintain electric range.

Figure 9.6 Battery pack (Source: GM Media)

Based on a GM study of more than 300 model year 2011 and 2012 Volts in service in California for more than 30 months, many owners are exceeding the EPA-rated label of 35 miles of EV range per full charge, with about 15% surpassing 40 miles of range. Current generation Volt owners have accumulated more than 600 million EV miles.

9.4.3 Two-motor drive unit

A new, two-motor drive unit is at the heart of the 2016 Volt's greater performance efficiency and expanded all-electric driving range. The motors are smaller and lighter than the previous motor-generator drive unit, while delivering more torque and power capability. The new drive unit was also designed with improved noise and vibration characteristics that contribute to a quieter driving experience. Total motor mass reduction is more than 33 lb (15 kg).

Figure 9.7 Motor (Source: GM Media)

The motors can be used individually or in tandem, effectively delivering two torque paths to make the most of performance and efficiency. The new Volt can operate on a primary motor at lower speeds such as city driving, split power between the motors at moderate speeds or fully engage both motors for higher load/higher speed driving, such as passing on the highway. The Traction Power Inverter Module (TPIM), which manages power flow between the battery and the electric drive motors, has been built into the drive unit to

Figure 9.8 Motors and transmission unit (Source: GM Media)

reduce mass, and size, which contributes to greater efficiency.

9.4.4 Range extender

A range-extending engine is the key feature that makes the Volt a no-compromises electric vehicle, providing owners the assurance they can go anywhere, anytime without having to worry about whether they have enough battery power to go through mountains or longer range for a spontaneous weekend getaway.

Energy for extended-range operation comes from an all-new, high-efficiency 1.5-litre naturally aspirated four-cylinder engine, rated at 101 hp (75 kW). It features direct injection, a high-compression ratio of 12.5:1, cooled exhaust gas recirculation, wide authority cam phasers and a variable-displacement oil pump to make the most of performance and efficiency. It also features a lightweight aluminium block, compared with the current engine's iron block.

Figure 9.9 Range-extending engine (Source: GM Media)

The new range extender also runs on less-expensive regular unleaded fuel and delivers a GM-estimated combined fuel economy rating of 41 mpg. The 1.5-litre engine will be manufactured at GM's Toluca, Mexico engine plant for the first year of production, then shift to the Flint, Michigan engine plant.

2

9.5 Tesla Roadster

9.5.1 Overview

I have chosen this EV as a case study because of its world-class acceleration, handling and design. It is a cool sports car that also happens to be an electric car, which was a major step forward in the public's perception of these vehicles. It is also a pure EV in that it uses rechargeable batteries. Tesla has now further increased its impressive range with the Model S.

Figure 9.10 Tesla drive components

Figure 9.11 Tesla Roadster – available in several colours including racing green! (Source: Tesla Motors)

9.5.2 Motor

The Roadster is powered by a three-phase AC induction motor. Small, but strong, the motor weighs just over 52 kg (115 lb). The batteries

produce 375 V to push up to 900 A of current into the motor to create magnetic fields. It delivers 288 peak hp and 400 Nm (295 lb-ft) of torque at the driver's command. At top speed, the motor is spinning at 14,000 rpm.

Safety First

The batteries produce 375 V. Do not work on high voltages unless trained.

Key Fact

The Roadster is powered by a three-phase AC induction motor.

The motor is directly coupled to a single-speed gearbox, above the rear axle. The simplicity of a single gear ratio reduces weight and eliminates the need for complicated shifting and clutch work. The elegant motor does not need a complicated reverse gear – the motor simply spins in the opposite direction.

Figure 9.12 Tesla's AC induction motor (Source: Tesla Motors)

The internal combustion engine (ICE) is a complex, amazing machine. Unfortunately, this complexity results in wasted energy. At best, only about 30% of the energy stored in fuel is converted to forward motion. The rest is wasted as heat and noise. When the engine is not spinning, there is no torque available. In fact, the engine must turn at several hundred rpm (idle speed) before it can generate enough power to overcome its own internal losses.

An ICE does not develop peak torque until many thousand rpm. Once peak torque is reached, it starts to drop off quickly. To overcome this narrow torque range, multi-speed transmissions are employed to create gear ratios that keep the engine spinning where it is most effective.

Internal combustion engine power output can be improved with faster rotation. However, combustion engines have a limit to how fast they can spin – as engine speed exceeds 5000 or 6000 rpm, it becomes challenging and costly to keep the timing of the engine on track and keep all of the parts together.

Electric motors are by comparison very simple. The motor converts electricity into mechanical power and also acts as a generator, turning mechanical power into electricity. Compared with the myriad parts in an engine, the Roadster motor has only one moving component – the rotor. The spinning

rotor eliminates conversion of linear motion to rotational motion and has no mechanical timing issues to overcome.

With an electric motor, instant torque is available at any speed. The entire rotational force of the motor is available the instant the accelerator is pressed. Peak torque stays constant to almost 6000 rpm, only then does it start to slowly roll off.

Key Fact

With an electric motor, instant torque is available at any speed.

The wide torque band, particularly the torque available at low speed, eliminates the need for gears – the Roadster has only a single speed gear reduction; one gear ratio from zero to top speed. Switch two of the phases (this can be done electronically), and the motor runs in reverse. Not only is this design incredibly simple, reliable, compact and lightweight,

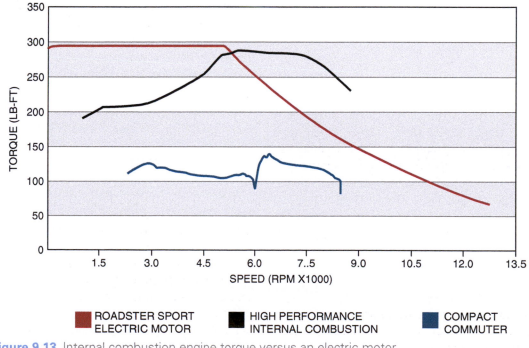

ROADSTER SPORT ELECTRIC MOTOR   **HIGH PERFORMANCE INTERNAL COMBUSTION**   **COMPACT COMMUTER**

Figure 9.13 Internal combustion engine torque versus an electric motor

but it allows a unique and exhilarating driving experience. The Roadster accelerates faster than most sports cars.

Tesla's electric motor is also able to create torque efficiently. The Roadster achieves an overall driving efficiency of 88%, about three times the efficiency of a conventional car.

As driving conditions permit, the motor acts as a generator to recharge the battery. When the accelerator pedal is released, the motor switches to 're-generative braking' mode and captures energy while slowing the car. The experience is similar to 'engine braking' in a conventional car.

The Tesla Roadster uses a three-phase AC induction motor. The induction motor was, appropriately, first patented by Nikola Tesla in 1888. These motors are widely used in industry for their reliability, simplicity and efficiency.

Key Fact

The Tesla Roadster uses a three-phase AC induction motor, first patented by Nikola Tesla in 1888.

The Roadster motor has two primary components: a rotor and a stator. The rotor is a shaft of steel with copper bars running through it. It rotates and, in doing so, turns the wheels. The stationary stator surrounds, but does not touch, the rotor. The stator has two functions: it creates a rotating magnetic field and it induces a current in the rotor. The current creates a second magnetic field in the rotor that chases the rotating stator field. The end result is torque. Some motors use permanent magnets, but not the Roadster motor – the magnetic field is created completely from electricity.

The stator is assembled by winding coils of copper wire through a stack of thin steel plates called laminations. The copper wire conducts the electricity fed into the motor from the power electronics module (PEM). There are three sets of wires – each wire conducts one of the three phases of electricity. The three phases are offset from each other such that combining the rises and falls of each phase creates a smooth supply of current – and therefore power. The flow of alternating current into the copper windings creates an alternating magnetic field. Because of the way the copper coils are placed within the stator, the magnetic field appears to move in a circular path around the stator.

The copper bars mentioned above are 'shorted' to each other (referred to as a 'squirrel cage'), which allows current to flow with little resistance from one side of the rotor to the other. The rotor does not have a direct supply of electricity. When a conductor (one of the copper bars) is moved through a magnetic field (created by the AC in the stator), a current is induced.

Because the stator magnetic field is moving, the rotor tries to catch up. The interaction of the magnetic fields creates torque. The amount of torque produced is related to the relative position of the rotor field to the rolling 'wave' of magnetism in the stator (the stator field). The further the rotor field is from the 'wave', the more torque is produced. Since the stator field is always ahead of the rotor when the accelerator is depressed, the rotor is always spinning to catch up, and it is continuously producing torque.

When the driver releases the accelerator pedal, the PEM immediately changes the position of the stator field to behind the rotor field. Now, the rotor must slow down to align its field with the stator field. The current in the stator switches direction, and energy starts to flow, through the PEM, back to the battery.

9.5.3 Motor control

When the accelerator pedal is pressed, the power electronics module (PEM) interprets a request for torque. Flooring the pedal means a request for 100% of the available torque. Half-way is a request for partial torque and so on. Letting off the accelerator pedal means a request for re-generation. The PEM interprets the accelerator pedal input and sends the appropriate amount of alternating current to the stator. Torque is created in the motor and the car accelerates.

Definition
PEM: power electronics module.

The PEM supplies as much as 900 A to the stator. To handle such high current levels, the stator coils in a Tesla motor employ significantly more copper than a traditional motor of its size. The copper is tightly packed in a proprietary winding pattern to optimize efficiency and power. The copper loops are encapsulated by special polymers that facilitate heat transfer and ensure reliability under the demands of high-performance driving in extreme conditions.

Key Fact
The PEM supplies as much as 900 A to the stator.

High stator currents mean high rotor currents. Unlike typical induction motors, which employ aluminium for their conductors, the Roadster rotor conductors are made of copper. Copper, while harder to work with, has a much lower resistance and can therefore handle higher currents. Special care is taken in the motor design to handle the high speed (14,000 rpm).

Though highly efficient, the motor still generates some heat. To keep within acceptable operating temperatures, specially engineered cooling fins have been integrated into the housing and a fan is employed to blow air across the fins to most effectively extract the heat. This helps keep the overall package light and tight.

9.5.4 Battery

The battery pack in the Tesla Roadster is the result of innovative systems engineering and 20 years of advances in lithium-ion battery technology. The pack contains 6831 lithium-ion cells and is the most energy dense pack in the industry, storing 56 kWh of energy. It weighs 990 lb and delivers up to 215 kW of electric power. The car will charge from almost any 120 V or 240 V outlet. Most Roadster owners find they rarely use a complete charge, and charging each night means their car is ready to drive 245 miles each morning.

Figure 9.14 Battery pack in production (Source: Tesla Motors)

To achieve the required energy density, Tesla starts with thousands of lithium-ion cells and assembles them into a liquid-cooled battery pack, wrapped in a strong metal enclosure. The battery is optimized for performance, safety, longevity and cost. With lithium-ion chemistry, there is no need to drain the battery before recharging as there is no memory effect. Roadster owners simply top-up the charge each night.

The cells used in a Roadster battery pack are referred to as 18650 form-factor, because of their measurements: 18 mm in diameter by 65 mm length. Tesla uses versions of this form factor modified for use in EVs. The small cell size enables efficient heat transfer, allows for precise charge management, improves reliability and extends battery pack life. Each cell is enclosed in a steel case, which

153

effectively transfers heat away from the cell. The small size makes the cell essentially isothermal, and its large surface area allows it to shed heat to the ambient environment.

> **Definition**
>
> Isothermal: a thermodynamic process in which the temperature of the system remains constant. The heat transfer into or out of the system is at such a slow rate that thermal equilibrium is maintained.

Sixty-nine cells are wired in parallel to create bricks. Ninety-nine bricks are connected in series to create sheets, and 11 sheets are inserted into the pack casing. In total, this creates a pack made up of 6831 cells. Appropriate cell temperature levels are maintained by a proprietary liquid-cooling system, which includes sensors within the pack monitored by the car's firmware. Liquid coolant is pumped through the pack to enable effective heat transfer to and from each cell. The cooling system is so effective that the cells on opposite sides of the battery pack stay within a few degrees of each other. This is important for maximizing battery life, optimizing performance and guaranteeing safety.

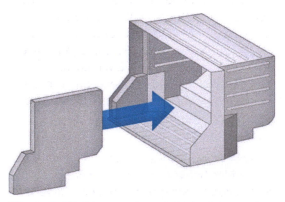

Figure 9.15 Construction of the battery pack

The Roadster's high-voltage systems are protected against accidental contact outside their protective enclosures and jacketed cables. Only with special tools may one gain access to the high-voltage components. In the event of significant impact or rollover, the high-voltage supply is automatically disconnected inside the pack to reduce risk of exposure to high voltage. Air bag deployment causes the high-voltage circuits in the vehicle to immediately shut down. The high-voltage systems are enclosed, labelled and colour-coded with markings that service technicians and emergency responders are trained to recognize.

> **Key Fact**
>
> Air bag deployment causes the high-voltage circuits in the vehicle to immediately shut down.

The pack enclosure is designed to withstand substantial abuse in the vehicle, while maintaining the integrity of the internal components. The pack is a stressed member of the chassis and helps provide rigidity to the rear of the car. The Roadster has been tested in standard frontal, rear and side impact crash tests.

In general, lithium-ion cells cannot be charged below 0ºC, which would theoretically prevent charging in cold environments. To overcome this cold weather charging obstacle, the Roadster is designed with a heater to warm the cells (when plugged in) to an appropriate charging temperature. If there were no battery pack heater, drivers living in cold environments would have difficulty charging and would experience stunted driving performance.

Likewise, the cells are designed to operate in high-temperature environments. High-performance driving is possible in even the hottest environments of the world. If the temperature rises above a set threshold, the air conditioning unit sends chilled coolant through the pack. Similar to the radiator fan of ICE cars, the chilled coolant continues to circulate after the motor has been turned off to keep the temperature at an appropriate level. Cooling the pack enables a driver to quickly charge immediately after hard driving in hot climates. Without such a cooling system, recharging in hot weather would be delayed after each drive.

The battery charger is located on-board the car. This means the Roadster can be plugged into any outlet, anywhere in the world. Charge times vary based on the outlet voltage and amperage. With the Tesla high-power wall connector, a Roadster charges in as little as 4 hours from empty. Most owners simply charge overnight.

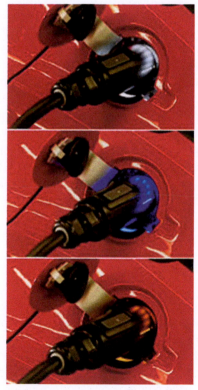

Figure 9.16 Charging port and coloured indicator

The PEM processor manages charging. When the charge port door is opened, charging systems come online and begin coordinating with the vehicle management system (VMS). The PEM is instructed to send current to the light ring in the charge port and white LEDs turn on. When the driver attaches the connector and slides the pilot switch closed, the lights turn blue. Once the connector is attached, the PEM processor detects the current available from the wall and the VMS checks if the driver had previously set charge preferences for the location.

When the car determines which level of current to use, the contactors between the motor and battery begin to close in a series of audible clicks. This function ensures that the high voltage from the wall does not flow to the battery until every connection is properly mated. The battery processor, PEM processor and VMS work together to flash the LEDs in the light ring – if the battery is empty, the lights flash quickly. As the battery charges, the rate of flashing slows. When the battery is completely charged, the lights turn green. The battery processors help preserve battery life if the car is plugged in for long periods of time by checking the state of charge every 24 hours, topping up the battery as needed to maintain a healthy state of charge.

The PEM processor also controls the Roadster when in drive mode. The processor monitors the accelerator pedal and uses the information to control current to the motor. To ensure that generated torque is appropriate for the state of other components in the car, many other processors monitor the status of the car and send outside requirements to the PEM. For example, if the battery processor and VMS calculate that the battery is full, regenerative torque is reduced; if the PEM processor detects that the motor has exceeded an ideal temperature, current to the motor is reduced.

9.5.5 **Power control**

The power electronics module (PEM) functions as a bridge between the charge port, battery and motor. It manages and converts current during driving and charging. As AC flows into the car from the wall (anything from 90 to 265 V between 50 and 60 Hz), the unit converts it to DC for storage in the battery. When driving, the module converts DC back to AC, which the motor uses to generate torque. At many operating points, it is 97–98% efficient: less than 2% of converted energy is lost.

Figure 9.17 Power electronics module (Source: Tesla Motors)

The voltage to the motor is varied by turning switches called IGBTs on and off very quickly. As the IGBTs allow more current from the battery to the motor, the AC waveforms grow in amplitude until peak torque is produced in the motor.

Definition

IGBT: insulated gate bipolar transistor.

In drive mode, the PEM responds to information from the accelerator pedal, motor speed sensor, ABS speed sensors and other powertrain sensors. It determines requested torque from the pedal position and monitors the ABS speed sensors to detect if tyres are slipping. Based on sensor feedback, it produces torque by converting the DC voltage stored in the battery to the appropriate AC voltage at the motor terminals. As the driver steps on the accelerator pedal, the PEM begins to control increasing motor current and voltage to produce the torque required to accelerate from 0 to 60 mph in just 3.7 seconds.

Key Fact

The Roadster can accelerate from 0 to 60 mph in just 3.7 seconds.

Inside the PEM, there are three major systems:

1 power stages
2 a controller
3 a line filter.

The most complex are the power stages, called megapoles. These are large semiconductor switch arrays that connect the charge port or motor to the battery depending on if the car is charging or driving. Within the megapoles, there are six different switches, grouped into three pairs known as half bridges. In drive mode, each bridge forms a phase. Each phase connects to a phase of the three-phase AC induction motor. In charge mode, only two bridges are required, one for each wire in the AC line. The charge and drive modes are configured using a set of four large relays known as contactors. The contactors allow the semiconductor switches to be used to connect the battery to either the charge port or the motor. When the Roadster is turned on, a series of clicking sounds can be heard as the contactors close the connection to the motor.

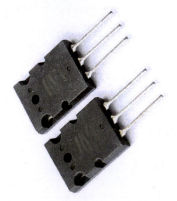

Figure 9.18 Insulated gate bipolar transistors (Source: Tesla Motors)

Each switch is composed of 14 insulated gate bipolar transistors (IGBTs). In total, 84 IGBTs are used in the PEM. Each IGBT is less than 25-mm square and about 6-mm thick. Inside the IGBT package is a small piece of silicon, about the thickness of a few sheets of paper and 6-mm per side.

The second major component of the PEM is the controller board that turns the switches on and off. The switches can turn on and off up to 32,000 times per second. The controller contains two processors: the main DSP and a secondary safety processor. The DSP controls torque, charge behaviours and interprets requests from the VMS. The safety processor monitors the accelerator pedal and the motor current to detect unexpected behaviours. If the safety processor measures motor current inconsistent with accelerator pedal position, it can stop the system. While this behaviour is extremely unlikely, this redundancy means a glitch in the main DSP can't produce unexpected torque.

The third major component of the PEM is the charge input filter. When the car is charging and the IGBTs are switching at 32 kHz, a large amount of electrical noise is created on the AC side of the power stages. If the noise were allowed to conduct back into the power lines, it could interfere with other appliances, radios, cell phones, etc. A group of large inductors called chokes are placed between the IGBTs and the charge port to filter out the noise and avoid unwanted interference.

Tesla power control enables a traction control system with amazing improvements over systems in internal combustion cars. Traction control systems for internal combustion vehicles have a few options to maintain traction at prescribed levels: kill engine spark, reduce fuel supply, use electronic throttle control to actively modulate throttle requests or apply the brakes. Fundamentally, it is practically impossible to maintain near-zero output torque from an ICE, whereas zero torque is simple to maintain in an electric drivetrain. In the Roadster, the motor torque can be accurately reduced either gradually or quickly – resulting in better control with less noticeable loss of power. With on-board sensors, the car predicts achievable traction when cornering before the driver can even command a change in acceleration. It's much safer to avoid loss of traction than react to it. Expert test drivers have found they are able to achieve higher performance with the Roadster traction control system than in comparable internal combustion vehicles.

9.5.6 Software

The Roadster is controlled by state-of-the-art vehicle software. The code is developed in-house with an intense focus on constant innovation. The system monitors the status of components throughout the car, shares information to coordinate action and reacts to changing external conditions.

The Roadster employs many processors to control functions the driver often takes for granted, from battery voltage management and motor control to diagnostics, door locks and touchscreen interaction. Many different operating systems and programming languages are used to optimize each processor for completing its designated function. The processors work together to monitor the status of components throughout the car, share information to coordinate action, and react to changing external conditions.

The vehicle management system (VMS) enables functions the driver is most aware of while driving. It manages the security system, opens the doors, communicates warnings (seatbelt, door ajar, etc.), manages the owner's PIN and initiates a valet (parking) mode.

The VMS compiles information from many of the other processors to coordinate the necessary actions for driving. When the key is inserted into the car, the VMS turns on the touchscreen. When the key is switched to the ON position, it readies the car for driving by instructing other processors to initiate their functions. It computes available range and prepares the PEM to send power to the motor from the battery. The VMS manages the driving modes (performance, standard or range) and works with the battery processor to charge and discharge appropriately. It

157

FIRMWARE PROCESSORS

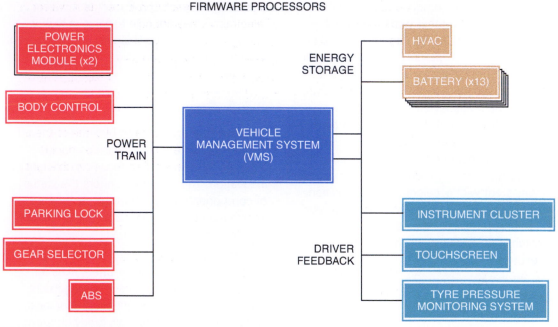

Figure 9.19 Firmware processors

Figure 9.20 Central control touch screen (Source: Tesla Motors)

computes ideal and actual range using a complex algorithm that considers battery age, capacity, driving style and energy consumption rate.

(Source: https://www.teslamotors.com)

9.6 Honda FCX Clarity

9.6.1 Overview

I have picked the Honda FCX Clarity zero-emissions hydrogen fuel cell electric vehicle (EV) as a case study because it has been in development for a while, and it is now at a mature technological level. Some innovative techniques are used and the result is a very useable Zero Emission Vehicle.

At the time of writing it is available for leasing in the USA, but not in the UK because of a limited refuelling infrastructure. However, this is expected to change soon. I am grateful to Honda for permission to use their materials.

To give an overview of the vehicle, some of the main features are as follows:

▶ Zero harmful emissions – the only exhaust emission is water vapour ($2H_2 + O_2 = 2H_2O$).
▶ The car generates its electricity on-board using compressed hydrogen as an energy carrier.

Figure 9.21 Honda FCS Clarity 2011 (Source: Honda Media)

- Crash tested and safety tested to the same standard as a conventional car.
- Range equivalent to a conventional petrol or diesel car.
- Improvement in fuel cell stack technology over previous versions – 180 kg lighter, 45% smaller than previous versions.
- Lithium-ion battery – 40% lighter and 50% smaller than previous versions.
- Start up at –30°C possible.
- Only one hydrogen tank, reduced from two in the previous model.
- An efficiency rating of around 60% (this is about three times that of a petrol-engine car, twice that of a hybrid vehicle, and 10% better than the previous model).

A fuel cell vehicle has a hydrogen tank instead of a petrol/gasoline tank. In the fuel cell, hydrogen is combined with atmospheric oxygen to generate electricity. The fuel cell is really a tiny electric power station, and generates its own electricity on-board rather than through a plug-in system.

> **Key Fact**
>
> In a fuel cell, hydrogen is combined with atmospheric oxygen to generate electricity.

Since the electricity required to power the vehicle's motor is generated on-board using hydrogen and oxygen, no CO_2 or other pollutants are emitted in this process. The only

emission is the water produced as a by-product of electricity generation.

A compact and efficient lithium-ion battery stores electricity generated during braking and deceleration in regenerative braking (just like a mild hybrid). The battery works with the fuel cell stack to power the vehicle.

As well as emitting no harmful exhaust gases, fuel cell electric vehicles offer good driving range, short refuelling time and a flexible layout and design:

- short refuelling time of 3–5 minutes
- vehicle range of 270 miles, comparable to that of a conventional car
- performance similar to a current mid-size car
- zero harmful emissions or pollutants.

9.6.2 Hydrogen

Hydrogen can be produced from renewable sources such as solar, wind or hydroelectric power (using electrolysis to extract hydrogen from water). Certain production methods are better suited in different areas of the world, but nevertheless it is possible to achieve a stable supply of hydrogen from renewable energy sources.

Currently, the most common way of producing hydrogen is steam reforming from natural gas. There is an environmental cost of extracting hydrogen in this way, but it is the most widely available approach. However, the same issue applies to battery electric vehicles (BEV). There is clearly an environmental cost of a BEV running on electricity made from a coal- or gas-fired power station.

Hydrogen is the most abundant element in the universe, and it is extremely efficient as an energy carrier. These are the key reasons why it is such a suitable fuel for fuel cell cars and clean motoring. Hydrogen can also be produced sustainably using electricity generated from renewable energy sources such as solar, wind and hydroelectric power.

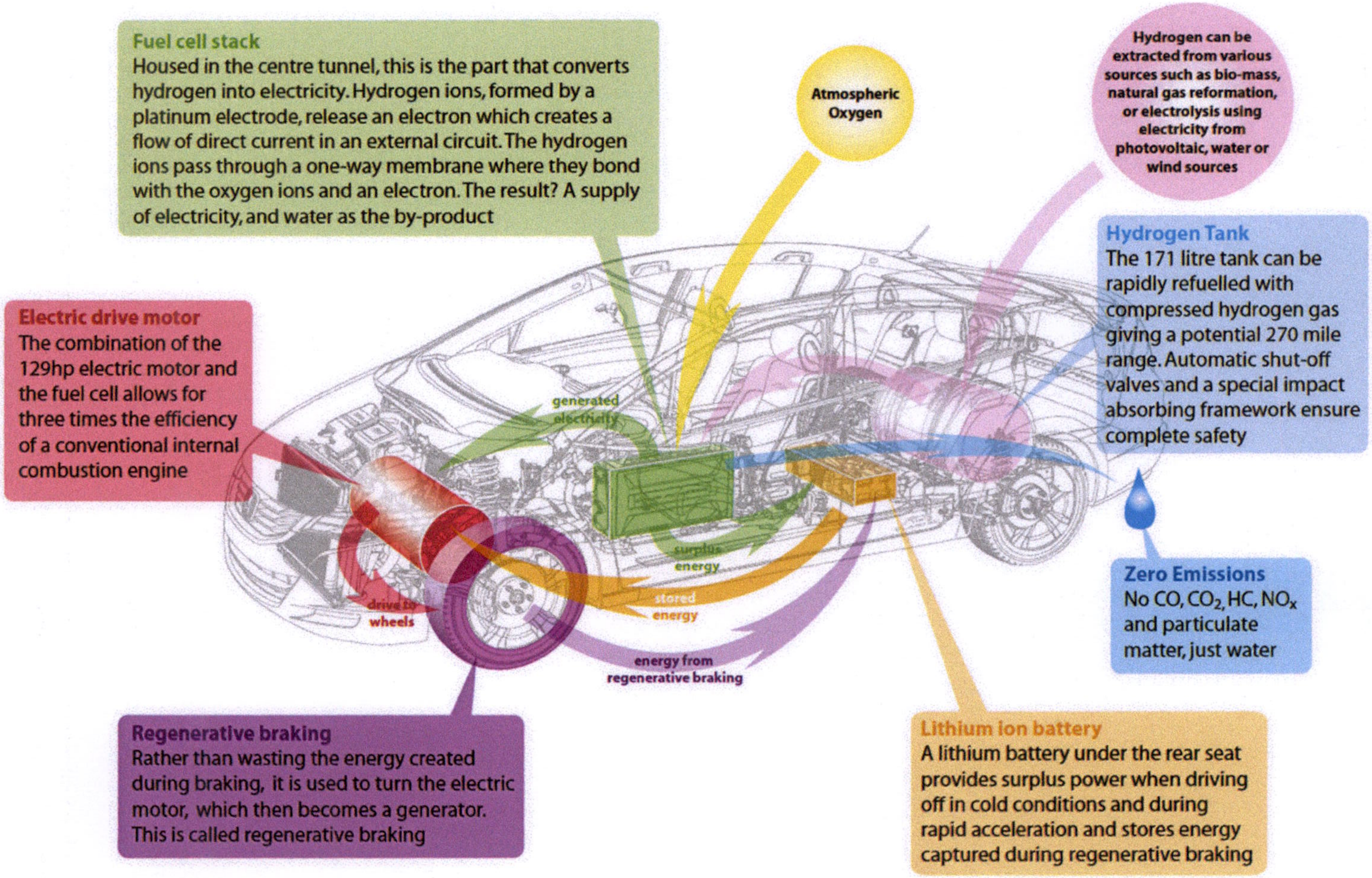

Hydrogen can be extracted from various sources such as bio-mass, natural gas reformation, or electrolysis using electricity from photovoltaic, water or wind sources

Hydrogen Tank
The 171 litre tank can be rapidly refuelled with compressed hydrogen gas giving a potential 270 mile range. Automatic shut-off valves and a special impact absorbing framework ensure complete safety

Zero Emissions
No CO, CO_2, HC, NO_x and particulate matter, just water

Lithium Ion battery
A lithium battery under the rear seat provides surplus power when driving off in cold conditions and during rapid acceleration and stores energy captured during regenerative braking

Atmospheric Oxygen

Fuel cell stack
Housed in the centre tunnel, this is the part that converts hydrogen into electricity. Hydrogen ions, formed by a platinum electrode, release an electron which creates a flow of direct current in an external circuit. The hydrogen ions pass through a one-way membrane where they bond with the oxygen ions and an electron. The result? A supply of electricity, and water as the by-product

Electric drive motor
The combination of the 129hp electric motor and the fuel cell allows for three times the efficiency of a conventional internal combustion engine

Regenerative braking
Rather than wasting the energy created during braking, it is used to turn the electric motor, which then becomes a generator. This is called regenerative braking

surplus energy

stored energy

energy from regenerative braking

generated electricity

drive wheels

Figure 9.22 Honda FCX Clarity features and operation (Source: Honda Media)

■ How power is managed

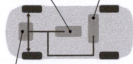

• **Startup and acceleration**

Power supplied to the motor from the fuel cell stack is supplemented with electricity from the battery for powerful acceleration.

Fuel cell stack   Lithium ion battery

Electric drive motor

• **Gentle acceleration and cruising**

The vehicle operates on electricity from the fuel cell stack alone, for fuel-efficient, high-speed cruising.

• **Deceleration**

The motor acts as a generator, converting the kinetic energy normally wasted as heat during braking into electricity for storage in the battery, which also stores excess electricity produced by the fuel cell stack.

• **Idling**

The auto idle stop system shuts down electrical generation in the fuel cell stack. The lithium ion battery supplies electricity required for the air conditioner and other devices.

Figure 9.23 Power management (Source: Honda Media)

Table 9.1 Fuel cell electric vehicle (FCEV), battery electric vehicle (BEV) and internal combustion engine (ICE) compared

	FCEV	BEV	ICE
Time required to refuel	Short	Long	Short
Vehicle range	Long	Short	Long
CO_2 emissions while driving	No emissions	No emissions	Emissions
Renewability of energy source	Renewable	Renewable	Non-renewable
Current common energy source	Steam reforming of natural gas	Coal-fired power stations	Oil

Table 9.2 Hydrogen production methods

Potential energy sources used in hydrogen production	Production method	Amount of CO_2 released during production	Renewability
Oil/coal	Gasification and reforming	Large	None
Electricity produced from coal-fired power stations	Burning	Large	None
Natural gas	Steam reforming	Medium to small	Limited
Electricity produced from nuclear energy	Water electrolysis	None	None
Electricity produced from solar, wind, hydroelectric power	Water electrolysis	None	100%

Key Fact

Hydrogen is the most abundant element in the universe.

Another advantage of using hydrogen is that it can be compressed or liquefied for delivery via a pipeline or for storage in tanks. Hydrogen can even be manufactured at conventional filling stations.

Honda uses hydrogen as a compressed gas because, in simple terms, more gas will fit in the tank that way. However, the tanks have to be able to cope with the pressure and it does require energy to compress the gas in the first place. Some critics say this compression process reduces the margin on zero-emission driving. However, Honda has made a number of developments in this area to ensure the car is still as efficient as possible.

The high-capacity hydrogen tanks use a newly developed absorption material to increase the amount of hydrogen they can store. This means it is not necessary to compress it to such a high degree to fit it in the tank, again saving energy at the compression stage. The high-capacity hydrogen tanks are so effective that the hydrogen can be compressed to 350 bar, compared with other fuel cell cars that use hydrogen compressed to 750 bar.

9.6.3 Energy efficiency and the environment

Because the FCX Clarity has an efficient power plant and energy management, it has an efficiency rating of around 60%. Figure 9.24 shows a comparison between different types of car.

Hydrogen is not found on its own in nature, but exists as a component within many different materials from which it can be extracted – like H_2O, for instance.

The ideal hydrogen cycle uses renewable energy sources, such as solar, wind or hydro, to extract hydrogen from water via electrolysis. The water produced as a by-product of the fuel cell process would then return to the rivers and oceans before once again being converted into hydrogen via electrolysis.

Definition

Electrolysis: a method of using a direct electric current (DC) to drive an otherwise non-spontaneous chemical reaction.

In a fuel cell, hydrogen is converted into electricity on demand, so just the right amount of electricity is produced. Using hydrogen to create electricity removes the challenge of storing it in large quantities in batteries.

There are two key measures when looking at the environmental cost of producing hydrogen,

■ Energy efficiency comparison

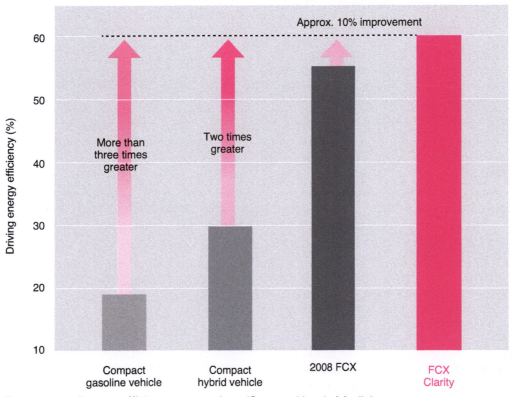

Figure 9.24 Energy efficiency comparison (Source: Honda Media)

■ Renewable Energy Cycle

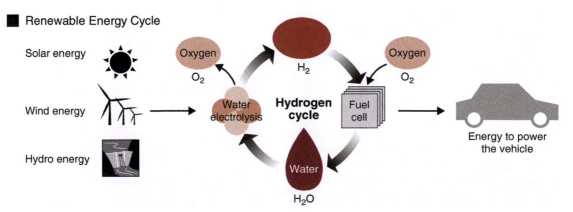

Figure 9.25 Renewable energy cycle (Source: Honda Media)

electricity or indeed any other fuel used for mobility.

- ▶ well-to-tank (getting it out of the ground)
- ▶ tank-to-wheel (using the fuel to provide mobility).

In a fuel cell car or a battery-powered electric car there are zero emissions tank-to-wheel, regardless of how the hydrogen or electricity is produced. However, the key question becomes: what is the environmental cost of producing the fuel?

The most common process for producing hydrogen at present is to steam it out of natural gas. This process is more readily available, and while there is an environmental cost, it is limited. To put it into perspective, if a customer were to run an FCX Clarity (fuelled on hydrogen generated from natural gas) there would still be a 60% reduction in greenhouse gas emissions compared with driving a conventional car. That's a huge benefit over the car technology in widespread use at present.

> **Key Fact**
>
> The most common process for producing hydrogen at present is to steam it out of natural gas.

In addition, the manufacturing of chlorine (for industrial use) generates hydrogen as a by-product. This can be stored in tanks and piped directly to a public fuel station. In Germany alone there's enough hydrogen produced as a by-product of chemical processes to fuel half a million cars.

Hydrogen can also be produced in a variety of other ways, including using renewable energy sources such as solar, wind or hydroelectric power. For example, Honda already produces ultra-efficient thin film solar cells, which can produce electricity in a sustainable way. That electricity can be used to electrolyse water and extract hydrogen via their solar-powered

refuelling station, which reduces the well-to-tank environmental cost even further.

It is the combination of environmental benefit and practicality of a fuel cell vehicle that means it excels at meeting customer demands and requirements – and those benefits are because it uses hydrogen as a fuel.

9.6.4 Core technologies

The previous FCX had two hydrogen tanks, but the FCX Clarity has only one. This creates more space for the rear seats and boot. The shut-off valve, regulator, pressure sensor and other components in the refuelling and supply system are integrated into a single in-tank module, reducing the number of parts considerably.

The main components of the vehicle's power plant are the fuel cell stack, the hydrogen tank, the lithium-ion battery, the electric drive motor and the power drive unit (PDU), which governs the flow of electricity.

At the heart of the system is the fuel cell stack – a device that uses an electrochemical reaction between hydrogen (H_2) and oxygen (O_2) to convert chemical energy into electrical energy. In effect, this is the reverse of the principle of electrolysis, in which an electrical current is used to separate water (H_2O) into hydrogen and oxygen. When supplied with hydrogen and oxygen, the fuel cell (FC) stack simultaneously generates electricity and water, with no CO_2 or other harmful emissions.

> **Key Fact**
>
> The fuel cell stack is a device that uses an electrochemical reaction between hydrogen (H_2) and oxygen (O_2) to convert chemical energy into electrical energy.

The Honda V Flow FC Stack uses a proton exchange membrane fuel cell (PEMFC) electrical generation system that directly converts chemical energy produced in

■ Hydrogen tank comparison

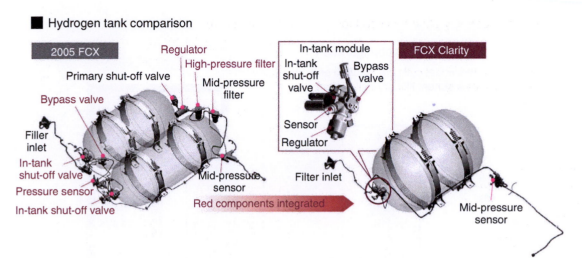

Figure 9.26 Hydrogen tank developments (Source: Honda Media)

Figure 9.27 Fuel cell stack (Source: Honda Media)

hydrogen–oxygen reactions into electrical energy. The extremely thin proton exchange membrane (electrolytic membrane) is sandwiched between pairs of electrode layers and diffusion layers (the hydrogen and oxygen electrodes) to form a membrane electrode assembly (MEA). The MEA is enclosed between two separators to form a cell – a single electrical generation unit. Several hundred cells are stacked together to form a fuel cell stack. As with batteries, these individual cells are connected in a series to produce a high voltage.

Hydrogen gas is passed over the hydrogen electrode. Each hydrogen atom is converted into a hydrogen ion in a catalytic reaction with the platinum in the electrode, releasing an electron. Having given up its electron, the hydrogen ion passes through the electrolytic membrane, where it joins with oxygen from the oxygen electrode and an electron arriving via an external circuit.

The released electrons create a flow of direct current in the external circuit. The reaction at the oxygen electrode produces water as a by-product. Because the electrolytic membrane must be kept continually damp, it is necessary to humidify the supply of hydrogen and oxygen. The water by-product is recycled for this purpose. Unneeded water and air are released via the exhaust.

Until more recently, hydrogen and air flowed horizontally through the cells of Honda fuel cell stacks. The new V Flow FC Stack introduces a cell structure in which hydrogen and air flow vertically, and gravity is used to facilitate more efficient drainage

165

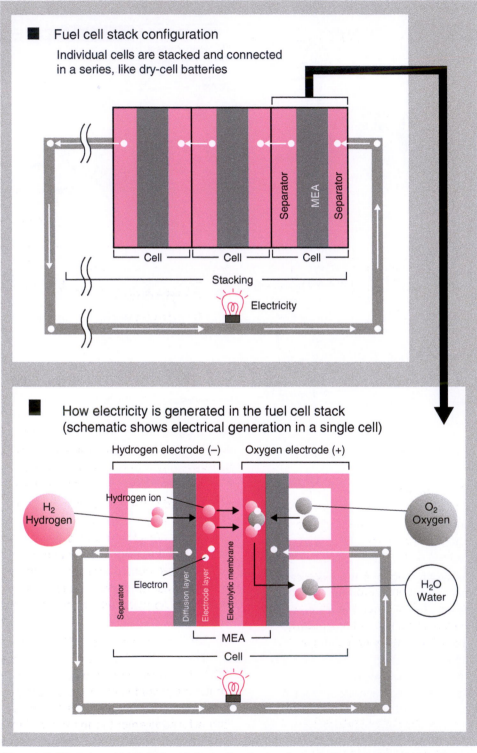

Figure 9.28 Generation of electricity in the fuel cell stack (Source: Honda Media)

■ Cell structure comparison

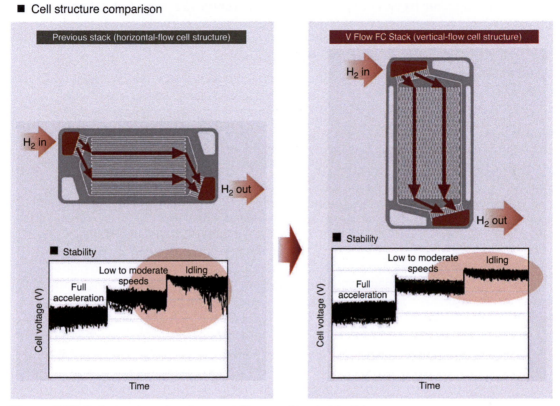

Figure 9.29 Cell structure development (Source: Honda Media)

of the water by-product from the electricity-generating layer.

The result is greater stability in power generation. The new structure also allows for a thinner flow channel and reduction in the stack's size and weight. The innovative and original wave flow-channel separators provide a more even and efficient supply of hydrogen, air and coolant to the electricity-generating layer. The results are higher generating performance, optimal cooling characteristics and major reductions in size and weight.

Key Fact

The wave flow-channel separators provide a more even and efficient supply of hydrogen, air and coolant to the electricity-generating layer.

Improved water drainage due to the V Flow cell structure helps to achieve better output immediately after start-up. The reduced coolant volume and single-box design made possible by the wave flow-channel separators result in heat mass 40% lower than previous stacks. As a result, the amount of time required to achieve 50% output after start-up at –20°C is only one-quarter that of the previous stack. Start-up is now possible at temperatures as low as –30°C.

The lithium-ion battery is 40% lighter and 50% smaller than the ultra-capacitor of the previous FCX, allowing it to be stowed under the rear seat. This gives the car more passenger and boot space. The advanced battery provides a powerful supplement to the fuel cell stack's output, improving the motor torque, for better acceleration. In addition to increasing the total energy capacity, the battery efficiently stores energy generated by the intelligent regenerative braking system, capturing 11% more kinetic energy than the ultra-capacitor used in the 2005 FCX; 57% of the energy of deceleration is regenerated with the new system.

Key Fact

The battery provides a supplement to the fuel cell stack's output, improving the motor torque, for better acceleration. It also stores energy from the regenerative braking system.

The drive motor configuration delivers powerful acceleration and a high top speed, along with a quieter, more luxurious ride. The new rotor and stator (stationary permanent magnets) feature a combined reluctance torque, low-loss magnetic circuit and full-range, full-digital vector control to achieve high efficiency and high output over a wide speed range.

The innovative shape and layout of the magnets in the rotor result in high-output, high-torque, high-rpm performance. These innovations deliver a maximum output of 100 kW along with impressive torque and power output density. At the same time, resonance points in the high-frequency range have been eliminated for quieter operation.

A newly designed rotor features an interior permanent magnet (IPM) to lower inductance, improving reluctance torque for high-torque performance. The magnet's high-energy characteristics also contribute to high torque and a more compact design. These innovations result in 50% higher output density and 20% higher torque density. The number of poles has also been reduced and the magnet widened to better withstand

■ Main components of the fuel cell vehicle

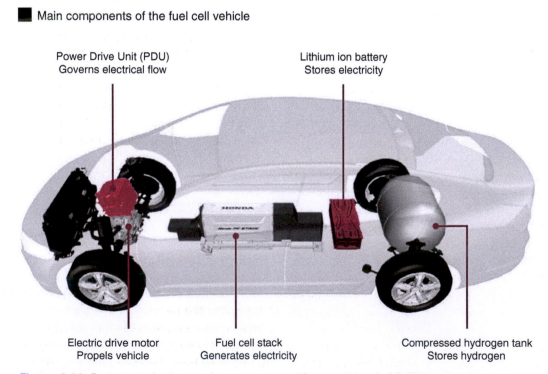

Power Drive Unit (PDU)
Governs electrical flow

Lithium ion battery
Stores electricity

Electric drive motor
Propels vehicle

Fuel cell stack
Generates electricity

Compressed hydrogen tank
Stores hydrogen

Figure 9.30 Battery and other main components (Source: Honda Media)

Figure 9.31 Induction drive motor, differential and final drive components (Source: Honda Media)

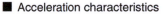

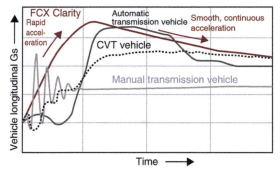

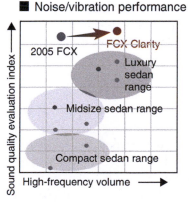

Figure 9.32 Performance and characteristics (Source: Honda Media)

stress, allowing the yoke to wrap around the outside of the IPM. A centre rib has been installed for greater rigidity. This more robust construction allows for operation at higher rpm.

The stator features a low iron-loss electrical steel sheet and higher density windings that decrease resistance and contribute to high torque and higher output. The number of magnetic poles in the rotor has been reduced from 12 to 8, eliminating resonance points within the operating rpm range.

9.6.5 Driving dynamics

The electric motor-driven FCX Clarity delivers a completely different driving sensation from a conventional car powered by an ICE.

There are no gear changes to interrupt power delivery and the torque characteristics are smooth, making acceleration seamless. There is none of the vibration that comes from reciprocating pistons. Acceleration times are around the same as a 2.4-litre petrol- or diesel-engine car of a similar size.

The vehicle's fixed gear ratio allows for simple operation: there's an easy-to-use shift control for forward, reverse and park that has a light touch and a short stroke. The compact shift unit features electronic control, allowing the shift lever to be installed on the dashboard.

The shifter, start switch and parking switch are all easy to operate.

Along with a new brushless motor with increased output, the front double-wishbone suspension helps facilitate tight cornering and delivers a 5.4-m turning radius; very tight

169

Figure 9.33 Dashboard and controls

given the vehicle's long wheelbase. The low inertia of the motor and minimal friction of the suspension when turning contribute to smoother steering. And a tilt-and-telescopic steering wheel provides an optimal steering position for a wide range of drivers. The FCX Clarity has Adaptive Cruise Control as standard.

The FCX Clarity features an integrated braking, traction control and electric-controlled steering system that works together to help the driver maintain control of the vehicle in emergency situations and in varying road conditions.

Working in conjunction with the vehicle's anti-lock brakes, traction control system (TCS) with slide slip control and vehicle stability assist (VSA), the electric power steering (EPS) enhances steering force for even better handling.

In controlling understeer, EPS provides supplementary steering force to prevent the steering wheel from being turned too far as motor torque is reduced and braking force is applied to the inner rear wheel by the VSA. In controlling oversteer, the EPS provides steering force to help the driver counter the spin-generating moment as braking is applied to the outer front wheel to stabilize the vehicle. When road conditions under the left and right tyres are different, torque and steering force are supplemented to help the driver maintain stability.

As a result of increased energy storage capacity and a broader range of regeneration control, it

has been possible to implement a system that regulates acceleration and reduces the need for pedal operation in downhill driving.

Assessing incline and vehicle speed, the system regulates acceleration when the driver first releases the accelerator pedal, minimizing the need for frequent braking. The system simultaneously adjusts the amount of regenerative braking to help maintain constant vehicle speed after brake pedal inputs. The function is similar to engine braking in a conventionally powered vehicle, but more intelligent, smoother and easier to use.

Key Fact

The system adjusts the amount of regenerative braking to help maintain constant vehicle speed after brake pedal inputs under downhill conditions.

Figure 9.34 Smooth performance (Source: Honda Media)

9.6.6 Safety: hydrogen and high voltage

Sensors are located throughout the vehicle to provide a warning in the unlikely event of a hydrogen leak. If a leak occurs, a ventilation system is activated and an automatic system closes the main cut-off valves on the hydrogen tanks or supply lines.

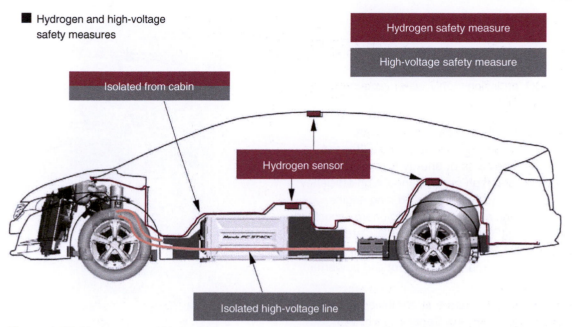

■ Hydrogen and high-voltage
safety measures

Hydrogen safety measure

High-voltage safety measure

Isolated from cabin

Hydrogen sensor

Isolated high-voltage line

Figure 9.35 Hydrogen and high-voltage safety measures (Source: Honda Media)

The high-voltage lines are electrically isolated
and sensors provide a warning in case of
grounding. In the event of a collision, high-
voltage contactors shut down the source
power line. Repeated flood and fire testing
have confirmed a very high level of safety and
reliability. Orange covers are used on all high-
voltage cables.

Safety First

In the event of a collision, high-voltage
contactors shut down the source power
line.

During refuelling, to prevent reverse flow
from the tank, the hydrogen filler inlet has
an integrated check valve. The fuel intake
mechanism is also designed to prevent
contamination by other gases or the
connection of nozzles designed for hydrogen
at incompatible pressure levels.

Figure 9.36 Fuelling pipe connection (Source:
Honda Media)

9.7 Toyota Mirai

9.7.1 Overview

This hydrogen fuel stack car is now available
to buy in the UK. Its outline features are as
follows:

▶ 100 kg proton-exchange membrane fuel cell
▶ 1.5 kWh 60 kg nickel–metal hydride battery
pack, single-speed gearbox, front-wheel
drive

- ▶ Power/torque: 153 bhp/247 lb ft
- ▶ Top speed: 111 mph
- ▶ Acceleration: 0–62 mph in 9.6 seconds
- ▶ Range: about 300 miles
- ▶ CO_2 emissions: only water vapour at the tailpipe.

The Mirai (which means future) was developed around Toyota's long-cultivated core technologies of energy recovery during braking, and high-performance, high-efficiency hybrid technology to assist during engine starting and acceleration. Two energy sources, a fuel cell (FC) stack and a battery, are used as appropriate to drive the motor to achieve more environmentally efficient and powerful running.

The Mirai is a hybrid that combines an FC stack with a battery. Generally, a hybrid car is a vehicle that runs efficiently using a combination of two drive sources: an engine and a motor. An FCV differs slightly from general hybrid vehicles in that it is a hybrid that uses a combination of an FC stack and a battery as the sources of energy to power the motor. The battery provides power support during acceleration, just as it does in other hybrid technologies used to achieve more powerful and efficient running.

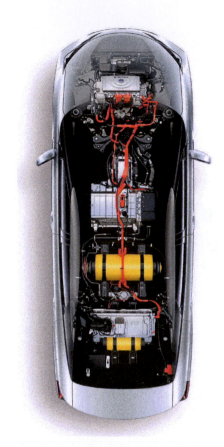

Figure 9.37 Components of the Mirai (Source: Toyota Media)

> **Definition**
> FCV: fuel cell vehicle.

9.7.2 Toyota fuel cell system (TFCS)

TFCS combines Hybrid and FC technologies developed by Toyota over many years and uses the latest compact, high-performance FC stack. The smallest element in a fuel cell (a cell) comprises an electrolyte membrane, a pair of electrodes (negative and positive) and two separators. Though each cell has a small voltage, of 1 V or less, large power output for running a vehicle can be obtained by connecting a few hundred cells in series, increasing the voltage. These combined cells form what's called an FC stack; this FC stack is usually what is meant when talking about fuel cells.

In a fuel cell, electricity is made from hydrogen and oxygen. Hydrogen is supplied to the negative electrode, where it is activated on the catalyst causing electrons to be released. The electrons freed from the hydrogen move from the negative electrodes to the positive electrodes, generating electricity. The hydrogen releases electrons that convert to hydrogen ions that move to the positive side while passing through a polymer electrolyte membrane. At the positive electrode catalyst, oxygen, hydrogen ions and electrons combine to form water.

Key Fact

In a fuel cell, electricity is made from hydrogen and oxygen.

9.7.3 Safety

The hydrogen that powers Mirai is stored at a high pressure (700-bar) in two compact, ultra-tough tanks. Toyota has been working on their design in-house since 2000 and is more than satisfied with their strength and safety performance.

The tanks' main source of strength is their carbon fibre shell, over which there is a further layer of glass fibre. Should the car be involved in an accident, any damage to the hydrogen tank will be clearly visible on the glass-fibre layer; tests can then be carried out to find out whether the carbon shell itself has been compromised. The glass fibre doesn't contribute to rigidity of the tank, but gives absolute confidence in its integrity. The whole tank is lined with plastic to seal in the hydrogen. The tanks have been subjected to extremely severe testing. They are designed to withstand up to 225% of their operating pressure, which is a very high safety margin.

In the unlikely event of a leak, the car is fitted with highly sensitive sensors that will detect minute amounts of hydrogen. These are placed in strategic locations for instant detection. Should a leak occur in the fuel system, the system will immediately close the safety valves and shut down the vehicle.

As a third layer of safety, the cabin is strictly separated from the hydrogen compartment to prevent the ingress of any leaking hydrogen, which would instead gradually disperse into the atmosphere.

9.7.4 Refuelling process

Refuelling is a critical process because it involves human action, which unfortunately

Figure 9.38 Cutaway view of the Mirai showing the fuel tanks in yellow (Source: Toyota Media)

can lead to unforeseen and unsafe scenarios, such as trying to drive off while the fuel nozzle is still connected to the car. For this reason, a number of safety precautions have been put in place.

1 The nozzle at the end of the hydrogen dispenser's flexible hose has a mechanical lock to form a perfect connection with the car's filling inlet. Unless this mechanical lock clicks into place securely, filling will not commence.

2 A pressure impulse checks for any leakage in the system between the filling station and the car. If a leak is detected, refuelling is aborted.

3 The rate of filling is carefully regulated, to avoid overheating during transfer. Temperature sensors in the car's hydrogen tanks, the nozzle and the pump constantly communicate with each other by infrared to control the rate of flow of hydrogen into the car so that the temperature rise is not excessive. This is probably the smartest refuelling system any driver will have experienced.

International SAE and ISO standards establish safety limits and performance requirements for gaseous hydrogen fuel dispensers. The criteria include maximum fuel temperature at the dispenser nozzle, the maximum fuel flow rate and the maximum rate of pressure increase.

> **Definition**
>
> International SAE and ISO standards establish safety limits and performance requirements for gaseous hydrogen fuel dispensers.

Should a driver attempt to drive off while the fuel nozzle is attached to the car, it will be immobilized until the nozzle has been replaced in its holster and the car's fuel cap is closed. To be absolutely sure, a safety system is embedded in the hose that locks the pump should an attempt be made to drive the car off in the middle of refuelling.

Hydrogen gas is the lightest thing known to man and considerably (14×) lighter than air. The consequence is that should a leak occur, the hydrogen will rise into the atmosphere. And thanks to its status as the smallest molecule in the universe, it disperses quickly in air or any other gas.

The fuel tanks have a pressure-relief device that releases the hydrogen gradually should there be an abnormal rise in temperature (for example, in a fire). This prevents any overpressure or explosion occurring.

Hydrogen is as safe as any other fuel used in a car. It's been used as an energy carrier for decades, and there is a vast amount of cumulative know-how and experience in Toyota and elsewhere to handle it safely. It is a carbon-free, non-hazardous energy source that can be produced from many renewable resources and emits no greenhouse gases when used as a fuel.

9.8 Honda light hybrids

9.8.1 Overview

This range of Honda cars are described as light hybrids because they do not run on electric only but do have an integrated motor for assistance. The motor also becomes a generator under braking conditions. It is in fact the classic hybrid where braking energy is collected and reused.

9.8.2 IMA battery

The Honda battery module uses nickel–metal hydride (NiMH) technology for high-energy density and long service life. The batteries are constructed in a modular form with a terminal voltage of 100.8 V to 144 V (or more on the Toyota Prius) and a rated capacity of about 6.5 Ah.

If servicing is required to the battery module, refer to the manufacturer's instructions because serious injury or even death can occur if the safety precautions are not observed. The batteries typically only weigh about 22 kg. The operating range is from −30 to +50°C.

> **Safety First**
>
> If servicing is required to the battery module, refer to the manufacturer's instructions – serious injury or even death can occur if the safety precautions are not observed.

The high-voltage batteries are fitted either behind the rear passenger seats or in some cases under the floor of the luggage compartment.

The battery module is used to supply high voltage to the electric motor during the assist mode. The battery module is also used to store the regenerated power while cruising, deceleration and braking. Current from the battery module is also converted to 12 V DC, which is supplied to the vehicle electrical system. A conventional 12-V battery located within the engine compartment is used for the vehicle's 12-V system.

Battery modules typically consist of:

▶ voltage sensors
▶ temperature sensors (thermistors)

Tank storage density *1

Lighter weight achieved through innovations of carbon fiber reinforced plastic layer structure.

Tank storage density of 5.7 wt% achieved (world top level *2)

Innovations to the plastic liner configuration and efficient layering pattern resulted in a reduction of approximately 40% in the amount of carbon fiber used.

Low centre of gravity

Fuel cell stack, high-pressure hydrogen tanks and other power unit components are placed under vehicle floor.

The lower centre of gravity raises handling stability and produces a comfortable driving experience by reducing body movements.

The front-rear weight balance is adjusted to produce a midship feel despite the front wheel drive design.

*3 November 2014, Toyota data

1 Fuel cell stack

Toyota's first mass-production fuel cell, featuring a compact size and top level output density.
- Type: Polymer electrolyte fuel cell
- Volume power density: 3.1 kW/L (world top level *2)
- Maximum output: 114 kW (155 DIN hp)
- Humidification system: Internal circulation system (humidifier-less; world-first *2)

2 Fuel cell boost converter

A compact, high-efficiency, high-capacity converter newly developed to boost fuel cell stack voltage to 650 V. A boost converter is used to obtain a higher voltage than the input. Number of phases: 4 phases

3 Battery

A nickel-metal hydride battery which stores energy recovered from deceleration, supplemented by energy produced by the fuel cell stack under low load driving conditions, to assist output during acceleration.

4 High-pressure hydrogen tank

Tank storing hydrogen as fuel. The nominal working pressure is a high pressure level of 70 MPa (700 bar).

Nominal working pressure	70 MPa (700 bar)
Tank storage density *1	5.7 wt% (world top level *2)
Tank internal volume	122.4 L (front tank: 60.0 L / rear tank: 62.4 L)
Hydrogen storage mass	Approx. 5.0 kg

5 Motor

Motor driven by electricity generated by fuel cell stack and/or supplied by battery.
- Maximum output: 113 kW (154 DIN hp)
- Maximum torque: 335 Nm

6 Power control unit

The component that optimally controls both fuel cell stack output under various operational conditions and drive battery charging and discharging.

7 Auxiliary components

Hydrogen circulating pump, etc.

*1 Hydrogen storage mass per tank weight

Figure 9.39 Details and key features of the Mirai (Source: Toyota Media)

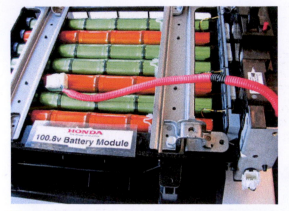

Figure 9.40 Battery module

Figure 9.42 Battery cells and groups

▶ battery cell groups; each cell group consists of six cells – one cell equals 1.2 V
▶ cooling fan
▶ terminal plate.

The battery cell groups are connected in series by the terminal plates, located on both sides of the battery module.

Charge and discharge are caused by movements of hydrogen when a chemical reaction takes place in the cells. The general construction of a cell is similar to that of a conventional battery, but the positive electrode is made of nickel hydroxide. The negative electrode is made of metal hydride (a hydrogen-absorbing alloy) and the electrolyte is potassium hydroxide, a strongly alkaline solution.

Follow safety procedures at all times – a strong alkali is just as dangerous as a strong acid:

▶ Wear protective clothing:
  – safety shoes
  – safety glasses
  – suitable rubber, latex or nitrile gloves.
▶ Neutralize electrolyte.

In a discharged state the surface of the positive electrode will contain nickel di-hydroxide ($Ni(OH)_2$) and there will be hydroxide ions (OH^-) in the electrolyte. As the battery is charged, the positive electrode loses a hydrogen atom and becomes nickel hydroxide (NiOOH). The freed hydrogen atom joins with the hydroxide ion to form water (H_2O), and a free electron is released.

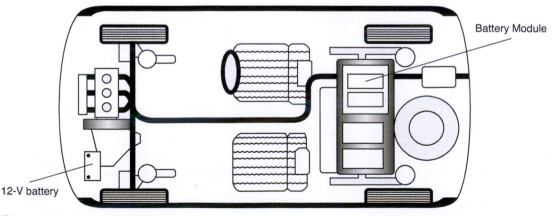

Battery Module

12-V battery

Figure 9.41 High-voltage battery location

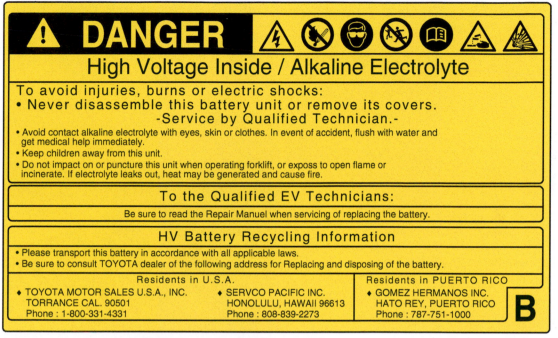

DANGER

High Voltage Inside / Alkaline Electrolyte

To avoid injuries, burns or electric shocks:
• Never disassemble this battery unit or remove its covers.
-Service by Qualified Technician.-
• Avoid contact alkaline electrolyte with eyes, skin or clothes. In event of accident, flush with water and get medical help immediately.
• Keep children away from this unit.
• Do not impact on or puncture this unit when operating forklift, or expose to open flame or incinerate. If electrolyte leaks out, heat may be generated and cause fire.

To the Qualified EV Technicians:
Be sure to read the Repair Manuel when servicing of replacing the battery.

HV Battery Recycling Information
• Please transport this battery in accordance with all applicable laws.
• Be sure to consult TOYOTA dealer of the following address for Replacing and disposing of the battery.

Residents in U.S.A.
♦ TOYOTA MOTOR SALES U.S.A., INC.
TORRANCE CAL. 90501
Phone : 1-800-331-4331

♦ SERVCO PACIFIC INC.
HONOLULU, HAWAII 96613
Phone : 808-839-2273

Residents in PUERTO RICO
♦ GOMEZ HERMANOS INC.
HATO REY, PUERTO RICO
Phone : 787-751-1000

B

Figure 9.43 Information plate from a Toyota

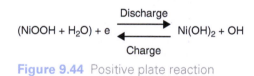

$$(NiOOH + H_2O) + e \underset{Charge}{\overset{Discharge}{\rightleftarrows}} Ni(OH)_2 + OH$$

Figure 9.44 Positive plate reaction

In a discharged state the negative electrode consists of the metal alloy, surrounded by H_2O and free electrons. As the battery is charged a hydrogen atom is dislodged from the water and is absorbed by the metal alloy to make metal hydride (MH). This leaves hydroxide ions (OH^-) in the surrounding electrolyte.

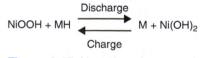

$$NiOOH + MH \underset{Charge}{\overset{Discharge}{\rightleftarrows}} M + Ni(OH)_2$$

Figure 9.45 Negative plate reaction

Nickel–metal hydride (NiMH) batteries are used because they are robust, long lasting, charge or discharge quickly, and have a high energy density.

The energy store of the future may be the lithium-ion battery. Bosch and Samsung are working together to further develop this technology for automotive applications. The main aim is to improve the energy density of this battery threefold, and to cut costs by two-thirds.

Key Fact
The energy store of the future may be the lithium-ion battery.

Figure 9.46 NiMH battery cells

177

Figure 9.47 Lithium battery pack
(Source: Bosch Media)

9.8.3 IMA motor

The thin design Honda IMA motor is located between the engine and the transmission. It is a permanent magnet type, brushless DC machine, which operates as a motor or a generator.

> **Key Fact**
>
> An IMA motor is usually located between the engine and the transmission.

Figure 9.48 Motor stator in position on a Honda engine

The functions of the IMA motor are:

▶ To assist the engine under certain conditions determined by the motor control module (MCM) for improving fuel economy, low emission and drivability.

▶ To regenerate power under certain conditions to charge the high-voltage battery module and the normal 12-V battery.

▶ To start the engine when the state of charge is sufficient.

The motor is located between the engine and transmission gearbox.

Figure 9.49 Power cable connected to the motor (remember, orange cables are high voltage)

The specifications for the Honda IMA motor shown here are as follows:

▶ type DC brushless
▶ rated voltage 144 V
▶ power 10 kW/3000 rpm
▶ torque 49 Nm/1000 rpm.

The rated voltage will vary between about 100 V and almost 300 V. These figures for power and torque are typical but other motors will vary.

In a conventional DC motor, the housing contains field magnets, the rotor is made up of coils wound in slots in an iron core and is connected to a commutator. However, in a brushless motor the conventional DC motor is turned inside out. The rotor becomes a permanent magnet and the stator becomes the wound iron core. The advantages are:

Key Fact

In a brushless motor the conventional DC motor is turned inside out.

▶ better cooling
▶ no brushes to wear out
▶ no maintenance.

The disadvantages, however, are:

▶ more complex motor control circuits
▶ expensive rare earth magnets have to be used because conventional iron magnets demagnetize when a large current is applied to them.

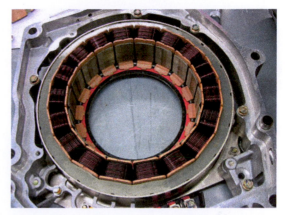

Figure 9.51 IMA motor stator removed from the vehicle

To maintain a constant field, the stator coils are divided into six groups of three. Each group has three electrical phases in each coil designated as U, V and W. Switching of current for each phase of these coils takes place in a power driver unit (PDU) when the motor is acting as a motor or as a generator. Maximum torque is produced when the rotor and the stator fields are at 90° to each other.

Figure 9.50 Permanent magnet rotor

The stator is constructed of 18 coils surrounding a rotor containing 12 poles. Although the motor is a DC type, note that the current supplied to it must be AC. This is because in normal DC motors (brush type) the current is reversed by the brushes and commutator. If the current is not reversed the rotor would come to a stop. The force that rotates the rotor is the interaction of the two magnetic fields produced by the stator coils and the rotor. These fields must remain constant in magnitude and relative orientation to produce a constant torque.

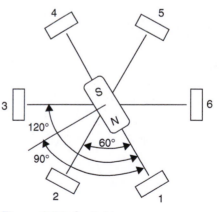

Figure 9.52 Switching sequence

To control the stator coil fields correctly, the relative position of the rotor must be known. A sensor disk is therefore attached to the rotor and is divided into 12 partitions – 6 high and 6 low. These are detected by three commutation sensors.

There are three commutation sensors. They act in a similar way to an ABS sensor where

Key Fact

A brushless DC motor is supplied with AC.

Figure 9.53 The sensor ring (just behind the stator coils) has high and low sections that are detected by the commutation sensors

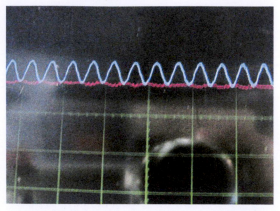

Figure 9.55 Sensor signal

metal teeth passing on a sensor wheel induce a signal current in the sensor. Each sensor is composed of two small magnetic reluctance elements that detect the presence of a high partition or low partition passing the sensor. The two variable magnetic reluctance elements transform their signal from a variable to a high (1) or low (0) signal.

Figure 9.54 Commutation sensor connection

Push-on or ring-and-screw-type terminals are used on the motor. Orange-coloured cables are attached, and make the connection between the IMA motor and the power drive unit (PDU) at the rear of the vehicle.

Developments are on-going in the hybrid motor field. However, the technology of stationary coils rotating permanent magnets seems to

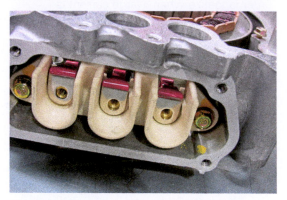

Figure 9.56 Motor terminals for the high-voltage cables (which always have an orange covering)

be well developed. A range of switching and control methods are used, but in simple terms the stator coils are energized in sequence to drive the rotor. When the rotor is driven by the wheels (on deceleration or braking), it induces electrical energy in the coils and this is used to charge the battery via suitable rectification and voltage controls.

This section has outlined a system used by Honda. An alternative Bosch hybrid transmission and the associated IMA system are shown below.

9.8.4 Hybrid IMA control system

Like any other complex control system, the control of the hybrid IMA system can be represented as a block diagram showing inputs and outputs. The IMA system can seem more complex because the motor changes to become a generator and back to a motor depending on road conditions. However, thinking of the system as shown here will help with your understanding of the operation.

The following diagram expands the basic block diagram. In this case the main component locations are shown.

Signals from the three commutation sensors are sent to the motor control module (MCM). The MCM is connected to the power drive unit, making it possible for the battery module and the IMA motor to interact.

The three signals coming from the commutation sensor on the IMA motor are sent to the MCM and transferred by the module into high and low signals for the stator's coil phases U, V and W. According to these signals, the circuits from the battery module to motor, or from motor to battery, are made by the power drive unit.

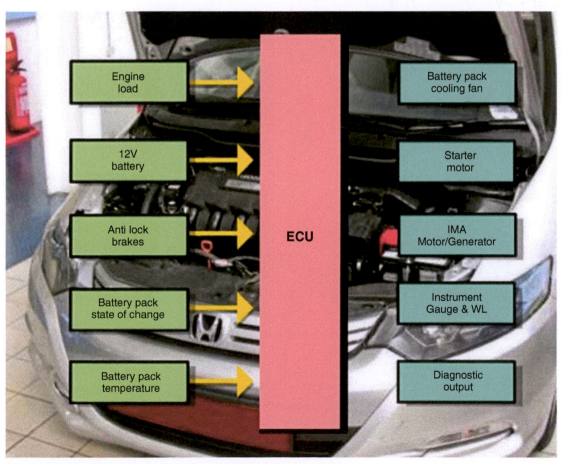

Figure 9.57 Basic input-control-output block diagram

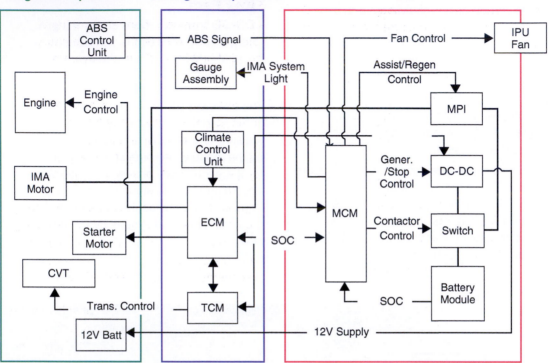

Figure 9.58 Block diagram showing all components and their locations

Figure 9.59 Motor control module

Figure 9.60 Inside a PDU

The power drive unit (PDU) consists of six power switches with a gate drive circuit. The switches are insulated gate bipolar transistors (IGBT), which are able to control a very large amount of power with a very small signal.

There are six motor commutation steps and as each step is made, another signal is generated. All six steps are different and none has a position where U, V and W are all low or all high. Two IGBTs in the same line never switch on together. It is always one IGBT in the upper side, and one in the lower side. This is very similar to how a stepper motor driver circuit works. Figures 9.61 and

9.62 show example switched paths that are the same when driving the motor or charging from the generator – except that current flow is reversed.

When the motor is acting as a generator, power is transferred from the stator through the PDU diodes controlled by signals from the commutations sensors. The PDU works in a similar way to a normal alternator rectifier.

The DC–DC converter takes the high battery-module voltage and converts it to charge the 12-V battery and run the system. Charging the battery and running the low-voltage system from the high-voltage system is more efficient than using a standard alternator.

The other key features used by many hybrid vehicles to improve efficiency are:

▶ Idle stop/start: to save fuel the engine is stopped, at traffic lights for example, and restarted almost instantly by the IMA.
▶ Braking control: the most important aspect of a hybrid is collecting energy normally lost on braking. If the normal brake operation is also electronically controlled so that more regenerative effect is used, efficiency is improved further.
▶ Engine valve control: to further enhance the regenerative effect, the braking effect of the ICE is reduced by preventing the valves operating.

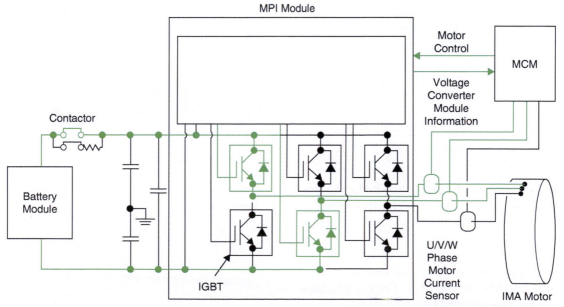

Figure 9.61 Motor circuit operation (example phase highlighted)

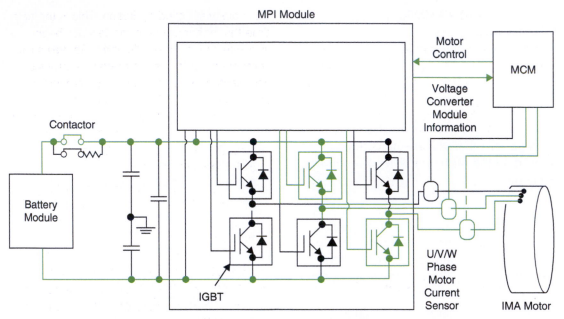

Figure 9.62 Generator circuit operation (example phase highlighted)

Figure 9.63 DC–DC converter

Figure 9.64 Valve control allows more braking to be done by the motor/generator

▶ Air conditioning control – on some systems the air conditioning is run by an electric motor so that it continues to work in stop/start conditions.

▶ Instrumentation feedback: it is well known that on any vehicle a significant effect on economy is driving style. Drivers who have opted for a hybrid tend to be looking for economy so are willing to change their style even further based on feedback. Some instruments show images such as growing green trees to indicate driving performance improvement!

The efficiency of the hybrid car has now improved significantly. Sophisticated control systems and highly developed and efficient component designs are the reason for this. However, remember that as with any complex system, it can be thought of as inputs and outputs –this makes it much easier to understand.

Figure 9.65 Feedback on economy/performance helps to change driving style and improve efficiency even more

9.9 Bosch parallel full-hybrid

9.9.1 Overview

The hybrid variants of the Volkswagen Touareg and Porsche Cayenne S feature hybrid technology supplied by Bosch. This is the first time that either of these models has been available as a parallel full-hybrid. As well as key components such as the power electronics and electric motor, Bosch is also providing the 'brain' of the vehicles in the form of the Motronic control unit for hybrid vehicles, which governs when the electric motor, internal-combustion engine or a combination of the two kick into action.

Volkswagen and Porsche both chose to equip their hybrid vehicles with a 3.0-litre V6 supercharged direct-injection engine and an eight-speed automatic transmission. The six-cylinder V-engine delivers 245 kW (333 hp) and a maximum torque of 440 Nm starting from 3000 rpm. The vehicle also features an integrated motor generator (IMG) developed by Bosch. The water-cooled electric motor includes a separate clutch. The hybrid module

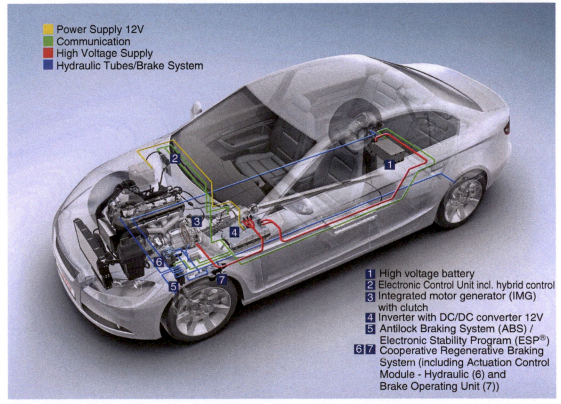

Power Supply 12V
Communication
High Voltage Supply
Hydraulic Tubes/Brake System

1 High voltage battery
2 Electronic Control Unit incl. hybrid control
3 Integrated motor generator (IMG) with clutch
4 Inverter with DC/DC converter 12V
5 Antilock Braking System (ABS) / Electronic Stability Program (ESP®)
6 7 Cooperative Regenerative Braking System (including Actuation Control Module - Hydraulic (6) and Brake Operating Unit (7))

Figure 9.66 Hybrid components and supply systems (Source: Bosch Media)

is positioned between the ICE and the transmission; it has a diameter of 30 cm and a length of just 145 mm. The IMG delivers 34 kW and a maximum torque of 300 Nm. That means the cars can cruise at a maximum of 50–60 km/h running on electric power alone, as long as the nickel–metal hydride (NiMH) battery has enough charge.

Key Fact

The IMG delivers 34 kW and a maximum torque of 300 Nm.

Figure 9.67 Integrated motor generator (Source: Bosch Media)

The battery has an energy capacity of 1.7 kWh with a peak of 288 V. During braking, the electric motor, now operating as a generator, recovers kinetic energy, which is then stored in the high-voltage battery.

Lifting off the throttle at any speed up to around 160 km/h activates what is referred to as 'sailing' mode: the ICE automatically shuts down and the vehicle coasts along without consuming fuel – obviously without

sacrificing any of the functionality of the systems required for a safe and comfortable drive. Braking is also a fully automatic process. The hybrid control unit monitors the pressure on the brake pedal to determine what brake torque should be electrically set by the IMG. This does not affect safety systems such as ABS and ESP®, which take precedence whatever the situation.

Figure 9.68 Braking control components (Source: Bosch Media)

9.9.2 Power boost

For drivers in a hurry, the electric motor and the combustion engine can also work in tandem, allowing the cars to sprint from 0 to 100 kilometres per hour in 6.5 seconds. This 'power boost' function increases the vehicle's performance to 279 kW (380 hp), offering the driver a maximum torque of 580 Nm. Compared with the first-generation V8 vehicles, these hybrid vehicles cut fuel consumption by up to 40%. EU cycle fuel consumption falls to 8.2 litres per 100 km, equivalent to CO_2 emissions of 193 grams per km. Both vehicles also comply with the Euro 5 standard and the US emissions standard ULEV 2.

Key Fact

This 'power boost' function increases the vehicle's performance to 279 kW (380 hp), offering the driver a maximum torque of 580 Nm.

Figure 9.69 Motor and clutch assembly (Source: Bosch Media)

9.9.3 Control system

The fact that the ICE and the electric motor work together so seamlessly stems from the perfectly tuned interaction between modern management and control technology and optimized hybrid components. Bosch can draw on many years of experience in this field thanks to its work on developing gasoline injection systems. The control unit is based on Motronic, which has already proved its worth in so many direct injection gasoline vehicles. The additional functions needed for hybrid operation were integrated. The control unit, for example, ensures that the electric motor and engine are turning at exactly the same speed when transferring the torque between them.

> **Key Fact**
> The control unit ensures that the electric motor and engine are turning at exactly the same speed when transferring the torque between them.

9.9.4 Hybrid and GDi engines

The supercharged V6 engine is a key part of the overall concept. The Motronic control unit manages the combustion engine with tremendous precision, right down to the rate

of individual injections. It employs an additional CAN bus interface to exchange all relevant data with the hybrid components, power electronics and battery, and the efficient direct injection system also reduces exhaust emissions. The combustion engine and electric motor complement each other perfectly, enabling parallel hybrids to offer a whole series of new features to improve driving comfort.

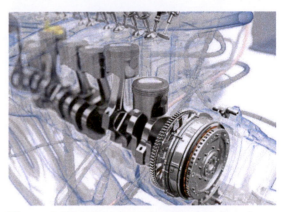

Figure 9.70 IMG in position (Source: Bosch Media)

9.9.5 Optimized components

Parallel full hybrid technology can be implemented as a more cost-effective solution in comparison with other hybrid concepts. For example, it requires just one electric motor, which operates as both a motor and a generator. The power electronics are a core component, providing an interface between the high-voltage electric drive and the vehicle's 12-V electrical system, and featuring an inverter that converts the direct current from the battery into three-phase alternating current for the electric motor, and vice versa. All components are optimized for space and performance.

> **Key Fact**
> All components are optimized for space and performance.

187

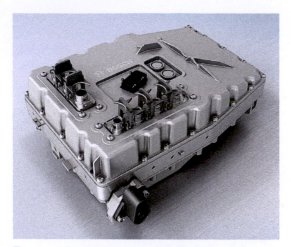

Figure 9.71 Inverter and DC–DC converter (Source: Bosch Media)

9.10 Volkswagen Golf GTE

9.10.1 Overview

The powertrain of the Golf GTE is a parallel plug-in hybrid (PHEV). Its electric motor and ICE are connected to each other in the hybrid mode. With a system output of 150 kW, the GTE is not only economical but also very dynamic. It has a claimed maximum range of 939 km and a 50-km electric-only range.

> **Key Fact**
>
> The powertrain of the Golf GTE is a parallel plug-in hybrid (PHEV).

Figure 9.72 Golf GTE main components (Source: Volkswagen Media)

Combustion engine	110 kW/150 hp
Electric motor	75 kW/102 hp
System	150 kW/204 hp
Maximum torque, combustion engine	250 Nm
Maximum torque, electric motor	330 Nm
Maximum torque, system	350 Nm
Electric range	50 km
Electric consumption	11.4 kWh per 100 km
Acceleration 0–100 km per hour	7.6 seconds
Maximum speed	217 kph 222 kph with boost function (138 mph)
Fuel consumption (NEDC)	1.5 litres per 100 km
CO_2 emissions	35 grams per km
Unladen weight	1540 kg

9.10.2 Motor and power electronics

The Golf GTE is equipped with a permanently excited synchronous machine with a maximum output of 75 kW. The permanent magnets in the rotor are alternating south- and north-poled magnets. The stator generates a rotating magnetic field, created by applying current to the three-phase copper coils. As a result of the interaction with the permanent magnets, the rotor turns at a speed synchronous to the rotating magnetic field of the stator. The compact e-machine in the Golf GTE is installed between the engine clutch and the transmission drive clutches.

> **Key Fact**
>
> The stator generates a rotating magnetic field.

The power electronics are responsible for the conversion of electric current. To do this, it is connected to the electric motor and the battery. In electric motor mode, six high-power transistors convert the direct current of the high-voltage battery into a three-phase alternating current that powers the electric motor. In generator mode, the power electronics rectify the alternating current generated. This supplies the electrical system and charges the high-voltage battery.

Figure 9.73 Electric drive and transmission (Source: Volkswagen Media)

9.10.3 Internal combustion engine and transmission

A 1.4-litre four-cylinder TSI engine with an output of 110 kW is part of the drivetrain. The power is transmitted via a six-speed dual clutch transmission (often described as direct shift gearbox or DSG). When the car is driven purely electrically, the engine remains switched off. It was constructed specifically to be able to provide full power instantly.

The six-speed dual-clutch transmission facilitates the combination of a transversely mounted ICE with an electric motor. The power flow is transferred over the input shaft into two separate transmissions, each with an upstream drive clutch.

9.10.4 Battery

The lithium-ion high-voltage battery is installed in the underbody of the car and connected to the power electronics. The battery

Figure 9.74 Engine, motor and transmission (Source: Volkswagen Media)

management system monitors and controls the battery and its energy flow. The battery must be charged in advance in order to provide energy for the drive. The high-voltage battery in the Golf GTE is fully charged within 3.5 hours, using a normal domestic 240 V outlet with a charging power of 2.3 kW. This only takes 2.5 hours if a wall box or a public charging station with a charging power of 3.6 kW is used. The battery charges using rectified alternating current.

Key Fact

The battery management system monitors and controls the battery and its energy flow.

Figure 9.75 Battery pack: 120 kg and 96 lithium-ion cells results in 8.8 kWh at 345 V (Source: Volkswagen Media)

9.10.5 Driver's control systems

The driver is able to maintain a good overview of the vehicle's technology. The

189

Figure 9.76 Power flow graphic

Figure 9.77 The option to set maximum charge current determines the charge time. The lower figure can be set, for example, when charging from solar panel output

Golf GTE is equipped with a touch screen, which always keeps the driver up-to-date during driving. In addition, owners can access a range of information from a distance on a smartphone using a special app. The range monitor shows the driver how far he can drive purely electrically. This function also explains how to increase the range by switching off auxiliary energy consumers, such as climate control or heated seats.

A power meter supplements the revcounter on the left side of the instrument panel. It

indicates if the high-voltage battery is currently charging via recuperation or if energy is being discharged.

Using the E-Manager, three different departure and charging times can be pre-set. The Golf GTE sets the required interior temperature as well as the battery's state of charge ready for these times.

Bibliography

Bosch (2011) *Automotive Handbook*. SAE

Electrical installations and shock information: http://www.electrical-installation.org/enwiki/Electric_shock

Flybrid flywheel systems: http://www.flybridsystems.com

Health and Safety Executive UK: https://www.hse.gov.uk

Institute of the Motor Industry (IMI): http://www.theimi.org.uk

Mennekes (charging plugs): http://www.mennekes.de

Mi, C., Abul Masrur, M. and Wenzhong Gao, D. (2011) *Hybrid Electric Vehicles*. John Wiley & Sons, Chichester.

Picoscope: https://www.picoauto.com

Renesas motor and battery control system: http://www.renesas.eu

Society of Automotive Engineers (SAE): http://www.sae.org

Society of Motor Manufacturers and Traders (SMMT): http://www.smmt.co.uk

Tesla Motors first responder information: https://www.teslamotors.com/firstresponders

Wireless power transfer: https://www.qualcomm.com/products/halo

ZapMap charging point locations: https://www.zap-map.com

References

Denton, T. (2013) *Automobile Electrical and Electronic Systems*. Routledge, London.

Larminie, J. and Lowry, J. (2012) *Electric Vehicle Technology Explained, Second Edition*. John Wiley & Sons, Chichester.

Index

Index

Index